More Advance Praise for
Language of the Spirit

"Reading Jan Swafford's *Language of the Spirit* is like taking a road trip through the land of classical music with your wickedly smart but charmingly self-deprecating best friend in charge of the map, stopping by must-see landmarks and hidden by-ways that are clearly personal favorites. Music to Swafford is not a dry, intellectual exercise, but rather an emotional experience touching on the full range of feeling of which humans are capable. Slip a copy of *Language of the Spirit* into your pocket the next time you attend a symphony performance and consult it before the lights dim—Swafford will help you hear all the richness and depth of the music he so loves."

—Elizabeth Lunday, author of
Secret Lives of Great Composers

"A perfect, lean compendium from a scintillating writer who knows profoundly where music comes from, and the geniuses who've made it best in the Western tradition. Composer and biographer on the grand scale, Jan Swafford has given us the last music book we'll ever need. The rest is listening!"

—Chris Lydon, host of Radio Open Source

LANGUAGE
OF THE SPIRIT
An Introduction to Classical Music

Jan Swafford

BASIC BOOKS
New York

Books published by Basic Books are available at special discounts for bulk purchases in the United States by corporations, institutions, and other organizations. For more information, please contact the Special Markets Department at Perseus Books, 2300 Chestnut Street, Suite 200, Philadelphia, PA 19103, or call (800) 810-4145, ext. 5000, or e-mail special.markets@perseusbooks.com.

Designed by Jack Lenzo

Library of Congress Cataloging-in-Publication Data

Names: Swafford, Jan.
Title: Language of the spirit : an introduction to classical music / Jan Swafford.
Description: New York : Basic Books, [2017] | Includes bibliographical references and index.
Identifiers: LCCN 2016036556 (print) | LCCN 2016037002 (ebook) | ISBN 9780465097548 (hardcover) | ISBN 9780465097555 (ebook)
Subjects: LCSH: Music appreciation.
Classification: LCC MT90 .S99 2017 (print) | LCC MT90 (ebook) | DDC 781.6/8—dc23
LC record available at https://lccn.loc.gov/2016036556

10 9 8 7 6 5 4 3 2 1

Contents

PART V: MODERNISM AND BEYOND

INTRODUCTION

This book proposes to do a number of things at once. It is an introduction to what we call classical music and its major figures, forces, and periods. It is intended to be a stimulus toward a better understanding of the music and the people who write and play it; a basic reference for facts and trends; a compendium of small biographies of important composers; and an examination of the presence of universal qualities in music: love, hope, exaltation, pain, and on through the catalog of qualities we experience and expect to be reflected in our art. After all, one of the prime functions of any art is to show ourselves to ourselves in moving and memorable ways.

Unlike my musical biographies, there are no footnotes—this is not a scholarly work. It is founded mainly on a particular motivation, which is the reason I got into classical music in the first place and the reason I'm still at it as a composer and writer: pleasure and emotion. As a teenager I took up this music because it excited me, made me *feel* more than any other kind of music, more than most other things in my life. It still does.

I got to age twelve in the 1950s listening to Elvis et al., like every other kid. Then I took up playing trombone in the school band and turned out to be good at it, which made music a more or less daily endeavor. Before long I was trying to compose, because listening to classical music gave me an almost painful yearning in the pit of my stomach that was assuaged only when I started writing it myself. In the process I lost interest in being like every other kid. I began to find that a lot of pop tunes I thought I liked got boring after a few listenings, while many classical pieces seemed to open endless vistas of sensation and mystery. So, this book is also a love song to the art I love and to which I have devoted my life. After that, for me, is the fascination of how music is made, in so many times and places. That fascination will be fundamental here, too: how sounds are organized by ear and by rule, how instruments inflect music, how forms shape it, how emotions are portrayed, and so on.

From the book's occasional forays into musical technique I hope the reader will leave with a basic understanding of the mechanics of music, because these play into the artistry. Overall, the book forms a brisk narrative history of the music, providing an introduction for novices and a reference for the familiar repertoire. It will work best when you listen along with the reading. Essentially every work I mention can be found on Spotify or a comparable online music service; the few that aren't there are usually on YouTube (with its generally mediocre fidelity and sometimes scraggly performances). Somebody once said that writing words about music is like dancing about architecture. I think that's about half right, but the words here will at least make better sense when related to the sounds.

There will be a certain irony hanging around these pages, because I look at music with a tincture of irony, likewise the whole of human life and the great globe itself. As a writer on music I've sometimes been accused of irreverence, which I admit, and add that my larger reverence is deep and plainly in view. I believe in genius and greatness, though like love and compassion and God, those are elusive and indefinable qualities. But music is made by and for human beings, and a certain amount of human life appears to me, to put it generously, nuts. Nobody, including great geniuses, is immune to that. To mention a few examples: Isaac Newton, who founded modern science, spent much of his life involved in alchemy. Franz Schubert, one the greatest born talents in music, spent much of his short life writing operas, the one medium he wasn't all that good at. Ludwig van Beethoven, who was reliably brilliant at every aspect of music, including playing and selling it, said accurately of himself: "Outside music everything I do is badly done and stupid."

As you can see, the book will be personal to a degree, but I won't be wallowing in my own presumed wisdom. I've taught music for some thirty-seven years, to students from eleven-year-olds to conservatory grads, and this book is intended to educate. My music biographies come from years of research and thinking; this book comes from decades of teaching. Much of the wisdom here is common wisdom, both that of musicians and of audiences over centuries. I have a certain respect for common wisdom; it never goes far enough, but often it's common for good reason. Likewise, with a given composer most of the pieces I suggest you start with are familiar ones to the initiated. Beethoven's Fifth Symphony may be all too familiar in some respects, but there are reasons it's been loved for a long time. (Besides, as I'll get to, in its day the Fifth was one of the oddest pieces ever written.)

You may find sins of omission or commission here: "How could you have left out [   ]!" Nothing to be done about that. I will say that the recommended composers and pieces do not predictably have to do with my own enthusiasms. I can't say

I'm crazy about every one of them (some I used to be crazy about but no more), but there's no piece mentioned in this book that I don't respect. You won't be crazy about them all, either. When I was young I made a point of never disliking anything, but that happy and hippie all-embracingness is long gone. Still, if I'm a bit of a snob it doesn't mean you have to be. I advise you to take in all new composers and works with absolute openness, and wait for your own taste to form as you get deeper into the territory. If something new surprises or shocks or perplexes you, I suggest going back to it. Some of those pieces will turn out to be favorites; some will upgrade your sense of what music is about; some may upgrade your sense of what *you* are about.

So while here and there I'll present a perhaps offbeat work and composer and point of view, most of the music will be from what we, with a sigh, call the standard repertoire, because many of those pieces are beloved for good reason. It's the word *standard* that rankles, because it doesn't evoke the excitement in these pieces that was manifest when they were new. A lot of today's standard was yesterday's revolutionary. At the same time, there is a body of works and composers out there who are lesser known but wonderful, and I'll dip into those. As one example, for years I've played for friends the final chorus of the oratorio *Jephte* by the relatively obscure baroque composer Giacomo Carissimi, and watched their jaws drop, and sometimes their tears flow.

I'll only suggest a few pieces for each composer, a starter package of familiar works, with a few more suggestions at the end of each essay. The idea is that when a piece or a composer grabs you, go out and look for more on your own. The Internet is a tremendous resource for finding information and further listening. If you like a piece I cite here, compare performances of it, and look for more pieces by that composer. On the whole I won't be dealing here with opera, which really requires a book of its own, though there is a chapter on Richard Wagner and his operas because he influenced music across the board. I also will not regularly be citing specific recordings; that would get voluminous, and there's no way to know what recordings will be available years from now. But here and there I will cite a recording for one reason or another, or because I couldn't resist. I also mention recordings sometimes to make you aware to what extent a performance can make or break a piece. Getting choosy about performers is as worthwhile as getting choosy about composers and pieces.

In the end, I believe that music is a language of the spirit—its essence can't be captured in words (though it can be useful to try). I like the conclusion of philosopher Suzanne Langer, who called instrumental music "an unconsummated symbol."

The extent of what Langer means by *symbol* is too much to get into here, but the basic idea is that a symbol is a story, painting, image, event, and so on, to which we respond in a complex emotional rather than a directly informational way. That's the difference between *denotation* and *connotation*. A stop sign at an intersection denotes that we should stop. At the same time, it may represent to us all the damn things in the world that tell us what to do, that get in our way, that mess with our lives. Or, on the other hand, it may elicit a comforting feeling of order, the social contract, the need for caution. In each of these cases we're responding to the stop sign's connotations. In other words, we're responding to it as a symbol.

Langer felt that our response to art and much of the rest of life is a texture of symbols, but that instrumental music, lacking words or clear imagery, is a kind of blank slate that we nonetheless respond to *as if* it were a tangible symbol. *What* the symbol is, in any given piece, is largely up to our own responses. So, "an unconsummated symbol."

This is an idea I subscribe to. The thing is, however, that in practice the emotional side of music is much, much more complicated than that. In most vocal music, for example, the words tell us the subject and imply feelings, and most composers want to express the emotional and even physical sense of the words (though sometimes they might write music that inflects or even contradicts the words). In a Schubert song, when the story turns sad, he usually shifts from a major to a minor key; meanwhile he jumps on every image in the text, from a spinning wheel to a tree in the wind, and paints it viscerally in the music.

So, music is expressive of emotion, sometimes in more concrete ways and sometimes in less concrete. Some of that response is cultural, some of it innate. After all, even one-celled animals respond to sound. I suspect that our response to music starts at the cellular level and resonates all the way through our mind up to the higher brain functions. And the most important part of our emotional response is unique to each listener. We can sometimes agree on *what* a piece expresses, but we'll each fill in the details differently. What we feel from music is like what we feel from a sunset. The sunset contains no emotion; it's a physical phenomenon that has nothing to do with us. Maybe the dinosaurs enjoyed them, too. In any case, the feelings are ours, some of them universal to humans, some individual. In the end, the source of such responses is a matter of magic and mystery, and so music echoes the magic and mystery of the universe.

All this is by way of putting gas in the tank. Let's get going on what will be an ambitious but distilled historical journey, starting more or less at the beginning.

PART I

MUSIC FROM THE BEGINNING

Chapter 1

Through the Middle Ages (up to 1400)

Wherever and whenever we find people, we find music. Likely an integral part of human life from the beginning, music has left its traces in instruments and in art dating back to the dawning of our species. The oldest instruments found from the cave days are flutes made from mammoth ivory and bird bones, over forty thousand years old. They have four holes, enough to provide a simple scale. Earlier bones with drilled holes that may be flutes date back over eighty thousand years; their makers were Neanderthals.

All the arts have a primeval connection to magic and mystery, and music is no exception. Animals painted on the walls of caves sanctified shrines that were in use sometimes for thousands of years. Whenever music has emerged from the obscurity of time, it has been connected to ritual, to ceremony, to what we call religion, but to ancient humanity was simply the ambience in which they lived. Instruments and song and painting and poetry and dance probably evolved together. All of them were linked to mystery, the uncanny, the holy.

Sumerian artifacts from the third millennium BC include a lyre whose body is the image of a sacred bull in gold and lapis lazuli. The walls of Egyptian tombs are full of music. In paintings and reliefs we see an array of sophisticated Egyptian instruments: harp, lyre, lute, flute, oboe, trumpet, percussion instruments. We see little bands of servants playing harp and lyre and flute for their mistress; men sitting on the ground, their arms raised in supplication, singing to the accompaniment of a harp; naked girls dancing to the music of a double flute. Singers ushered the dead into the afterlife, their lyrics sometimes written on the tomb:

> *O Royal Seal-bearer, Great Steward, Nebankh!*
> *Yours is the sweet breath of the north wind!*
> *So says his singer who keeps his name alive,*
> *The honorable singer Tjeniaa, whom he loved,*
> *Who sings to his ka every day.*

We don't know what the music of ancient Greeks or Romans sounded like, any more than we do Egyptian music, but again we know their instruments and the lyrics of their songs. Singers and players and dancers disport themselves around Greek pottery. Epic poetry, such as the *Iliad* and *Odyssey*, was meant to be sung, often accompanied by lyre. Every ceremony from temple to marriage to Olympic games had its music, in the approved scale pattern, using the traditional instruments. The choruses of Greek drama danced and sang their poetry (millennia later, Greek theater inspired the creation of opera). There survives a story of a performer on the aulos, a double-piped oboe, who in an amphitheater played a depiction of a battle so powerful that people were still speaking of it two hundred years later.

The Greeks founded musical theory as it exists to this day. The philosopher Pythagoras was the first person we know of to define musical intervals in terms of mathematical divisions of a string: stop a string in the middle and pluck it, and you have an octave; stop it a third of the way and you have a fifth above that, and so on. In white notes on the piano, starting on C is the major scale and A the minor; *modes* are scales starting on the other notes. Greek names for various forms of scales are still with us: the Dorian mode, which Plato says inspires bravery in battle; the Phrygian, which inspires peace; the Lydian, which promotes languor so ought to be avoided. The modes, their names and connotations, survived into the sacred music of the medieval and Renaissance periods.

Later in the West, the Christian Church provided the impetus for the systematic development of music. What we call Gregorian chant, named after Pope Gregory who according to legend codified it in the sixth century, is a pure, unaccompanied repertoire of vocal melody sung in Latin that has graced religious services for over a thousand years. For a sample, look for a chant version of *Veni sancte spiritus*. (If you hear chords in the background, find another version—authentic chant is unaccompanied.)

In the early history of Western music, there have been two epochal developments whose reverberations continue into the present. The first was the development of the world's first effective system of musical notation. Notes finally could be written down like words, reproduced faithfully, and disseminated widely. Earlier civilizations, including the Greeks, had made efforts at notation, but the notes were skimpy and in any case now indecipherable. Around the eleventh century Christian monks developed the basics of writing down notes and rhythms; over the next centuries that evolved into the system of notation we use today.

Notation was more than a practical method for preserving an expanding repertoire of music. It changed the nature of the art itself. To write something down means that people far away in space and time can re-create it. At the same time, there are downsides. Written notes freeze the music rather than allowing it to develop in the hands of individuals, and it discourages improvisation. Partly because of notation, modern classical performance lacks the depth of nuance that is part of aural tradition. Before notation arrived, in all history music was largely carried on as an aural tradition. Most world music is still basically aural, including sophisticated musical traditions such as Indian and Balinese. Most jazz musicians can read music but often don't bother, and their art is much involved with improvisation. Many modern pop musicians, one example being Paul McCartney, can't read music at all.

As a young composer I thought about trying to notate the way jazz legend Miles Davis plays a single note: he might fuzz into it with a half-valve attack, bend the note en route, and/or inflect the pitch as a "blue note," and end with a small slide down. Soon I realized that I would need three or four levels of notation to get all that down, and somebody reading it would never have the fluidity that Davis does in playing from his head. Notes are irreplaceable in our music, but at the same time they can be an obstacle.

In the end, though, the invention of a sophisticated musical notation was a unique event in history that fundamentally changed the equation. When the West committed to notation, it made possible another fundamental development in the history of the art: the invention of counterpoint and harmony. These require a little explanation.

The most common way to understand a piece of music is as a melody with some kind of accompaniment: guy singing with a guitar, soprano with an orchestra, a tune in a string quartet, that sort of thing. This covers most of the music we hear, including essentially all popular music. But in fact there are three ways of presenting melody in a piece, and the name for them is *textures*.

The simplest texture, the kind of music that dominated the world for countless ages and in many places still does, is *monophony*, meaning a single melodic line with no integral accompaniment. One may add drums or a drone or the like, but no harmonies; the tune is essentially the whole thing. This covers everything from the ancient *Iliad* and *Odyssey*, which were sung, to Gregorian chant, including the troubadours of the Middle Ages, most world and folk music from time immemorial, and you singing in the shower (unless you have a guitar in the shower). If the tune's the thing and accompaniment is ad hoc and optional, it's monophony.

When music in more than one part began to happen—which in the West took place around the 800s, because people had only heard monophony, they first developed a new kind of music that was still basically all melody. It happened in stages. Some monasteries began singing monophonic chant in two levels: the same tune sung in parallel lines a fourth or fifth apart. This was called *organum*. An example of later and more sophisticated organum is the beautiful and otherworldly **Winchester Troper**, from the eleventh century.

Over the next centuries these added lines gradually grew more independent. Meanwhile the art of notation became steadily more sophisticated to keep up with pieces that were getting too long and complicated to remember. Finally, music arrived at *polyphony*, meaning two or more melodies that are superimposed, all more or less equally important. The first polyphonic composer whose name we know was a monk named **Léonin**, who worked in Notre Dame in Paris in the twelfth century. In his *Viderunt omnes* you'll find simple but lovely proto-polyphony, much of it florid lines written above drones, those drones being stretched-out notes of a Gregorian chant. Mixed in are stretches of traditional monophonic plainchant and also simple two-part polyphony. It appears that Léonin also made some important advances in notating rhythm.

By the next century at Notre Dame, the monk **Pérotin** was writing elaborate polyphony in four parts. In many ways Pérotin set the pattern for much polyphonic music for centuries to come: you take an existing melody, in his case Gregorian chant, and compose more melodies around it. In Pérotin's case, the chant lines are again stretched out into long drones, over which he wove his voices. (Note that in polyphony each part is called a *voice* whether it is sung or played on an instrument.)

Like the other arts, Renaissance polyphony flourished in splendid and enormously sophisticated forms. This was the golden age of pure polyphony, most of it composed for church (though there were plenty of secular songs and dances, too).

So, that's polyphony, which is a Western invention and specialty. What, then, is *counterpoint*? Actually, sort of the same thing. The terms are often used interchangeably, but strictly speaking, polyphony is the name of a musical texture, and counterpoint is the technique of writing polyphony. In practice, many musicians tend to use *polyphony* to refer to such music written during the Middle Ages and the Renaissance, and *counterpoint* for the baroque period and later. That's how I'll use them here.

So, again: monophony is a single melody; polyphony/ counterpoint is music made of intertwined melodic lines. The third kind of texture, *homophony*, is a single melodic line with chordal accompaniment—back to guy with guitar, leading tune in an orchestral piece, and so forth. In other words, most of the music we hear is homophonic: melody and some kind of harmonic accompaniment.

As soon as polyphony developed, composers realized that you can't just slap tunes together; the results have to sound good, the melodies complementing one another instead of getting in one another's way. Musicians began to develop rules about what kinds of sounds were desirable—in our terms, rules about harmony. In the West, at first, harmony was seen as an incidental effect of polyphony. It was hundreds of years before the kind of harmony we're familiar with had evolved. Early polyphony has an exotic, visceral sound with delicious harmonic clashes that would later be banned. For a sample, try the *Sederunt principes* of the aforementioned twelfth-century monk Pérotin. (One of my favorite versions is one from 1976 by David Munrow and the Early Music Consort of London.) Note that this kind of polyphony, long pieces with thousands of notes, would have been impossible to realize or even conceive of without notation. Here is sacred music joyous and dancing, as if exulting in the boundless potentials of a newly redefined art. Music has been exploring those possibilities ever since.

Again partly thanks to notation, the ensuing music of the medieval period saw an expanding repertoire, much of it with an experimental cast as composers explored techniques of organizing and rationalizing the new polyphony. One early and lasting device was *canon*, meaning a single melody sung or played in staggered entrances, so it makes polyphony with itself. Call canon a kind of grown-up round, such as "Frère Jacques": one voice sings a melody, soon another voice starts the same melody, and in the overlap the single melody makes harmony with itself. A canon does the same thing, but without going around and around. Here's a diagram of a three-voice canon:

MELODY——————————————————————————————————

MELODY——————————————————————————————

MELODY——————————————————————————

This is a straightforward canon, but there are many possible variations. The echoing entries of the melody can start on the same note or on a different degree of the scale. Among the more arcane types are the *inversion canon*, which has the melody alternating right-side up and upside down. There is the odd beast called the *crab canon*, in which the second entry of the melody is backward. (For a composer, this is absurdly difficult to do well.) There are *puzzle canons*, in which a single melody is written out and you have to figure out for yourself where the later entries of the melody start, and/or on what degrees of the scale. In all cases, the result has to make coherent harmony. There are more arcana involved, but let's leave it at that.

The Middle Ages have a reputation for general dreariness and violence, and to be sure, there was a lot of that around. If you were a serf in the fields, life could be pretty nasty, but even serfs had their bagpipes and dancing on feast days.

Those with money and position, however, knew how to have a splashier good time, and music was inevitably involved. This was the time of troubadours and minstrels, wandering singers who made the rounds of town and castle and were vital to any proper whoop-de-do. We know some of their songs and dances because sometimes a monk liked one enough to write it down.

It was in the poetry and song of the Middle Ages that the modern Western idea of love developed, an almost mystical union of two lovers that came to be called courtly love. The highest expression of courtly love was in poetry and music. We've been singing about this stuff ever since.

It was in the context of courtly love that the greatest composer of the Middle Ages emerged: **Guillaume de Machaut**, who was born around 1300 and died much celebrated in Reims in 1377. He was a musician and composer, poet, priest, and courtier; served as secretary and chaplain for the king of Bohemia; and became canon of Reims cathedral. Machaut wrote the first integrated polyphonic setting of the Catholic Mass. My favorite performances of the result, the *Messe de Nostre Dame* are sung in a bright, natural style aiming at how the old monks might have sounded. (The Taverner Consort recording is in that direction, and there's a nicely reedy version by the Ensemble Organum.)

Machaut is most admired for his secular love songs both monophonic (in one voice) and polyphonic. Of his monophonic songs in the troubadour tradition, most famous is the lilting **"Douce dame jolie"** (Fair sweet lady), one of the hits of the era. Fluent in the stylized passion of courtly love poetry, Machaut was also a vital experimenter with technique, including the complex arcana of polyphony. His polyphonic music, far from the tamer and more rule-bound harmony of later centuries, sounds exotic to our ears. The text of his celebrated **"Ma fin est mon commencement"** begins, "My end is my beginning, and my beginning is my end." And indeed one of the parts is a palindrome, in which one voice goes halfway and then reverses course backward to its beginning. This kind of game is plenty hard to master, but to make it elegant and attractive, as Machaut does, is far harder. Rather than recommend particular pieces for this prolific composer, I suggest trying several recordings of his work and looking for the liveliest, most colorful, most beautiful-sounding renditions you can find. One starting place could be his enchanting collection of love songs and poems *Le remède de fortune* (The Cure of Ill Fortune).

How to summarize medieval music as a whole? While a crucial moment in the evolution of classical music, medieval music is much more than a stepping stone to bigger and better pieces. Whether sacred or worldly, the music has a distinctive archaic timbre, often kind of hollow in sound—in many ways the musical equivalent of medieval painting, with its stylized saints and Madonnas in primal colors. It often uses modes rather than our major and minor scales. You'll find Renaissance music richer in sound and more familiar in its harmonies, but if you can get on the wavelength of medieval music, it's as compelling as any—and the dances are robust and irresistible.

Chapter 2

The Renaissance (ca. 1400–1600)

By the fifteenth century the medieval period had given way to the Renaissance, with its revival of learning and humanism. Life in the West did not exactly get less dangerous, but it did get more colorful, maybe even more fun. Epochal developments of the time included the printing press, which revolutionized the dissemination of knowledge. There was a comparable revolution in the arts. Painting saw the development of perspective and an unprecedented realism. In music there was a flowering of magnificent polyphonic sacred works, bolstered by the continuing development of notation. Popular music burgeoned as well; often the same composers wrote both sacred and secular pieces. All composers of the Renaissance wrote music we call *modal*, that is, based on scales beyond the major and minor ones that music largely settled into after the seventeenth century. Modes tend to leave the music less tonally clear, sometimes giving it a floating quality.

The sacred choral works of the Renaissance have a distinctive purity and ethereal beauty. If you died and went to heaven and it sounded like that, it would seem just right—and that was essentially the intention of the composers. The secular music, on the other hand, the dances and love songs, have a fullness of sound that sets them off from medieval music. The work ranges from the sexy chansons of Josquin and others to the variously rowdy and tender work of the English madrigalists, who splendidly set to music some of the finest poetry in the language.

At the summit of the Renaissance musical repertoire stands the art of Franco-Flemish genius **Josquin des Prez**, whose work epitomizes these changes. Josquin absorbed the polyphonic art he inherited from the past and added his own innovations. Dazzling whether writing a traditional polyphonic sacred work or a ribald chanson, Josquin turned away from the exquisite but relatively impersonal church music of the time, bringing to everything he did a distinctive voice that marked him off not only as a master but as a striking personality.

Josquin was born ca. 1440 probably in Condé-sur-l'Escaut, and died there in August 1521, the most celebrated composer of his age. History first catches up with him in his early twenties, as he was beginning over three decades of wandering from one court and chapel job to another around Europe, including five years in the papal chapel in Rome. In his later years he returned to Condé and became provost of the collegiate church.

The few stories of Josquin that survive reveal him as somebody who knew his value and annoyed superiors when he did not jump as ordered. A letter putting forward another composer for a prince's chapel notes, "It is true that Josquin composes better, but he composes when he wants to and not when one wants him to, and he is asking 200 ducats in salary while Isaac will come for 120." (The prince had good taste; Josquin got the job.) Another story has him walking around his choirs as they rehearsed new pieces, making changes on the fly.

A familiar musical form in those days was the *motet*, a sacred choral work of moderate length. Josquin produced some of the greatest of the genre. For an ideal introduction to the depth and breadth of his art, begin with the exquisitely tender *Ave Maria, gratia plena*, one of Josquin's most celebrated motets, and add the elegaic **Absalon, fili mi**. From his secular work try the dashing little chanson **"El grillo"** (The Cricket), with its droll imitations of its subject. In another realm of feeling is the lovely love song, **"Mille regretz"**: "A thousand regrets at deserting you / and leaving behind your loving face."

On the more austere and churchly side of the Renaissance spectrum is the Franco-Flemish **Johannes Ockeghem** (1410–1497), once wrongly thought to have been a teacher of Josquin—though he was an influence on the younger man. Ockeghem was a wizard of a composer, adept in the polyphonic devices of the time, especially elaborate canons. His *Missa prolationum* is made entirely of mensuration canons, a difficult and esoteric technique in which the canonic answer enters faster than the original melody and catches up, so they end together. Ockeghem's *Ave Maria* shows the often dark and intense cast of his work, and his beautiful long-sustained melodies.

Have a listen also to the prolific Flemish master **Orlando di Lasso**, a.k.a. Orlande de Lassus (1530/32–1594). After various peripatetic jobs around Europe, he settled at the court of Duke Albrecht V of Bavaria in Munich. Lassus was another composer equally adept at sacred and secular music. For a sample of his lighter things, try a couple of his many irresistible madrigals. **"Bonjour mon coeur"** (Good day, dear heart) is an exhilarating stretch of verbal and musical flirting. The lyric of **"Matona, mia cara"** depicts an attempt at seduction by an occupying German soldier serenading an Italian lady—"Matona" is his attempt at "Madonna." He assures her that if she comes downstairs, he's man enough to *ficar tutte notte*. Some performances censor this text—avoid those. Among the sacred works of Lassus is the *Lagrime di San Pietro*, completed weeks before he died. Wielding the old polyphonic style with his customary vigor, he sets a collection of verses of eccentric religious obsession: each lyric concerns the same moment, when the disciple Peter meets the eyes of the risen Christ and feels the full weight of his betrayal. (All the aforementioned Renaissance composers and some of the noted pieces can be heard on the Hilliard Ensemble's recorded compendium *Franco-Flemish Masterworks*.)

Finally there's the legendary **Giovanni Perluigi da Palestrina** (1525–1594), whose sacred music is the distillation of Renaissance polyphony, the purest and most serene music of the era. In its polished perfection it became the main model for the study of writing polyphony, and it remains so today. The most famous of Palestrina's many mass settings is the *Missa Pappae Marcelli* (Pope Marcellus Mass), not just because of the music but because of an old myth that the piece forestalled an edict by the Council of Trent banning polyphonic music in services. That isn't so, but if anybody could have saved polyphony had it needed saving, Palestrina was the man.

Now we'll move on to more familiar territory, the grand and dramatic work of the baroque, whose leading figures are two of the giants of all time: Bach and Handel.

Part II

Baroque

Chapter 3

THE BAROQUE PERIOD (CA. 1600–1750)

The word *baroque*, originally referring to a misshapen pearl, eventually became a term of derision for the florid architecture of the seventeenth century, which was out of fashion in the next generation. Among other things, the grandiose style of baroque churches, with their cloudy decoration, their painted ceilings seeming to stretch up to a heaven teeming with angels, was part of an initiative by the Catholic Church to challenge the appeal of the Protestant Revolution with grandeur to dazzle the senses. As often happens, over time baroque lost its negative connotations and simply became a label for the period.

In music, the baroque we're concerned with started in Italy around 1600, when a group of intellectuals known as the Florentine Camerata resolved to re-create ancient Greek drama—which they understood to be stories entirely sung. Their historical knowledge was dicey, so in practice they created an entirely new kind of artwork: *opera*, sung drama. Along with this new medium came a revolution in musical texture. In early opera the music was considered entirely the servant of the text and story. Declaring that Renaissance-style polyphony was not able to express concise emotions in a drama, the Camerata created a style in which a text was recited in a kind of singsong over simple harmonies, what was called *recitative*.

In terms of musical texture the result was a generally new kind of music we call *homophony*, which as previously noted refers to a single tune with chordal accompaniment—in other words, what has been the main definition of a song or instrumental piece ever since. As a result, harmony, which had always been seen as a kind of by-product of polyphony, now took on a new significance in itself. Composers began to think of harmony as a progression of chords. Often in early opera only the voice part and the instrumental bass line were written down; from the bass line and number symbols representing the chords, keyboard players improvised the accompaniment. This "figured bass" was much like a modern song lead sheet, which has only the tune and chord symbols.

In the seventeenth century Claudio Monteverdi called the old polyphonic style "first practice" and modern homophony "second practice." Monteverdi did not write the first operas, only the first great ones—*Orfeo* and *The Coronation of Poppea*. He began the process of moving beyond virtually all-recitative operas, in which the text was king and the music relatively simple, to richer musical fabric: songful and expressive arias, choruses, colorful instrumental accompaniments. Recitative persisted in opera into the nineteenth century, but more and more the musical elements and therefore musical interest tended to edge it out, until by the late eighteenth century Mozart declared the music in his operas more important than the words.

Still, polyphony, a.k.a. counterpoint, never died out. Both homophony and counterpoint coexisted, often in the same piece. Baroque composer Handel wrote plenty of tuneful homophonic music but was also a master of counterpoint. The supreme genius of counterpoint was a contemporary of Handel: Johann Sebastian Bach, who died in 1750. Bach's dedication to counterpoint marked him as a backward-looking composer among his colleagues, though he was also intensely aware of opera and other contemporary trends.

Bach was history's greatest writer of the contrapuntal procedure called fugue, another term that requires explanation. A *fugue* is a contrapuntal procedure/genre that was often used in the baroque, but was so effective and flexible that it lasted into the twentieth century: high-modernist Béla Bartók began his Music for Strings, Percussion, and Celesta with a massive fugue. A fugue can have any number of voices/lines, but usually involves three to five. It is based on a scrap of tune called the *subject*. The idea is that the subject gets passed from voice to voice, each voice picking it up like a topic in a conversation.

In practice the matter is more complicated. For one thing, in some (not all) fugues there's a *countersubject*, which is another scrap of melody that accompanies the subject throughout. Each time a new voice picks up the subject, the preceding voice continues on with the countersubject. Here's a diagram of the beginning of a three-voiced fugue with countersubject:

SUBJECT————COUNTERSUBJECT——(FREE)————*etc.*
　　　SUBJECT——————COUNTERSUBJECT—*etc.*
　　　　　SUBJECT——————*etc.*

As you see, after each voice has stated subject and counter-subject, it goes on to mess around on its own. Meanwhile the entries of the subject are not all in the same key; the entries change keys as the fugue progresses. While all this pertains to the melodic lines, the whole shebang also has to make effective harmony, otherwise it would sound like random nonsense. As musicians put it, you have constantly to reconcile the demands of the *horizontal* (melody) and the *vertical* (harmony).

If all this seems complex and hard to manage for the poor composer, it bloody well is. Fugue and canon are some of the most difficult musical disciplines, which is why so many composers have been challenged and fascinated by them. And this is only the simplest form a fugue can take.

The diagram lays out what is called an *exposition* section in a fugue, which means a stretch where the subject is entering. Every fugue has several expositions, usually spaced by what are called *episodes*, which are sections of free counterpoint with no subject entries—but using material derived from the subject. So, in its large form a fugue will progress in the pattern exposition–episode–exposition–episode . . . , moving through various keys, for as long as you like. At the end there may be an exciting effect called a *stretto* (the Italian means "tight"), where the entries of the subject come in sooner, before each has finished, as if in its eagerness to be heard the subject steps on the heels of its twin. If a composer wants to end with a stretto, he or she has to plan it from the beginning in creating a subject that will allow for the effect. (Good counterpoint rarely happens by happy accident.)

There can also be *double fugues*, *triple fugues*, and so on, in which there is more than one subject in the course of the piece. All this describes a freestanding fugue. But any number of works, such as movements of symphonies and string quartets, have integrated fugal sections. Those sections often don't have complex structures involving episodes, strettos, and the like; they can be a *fughetta* (little fugue) or *fugato* (fugue-ish).

With enough brain-breaking practice and a modicum of talent, any composer can learn to write canons and fugues. Thousands have been written over the centuries, many of them clever and technically impeccable. The trouble is, most of them are boring, because in addition to the daunting technical requirements, the piece is of little use if it doesn't also manage to be expressive—to be moving, charming, amusing, those kinds of things that we expect of music.

This is where the supremacy of J. S. Bach in contrapuntal music comes in. He seems to have had an Einsteinian sort of mind that could handle the most outlandish difficulties of fugue and canon with ease: whole fugues that are heard rightside up, then upside down; he produced fiendishly obscure puzzle canons; and so on. But as Bach told his composer sons: *never do anything, not even a little chorale harmonization, that does not say something.* In other words, that is not expressive, and in the case of a text, expressive of the feelings and images of that text.

Very few composers have had the gift of making complex counterpoint warm and human, as Bach did. A wonderful example of this is in his jazzy and dazzling **Contrapunctus IX**, a double fugue with inversions of the subject, from **The Art of Fugue**. That latter collection, a chain of fugues of increasing complexity all featuring the same subject, is one of the most esoteric pieces ever written, and yet it speaks to audiences in the most compelling and visceral way.

Another important formal pattern of the baroque period was the *concerto grosso* (big concerto), which sets off a small group of instruments against a larger group. The full group is called the *tutti* (meaning "everybody"); the solo group, the *soli*. The form of a concerto grosso is simple. It begins with a tutti, everybody playing an expansive tune on which the whole piece will be based; then there is a section for the soli, answered by the tutti on a bit of the opening theme; and so on: tutti–soli–tutti–soli–tutti . . . until you're done. Meanwhile the music changes key here and there for the sake of tonal variety, and at the end, everybody joins in on a big restatement of the full theme in the home key. Baroque concertos for solo instrument follow the same pattern. Handel and Bach wrote some supreme examples, such as the latter's six Brandenburg Concertos.

The baroque also saw a new interest in instrumental music (without vocals) and with writing music particular to the instruments that are playing it. In the Renaissance the instruments used in a piece tended to be somewhat ad hoc, because vocal and instrumental lines were written pretty much the same. In the baroque arrived schools of violin playing, of keyboard playing, and the like. Composers were concerned for the first time with writing, say, idiomatic fiddle music as distinct from flute music, flute music as distinct from vocal music, and so on. In a natural corollary, there was a new emphasis on instrumental and vocal virtuosity. At the same time, however, while the baroque had lots of orchestral music (and the Renaissance none) there was as yet no standard makeup of the band. You picked the instruments you wanted for a given piece and/or what instrumentalists you had at hand—music in those days was often performed as soon as the ink was dry.

This new emphasis on instrumental music led to a new concern with ways of organizing music, which is to say with "abstract" musical form. The old procedures of fugue and canon were still around, but we also see the forms and rhythms of dance music getting into big pieces, leading to such things as Bach's solo violin and cello works put together in dance genres of the time—allemande, sarabande, gigue, chaconne, and the like, each with its allied rhythms and moods.

It was the florid grandeur of composers such as Bach and Handel in their large works that allied them with the atmosphere of baroque churches. Tonally, Baroque counterpoint was distinct from the older Renaissance polyphony in being richer in sound, more concerned with harmony and concise progressions of chords. To our ears baroque harmony sounds more modern than it did in the Renaissance; it uses the familiar major and minor scales rather than modes, and in its course it changes keys more often. Meanwhile, especially in eighteenth-century Germany, composers adopted a "doctrine of the affections," in which a vocabulary of gestures in the melody, harmony, and rhythm were used to represent more or less specific emotions. Each movement of a work was founded on one basic musical idea and one expressive affect. An example is the **Crucifixus of Bach's Mass in B Minor**, with its mournful descending bass line.

Baroque music ranges from grand and magisterial to intimate, depending on the forces and the expression. How to tell a baroque piece by ear? I can't provide a handy guide to that other than to say when you've listened to some Handel and Bach and Vivaldi, you'll learn to recognize the sound, because among them they epitomized the period. You'll notice that, after the Renaissance, music got bigger, grander, more colorful in sound and harmony, and more expressive. The Renaissance went for an exquisite realization of something within limited means; the baroque went for lavish.

In brief, to understand the baroque you need to look at the invention of opera and the musical chain of events it unleashed. The new emphasis on a single melodic line with some kind of accompaniment, whether simple or florid, led in turn to all kinds of developments: solo song in its many manifestations, more elaborate and idiomatic instrumental music, a more harmonically controlled kind of counterpoint, and a new concern with form. What we call a *song* had been born.

Chapter 4

CLAUDIO MONTEVERDI (1567–1643)

A rtistic genius comes in many flavors. Some blossom early, such as Schubert and Mozart; some late, such as Verdi and Dvořák. Some, such as Charles Ives, seem to come out of nowhere; others, such as Berlioz, are the distillation of their times. A special category belongs to the giants who bestride two ages, one foot in the past and the other in the future. One such genius was Claudio Monteverdi, who was a master of Renaissance polyphonic style he inherited from Palestrina and Josquin, but equally an innovator who brought unprecedented vitality to the revolutionary ideas of his time.

Born in Mantua in May 1567, Monteverdi began publishing his work in his teens. At twenty-three he entered the service of the splendiferous Gonzaga court in Mantua, working his way up through the ranks until he became head of court music at age thirty-five. Meanwhile he assimilated the ideas of the progressive composers around him who were moving beyond the old contrapuntal art toward a heightened emotional realism.

In 1603 and 1605 Monteverdi published two pioneering books of madrigals (small vocal pieces for usually two to five voices, intended for domestic music-making). Many of them are striking for their intense expressiveness, their angular

melodies and dissonant harmonies. Their radical emotionalism famously incited a bitter attack from a conservative
theorist named Artusi: "Such composers . . . have nothing but
smoke in their heads if they are so impressed with themselves
as to think they can corrupt, abolish, and ruin at will the
good old rules handed down from days of old." Monteverdi, a
feisty guy in the best of times, did not take the critique lying
down. In 1605 he published a robust defense of himself and
his fellow progressives that at once made history and cinched
his fame. There are two "practices," he said: one, the old polyphonic sacred style of Palestrina et al., in which the music is
more important than the text; the other, contemporary music
that aspires to a new directness and expressiveness in expressing its text. Monteverdi himself was master of both styles,
and used them all his life. He did not write the first operas,
but his *Orfeo* of 1607 is the first masterpiece of the genre. He
used pizzicatos (plucking the strings) to illustrate the clash of
swords; he later invented the string tremolo, a twitching of the
bow, to indicate trembling and intense emotion.

In listening to Monteverdi's madrigals, one can chart a path
to his mature operas and other dramatic works. As an introduction, try his scintillating madrigal *Zefiro torna* for two voices
and instruments (not to be confused with his five-voice madrigal
of the same name). The text talks about summer breezes, about
love and loneliness. Monteverdi set the poem in spiraling vocal
lines set over a vigorous repeating bass line. The singers portray
winds, longing, sex, in an impetuous and constantly changing
collaboration and competition. (I recommend the ripsnorting
version on YouTube by the L'Arpeggiata ensemble.)

After years of dissatisfaction in Mantua, the death of
his wife, periods of depression and fitful production, in 1613

Monteverdi secured the grandest musical job in Italy, director of music at St. Mark's Basilica in Venice. There, in his midforties, Monteverdi began the most remarkable and happiest phase of his life—or as happy as a depressive sort like him could manage. By then, more or less as a portfolio when he was looking for a job, he wrote the towering *Vespers of the Blessed Virgin*, a.k.a. the Vespers of 1610. It begins with a breathtaking fanfare alternating with a dance, announcing itself not as a work of inward piety, but rather a product of the Catholic Counterreformation, to dazzle worshipers with splendor and spectacle. The Vespers is a work ranging far in emotions, but its foundation is in joy, and the prime source of its musical style the dramatic and humanistic world of his operas. Listen to the lusty, lilting **"Laudate, pueri Dominum,"** the music shifting nimbly moment to moment to capture the text. In **"Duo seraphim"** the voices weave a quietly magical, hypnotic tapestry. For me and I suspect for many, there are four supreme landmarks among major choral works: Bach's Mass in B Minor and *St. Matthew Passion*, Handel's *Messiah*, and the Monteverdi Vespers.

Monteverdi's *Orfeo* of 1607 has a depth of passion and drama unprecedented in opera to that time. Here he showed his gift for painting character, story, and movement on the big stage. From the operas, try the astonishing *Coronation of Poppea*, part of what astonishes being that Monteverdi produced it at age seventy-five. Here on display is everything he could do: tender love songs and lively dances, humor, tragedy, you name it, all brought off with his characteristically versatile style. The story is no less astounding: the monstrous emperor Nero drives his mentor Seneca to suicide, puts aside his wife, and crowns the prostitute Poppea as his wife and empress.

Their final love song may actually be by another composer, but in any case it is one of the most beautiful pieces in the world. In the opera it represents the triumph of evil.

Monteverdi's many letters and their extravagant personality make him the first composer who seems to appear before us as a whole person. One overworked response to his employer: "My usual powers . . . are still in a weakened state . . . and so feeble that not medicine, nor diet, nor the interrupting of studies have restored them . . . I shall then entreat Your Serene Highness for the love of God not to burden me ever again with so much business at once."

At the end of his years, Monteverdi had lost none of his youthful brio, also none of his jaundiced view of life at the same time as he captured and celebrated every part of life in his music. He was the most celebrated composer of his age, but fifty years after he died, his work was largely forgotten and much of it lost. His revival only began in the late nineteenth century. Some of Monteverdi's output, groundbreaking at the time, is dated now, but the best of it has a vitality that will never get old.

More Monteverdi: The opera *Orfeo*.

Chapter 5

Johann Sebastian Bach (1685–1750)

Really, there is no explanation for Johann Sebastian Bach. He himself would have attributed his gift to God, but that only raises another mystery to account for what he achieved. He might also have mentioned science, because in one of his few surviving statements about music he called it "an art and a science." He considered music to be a matter of rules and definable phenomena: say, with a given fugue subject you can do this but you can't do that. But though Bach knew as much about notes as anyone ever has, and was clearly a gifted teacher because three of his sons became important composers, none of his pupils ever achieved anything like what he did. Which is to say that in the end, Bach himself didn't know how he did it.

If that sounds kind of moony, that's because for me and for many musicians, Bach is a figure of awe. The fact that we know so little about his life and personality only magnifies the mystery. How could he think in such complexities and make his music so moving, so delightful, so directly communicative?

Inevitably it is noted that Bach is a testament to the reality of inborn talent. He came from a family so prolific with musicians that in Thuringia, their home territory, musicians regardless of name tended to be called a "Bach." Yet none of the Bachs before him is much remembered in history. He likely had teachers in performance, but as a composer he seems to have been self-taught. He simply took to notes with the same kind of brilliance and instinctive understanding that Einstein did to numbers. Temperamentally conservative, he was not an inventor of genres and forms; instead, he absorbed the models around him and brought nearly the whole spectrum of baroque music into a unique synthesis.

Johann Sebastian Bach was born in the town of Eisenach, his father a town string player. The family was surrounded by Bachs in musical posts all over the map. His parents died during his childhood and he was taken in by his eldest brother, Johann Christoph, an organist in Ohrdruf. From this brother Johann Sebastian probably received his first keyboard training.

At eighteen, already a brilliant performer, he got his first church organist job in Arnstadt. He stayed there for four years, but failed to earn the affection of local authorities. Among other offenses, after he secured a month's leave to hear the celebrated organist and composer Dietrich Buxtehude in Lübeck, a walk of 200 miles, he lingered there for four months listening to his hero. There were some words when he got back. Meanwhile, his superiors complained that his hymn accompaniments were too complicated and confused the congregation, and besides, he wasn't writing enough music. Then there was his street brawl with an orchestra player whom he had called a "nanny-goat bassoonist." Bach seems to have been an affable man on the whole, sociable, a leader and a valued colleague, a fine dad to his children, but when it came to his music he was prickly and proud, especially if he felt undervalued by his employers.

In 1707 Bach escaped to a job in Mühlhausen, where he married his cousin Maria Barbara and they got busy making babies. (Of Bach's eventual twenty children, ten made it to adulthood, a normal percentage for the time.) In these years he wrote his first masterpieces, including the most famous organ piece in the world, the *Phantom of the Opera* one: **Toccata and Fugue in D Minor**. This hair-raising work is a good sample of Bach's youthful style: melodramatic, dissonant, the toccata stream of consciousness, all of it overflowing with passion and youthful bravado. Bach may have been the greatest organist who ever lived, noted for finding new colors on the instrument, and hearing him do this live must have been a devastating experience. He was also a phenomenal improviser, able to invent on the organ a six-voiced fugue on the spot.

Once again, though, in Mühlhausen Bach and the authorities got on one another's nerves; he didn't like the conditions or the pay. In 1708 he took a job at the court of the Duke of Weimar and stayed until 1717. It was during this period that he began studying and arranging the work of his Italian contemporary Antonio Vivaldi, who taught him clarity and directness, giving focus to his predisposition to complex counterpoint. (Try the sparkling **Concerto for Four Harpsichords BWV 1065**, his arrangement of a Vivaldi concerto, which he transforms into a kind of aviary excursion.) This job didn't end all that well, either. Disgusted at being passed over as court music director, Bach secured a plum job heading the music for a princely court in Köthen. After "too stubbornly forcing the issue of his dismissal," Bach found himself clapped in jail for a month before he could move on.

The years at Köthen may have been the happiest period of Bach's life. Prince Leopold loved music and admired his music director. In these years Bach wrote a huge quantity of mostly secular music, including some of his most celebrated works: the **Brandenburg Concertos**, the **sonatas and partitas for solo violin and solo cello**, and the epochal *Well-Tempered Clavier*, **Book 1**. All these works are splendid from first note to last, a kind of compendium not only of what instruments can do, but what music itself can do.

In relation to *The Well-Tempered Clavier*, we need a digression here. As part of his attention to every dimension of music, Bach was highly and historically concerned about the sticky issue of keyboard tuning. Explaining what I mean by *sticky* will take a while.

In dealing with tuning, there are two main terms to know. One is *interval*. It means the distance between notes. Intervals are also mathematical ratios. If you take an open guitar string sounding E, stop it with your finger in the middle, and pluck, you get E an octave above. The octave ratio, then, is 2:1. If you stop the string in the ratio 3:2, you get a fifth higher than the open string, the note B. The other intervals have progressive ratios; 4:3 is a fourth, and so on.

Now comes the gods' great joke on musicians. If you start with a C at the bottom of a piano keyboard and tune a series of twelve perfect 3:2 fifths up to the top, you discover that where you expect to have returned to a perfect high C, that C is overshot, intolerably out of tune. In other words, nature's math doesn't add up. A series of perfect intervals doesn't end at a perfect interval from where you started. It is this surreal irreconcilability of pitch that, through the centuries, has driven musicians nuts.

What all this means in practice is that in tuning keyboards and fretted instruments, you have to screw around with the intervals to fit the necessary notes into an octave. (None of this applies to instruments like violin or to singing, where you can tune each note on the fly.) In other words, as we say, on keyboard instruments you have to *temper* pure intervals, nudge them up or down a hair in some systematic way. Otherwise, you get chaos. So, there's the second word you need to remember: The business of adapting tuning to nature's messy math is called *temperament*. And now we're halfway to understanding Bach's *Well-Tempered Clavier*: it has to do with the art and science of keyboard tuning.

Before Bach's time, dozens of keyboard-tuning systems had been created, but they resulted in only fourteen workable keys. The rest of the twenty-four possible major and minor keys simply weren't used in keyboard music because they were intolerably out of tune. And no scale on a keyboard, not even good old C major, can be perfectly in tune. If you want your fifths nicely in tune, the thirds can't be; if you want pure thirds, you have to put up with impure fifths. Medieval tunings voted for pure fifths. By the late Renaissance, the tuning systems favored better thirds. The latter were various kinds of *mean-tone* temperament. In mean-tone, most of the accumulated fudges were dumped onto two notes, usually G-sharp (a.k.a. A-flat) and E-flat. The A-flat in particular sounded so out of tune that it was called the "wolf." You didn't write in the key of A-flat for keyboard, and generally tried to skirt the note entirely.

Between the sixteenth and eighteenth centuries a lot of splendid music was written in mean-tone tuning, within that range of fourteen acceptable major and minor keys. But the inability to write in all twenty-four possible keys ate at composers' guts. More and more, there was a demand for a tuning system that would render all keys usable.

One of those tuning systems was already known to the ancients: *equal temperament*. Here the poison is distributed equally through the system: the distance between each adjacent note is mathematically the same, so each interval is equally in, and slightly out of, tune. Nothing is perfect; nothing is terrible. So, now it's all fixed, yes?

Of course not. The gods don't let us off so easily. For centuries, equal temperament didn't catch on because musicians tended not to like it. Most especially, musicians didn't like the fat major thirds of equal temperament, which are way out of tune with nature. They preferred the sweet thirds of mean-tone temperaments, with all their limitations. For another thing, in mean-tone each key had an audible personality, from, say, the almost-pure and upstanding C major, suitable to moods of equanimity and celebration, to shadowy C minor, suitable for doubt and despair. Equal temperament leaves every key with exactly the same personality, which was widely felt to be boring. Musicians still preferred, then, the old varieties of what is generically called *unequal temperament*.

In the late seventeenth century, tuning geeks came up with a new idea: let's hair-split all over the keyboard, tweaking this and that in minuscule ways, letting, say, a third be a bit larger in one spot and a bit smaller in another. These kinds of flexible temperaments accomplished several things at once: (1) they made all keys usable; (2) yet they preserved the individual character of keys, because each still had its distinctive collection of intervals; and (3) they tamed the big bad wolf. Hey, said adherents of this more sophisticated unequal system, this really works well! So, they called it *well-temperament*. One of those adherents was J. S. Bach. He wanted, he said somewhat testily, to write in any damn key he felt like, and he tuned his harpsichord himself to make that possible. When a famous organ tuner who did mean-tone tuning showed up, Bach would play an A-flat major chord on one of his organs, with its howling wolf, just to torture the old man. Eventually, though, history stepped in: by the third decade of the nineteenth century equal temperament had more or less triumphed because it was best at handling the increasing harmonic complexity Beethoven and his heirs were exploring.

Back to *The Well-Tempered Clavier* (*clavier* meaning any kind of keyboard instrument), as art rather than science. Bach wrote the preludes and fugues of the *WTC* in all twenty-four possible keys. Not only does this collection show off this improved tuning system, but Bach helped make well-temperament mandatory by writing irreplaceable pieces in every key. Anybody who wanted to play from the *WTC* was pressured to use well-temperament, because many of the pieces sounded sour in any other tuning. However, heh-heh, there's no reliable record of which well-tempered system Bach used, though it probably was not equal temperament.

For a sample of the *WTC*, start at the beginning. The little Prelude in C Major that starts the set is one of Bach's most famous and beloved pieces (it was reportedly a favorite of his, too), yet what appears to be a simple rippling up and down on chords disguises a complex interweaving of melodies. It prefaces a gently lyrical fugue. Then the Prelude in C Minor explodes in a kind of faux-demonic fury, rattling strenuously from beginning to end, followed by an impish and intricate C-minor fugue. The Prelude in C-sharp Major that follows is one of the most happy-making pieces in the world. And so on. Looking further into the piece, listen to the massive Prelude in B-flat Minor, a long-breathed mournful aria. In these ways the *WTC* surveys the spectrum of human feeling, and the spectrum of what music can do in expressing it. It is one of the wellsprings of all Western music that followed it. One of the first musicians to grow up playing the *WTC* was Beethoven, and it's among the reasons he became what he did. (The many available recordings of the piece include both harpsichord and piano, and either can be equally effective. But I entreat you, skip the synths, Japanese kotos, didgeridoos, and other versions we used to call "schlock Bach." I'll allow an exception for the effervescent scat-sung Bach by the Swingle Singers, from the 1960s.)

Another of his legendary keyboard works is the **Goldberg Variations**, made up of thirty contrasting variations on an aria. Even before the Bach revival of the nineteenth century, this was considered the greatest of its genre; when Beethoven's *Diabelli Variations* were published, they were compared with the *Goldbergs*. The work's modern reputation was created practically overnight in 1955 in a crystalline recording by the young Glenn Gould.

In the summer of 1720 Bach returned from a journey with his prince to find his wife Maria Barbara had died. (Some have speculated that his tragic **Chaconne** for solo violin was a memorial for her.) The next year he married the young singer Anna Magdalena Wilcke. She bore him thirteen more children and beyond that was a fine helpmate; some of his later manuscripts are in her hand. His affection is shown in the collection of winsome little harpsichord pieces he assembled for her, the *Notebook for Anna Magdalena Bach.*

Spring of 1723 found Bach in a new job, as director of Lutheran church music for Leipzig. The city was an arts center rivaling Paris, the position extremely prestigious. Still, Bach had been the third choice for the job, securing it only after two more-famous composers had turned it down. From that point some of his employers tended to look at him as third-rate in general, which led to contrapuntal aggravations in the following decades. Bach never traveled far from home and did not publish much, so he never had the wide reputation of broadly popular composers such as Handel. Eventually he became the dominant musical figure in Leipzig, but elsewhere except for the occasional enthusiast, not much more than a name. In his last years Bach had the pleasure of being received and praised by one of his fans, Frederick the Great of Prussia, who was an avid flute player. Afterward Bach wrote *The Musical Offering,* a series of pieces based on a theme the king gave him.

Based at the Thomas Church, Bach had also to supply music for three other churches, and was expected to compose steadily. At the same time he was much involved in town music-making. In the first years he sometimes wrote a church cantata every week, meaning fifteen to twenty-five minutes of music composed, copied, rehearsed, and performed in the course of seven days. An oratorio is more or less an unstaged opera, with recitatives and arias and choruses, and a cantata is like a miniature oratorio. Of his over two hundred surviving cantatas inevitably some are less inspired, but there are countless glories in them. It was a killing job, but Bach carried it out with indefatigable energy and a burning determination always

to put out the best that he was capable of. Many of his manuscripts have tiny holes where revisions were pinned in; they
have all been lost.

A good introduction to his surviving cantatas is *Wachet
auf, ruft uns die Stimme* (Awake, the voice is calling). Like all
of them, this is based around a single Lutheran chorale melody; the cantata ends with the hymn. Throughout, this is Bach
at his most buoyant. It's worth looking up this piece on Wikipedia or the like to get the text and context: it's for a service
that symbolically joins Christ as bridegroom of the church, so
the whole thing is portrayed with matrimonial warmth.

As a sample of Bach's singular approach to expressing
a text, have a listen to one of my favorite of his arias, **"Wie
zittern und wanken"** from the cantata *Herr, gehe nicht ins
Gericht* (Lord, do not pass judgment). The text portrays sinners trembling before the judgment seat of God, repeating
themselves, accusing one another of their own sins—dark Lutheran stuff. Bach paints every part of that scene: the string
accompaniment is a tremolo, so they tremble; the solo oboe
repeats a phrase over and over, like the sinners; there is no
bass, so the sinners have no foundation. Yet this is some of the
most beautiful and touching music he ever wrote, its keynote
not vengeance but pity.

The largest works to recommend for Bach are the obvious
ones, because they stand at the summit of the entire choral
repertoire. Bach never took up opera, but he absorbed it along
with everything else, and put operatic drama and emotion
into his *St. Matthew Passion*, originally from 1727 and later
revised. A *passion* is an oratorio whose subject is the suffering
and death of Christ. Here his forces are vocal soloists, including an Evangelist who tells the story, with double choir and

orchestra for echoing effects. The throbbing opening chorus is a tapestry of mourning, beginning, "Come ye daughters, help me lament." Here and in all his sacred music Bach treats the familiar biblical story as a universal human drama. The *St. Matthew* evokes the universal experience of loss: we all lose loved ones, all suffer, all die. Bach rests his work on that inescapable tragedy. The music is alternatively sorrowful and gently consoling, held together by the recitatives of the Evangelist, the words of Jesus (always surrounded by a symbolic halo of strings), and the Lutheran chorales that turn up among the movements. We stand beside the cross, participate in Christ's suffering, grieve for his death. Listen to No. 75, the bass aria **"Mache dich mein Herze rein,"** with its poignant refrain "I will myself bury Jesus." (Avoid versions that take this sorrowful movement at lively dance tempo, which these days is common and unfortunate.) This is perhaps the greatest of oratorios, rivaled only by Handel's *Messiah*.

At the end of his life, in 1748–1749 Bach pulled together earlier movements written for various works, added new material, and created the **Mass in B Minor.** He probably never heard it complete in his lifetime because it is a full Catholic Mass, with movements the Lutheran service doesn't use, and at some two hours it's too long for a Catholic service. Why would Bach undertake such a thing? It may have been another tour de force like *The Art of Fugue* that he wanted to leave for posterity. For Bach, the mass was the most important of all musical genres. It was the perfect canvas for him to show everything he could do, musically and expressively. Its ancient text contains the deepest despair and the wildest joy, the mystical and the lyrical: every corner of life and of religion. And religion was at the center of Bach's life. Despite its checkered sources, the result is of a piece, for many of us not just the summit of sacred music but of all music.

Perhaps start not with the whole piece but a sampling to show its astonishing range. After an introduction the Mass begins with a massive and solemn fugue on Kyrie eleison. The No. 4 Gloria in excelsis is a dancing explosion of joy. It's a good test of a recorded performance: if it isn't one of the most glorious things you've ever heard, try another one. No. 8, Domine Deus, begins with an enchanting flute melody whose gentleness carries through the movement. In the center is the anguished Crucifixus, depicting the Crucifixion in grinding dissonances and perpetually falling lines. At the end it descends into the grave and silence. From that erupts the *Et resurrexit*, an ecstasy of joy flashing with trumpets.

Bach's end in July 1750 was sad, but he met it on his terms. He had been working on the epic **Art of Fugue**, a compendium of pieces all based on a single theme that was intended to demonstrate everything he had learned about fugue. He was not to finish the last piece. In it he had worked in his own name as a countersubject, which in German notation are the notes B-flat, A, C, and B. They were some of the last notes he wrote with his own hand. On his deathbed, blind and suffering, he dictated to a pupil a revision of one of his organ works, which he renamed **Vor deinen Thron tret' ich allhier** (Before Thy Throne I Stand). It was his calling card to God.

I was reared on the old tradition that said Bach was forgotten for a hundred years after he died. In fact, while the major works were not heard, *The Well-Tempered Clavier* and other smaller works kept his name alive. When Beethoven first arrived in Vienna, he made his early reputation as a virtuoso partly by playing the *WTC*, which was known to connoisseurs. Although he knew sadly little of the music, Beethoven understood Bach's significance: "He should not be named Bach [which in German means "brook"] but rather ocean!" The nineteenth-century Bach revival took off in earnest with Felix Mendelssohn's historic performance of the *St. Matthew Passion* in 1829, the first time it had been heard since Bach's lifetime. The first complete edition of Bach's music took the rest of the century to finish.

One more point. Many would agree that the supreme artists in the Western musical tradition are Bach, Mozart, and Beethoven. There is a nice symmetry to that group because they are three different kinds of composers: Bach the conservative, called old-fashioned in his time; Mozart, the au courant artist, completely involved in his time; Beethoven, who from early on was called a revolutionary (though he never called himself that). Which is to say that there is no pattern for genius and inspiration, any more than there is ultimately any explanation for them. We try to explain all we can, but in the end genius is a profound mystery, even to its possessors. We can only look on and marvel.

More Bach: Magnificat in D; the suites for solo cello and violin; the Brandenburg Concertos; Harpsichord Concerto No. 1 in D Minor; cantata *Ein feste Burg ist unser Gott*.

Chapter 6

GEORGE FRIDERIC HANDEL (1685–1759)

G eorge Frideric Handel was the first composer in Western history who never had to be rediscovered, mainly
because by the time he died his oratorio *Messiah* had already
attained the legendary status it has never lost. Up to Handel's time music was written for the present and was largely
expected to fade away after the creator died. But because of
him, the next generation of composers began to realize that
their music could become part of a permanent repertoire. In
his time Handel was something on the order of an international superstar, an opera composer and impresario and traveling virtuoso. Corpulent, slovenly, obstinate, he composed in
a manic frenzy often followed by collapse. In his last years,
when he was blind and ill but still performing, his audience
saw him as a myth still living before their eyes and ears.

There's an old story about Handel, perhaps apocryphal
but indicative. In the middle of the night, one of his librettists
was awakened by a German-accented ruckus in the street. He
staggered to the window to find Handel in a carriage shouting: "In your text, vot is 'billows'?" Shaking off sleep, the librettist explained that a billow is a wave on the ocean. "Aha!"
cried Handel. "Ze vafe! Ze big vafe!" And he went back home

to work. He couldn't compose the word until he knew what it meant, literally and viscerally. You can be sure that his music for billows was wavelike on a grand scale.

In the history of musical illustration, Handel looms large. He was the most extravagant of his time—and yet, as we see in *Messiah*, he was also capable of making his pictorial touches so thoroughly musical that many people never notice them. For instance, in the aria "Every valley shall be exalted," from *Messiah* those words are expressed by a melodic line mounting to exaltation. Then comes "the crooked straight"—a jagged line ending in a sudden held note—and "the rough places plain," another jagged section that smooths into a plain, drifting line.

When Handel got hold of a juicy image, he could not resist. In the oratorio *Israel in Egypt* he plays the plagues for comedy. "There came all manner of flies," declaims the chorus—and the strings erupt in buzzing. When the soprano sings, "Their land brought forth froooogs, froooogs," a singer in on the joke will croak in a musical yet illustrative manner. Meanwhile her accompaniment is hopping, hopping, hopping.

Born Georg Friedrich Händel in Halle, Brandenburg, he was a barber's son who early on showed a remarkable gift for music, but for a time had to pursue it in secret. His father discouraged music and wanted his son to study law. Musical studies were eventually allowed, but despite his father's death when Handel was eleven, he went through the motions of enrolling in law at the University of Halle in 1702. The next year, though, found him playing violin and harpsichord in an opera orchestra in Hamburg. In 1715 Handel produced an opera of his own in Hamburg, *Almira*, and his career as a composer was on its way.

In those days, Germany was considered the home of harmony and counterpoint, Italy home of song and opera. After Hamburg, Handel spent four years performing and composing in Italy, absorbing the country's music and enriching his own work with a compelling melodic style. From this point on, much of Handel's essence would combine a fluid gift for counterpoint with a great warmth and clarity of means.

Handel's Italian years reached their climax in 1710 when his opera *Agrippina* caused a sensation in Venice. That year the elector of Hanover, later King George I of England, hired him as director of court music. The following year Handel scored a success in London with another opera, *Rinaldo*. When his employer ascended the British throne in 1714, Handel saw his opportunity and took it, never looking back. By the time he moved to London Handel had written a great deal of music and a number of operas, and he was already famous around Europe, but it was in England that he truly came into his own. Georg Friedrich Händel was now George Frideric Handel, British gentleman (though his English remained a bit comical).

He quickly found his place in court and among the music-loving aristocracy. In 1727 he became a British subject and was named composer of the Royal Chapel. There are various stories about his quirks. It was noted that he had a propensity for prodigious and polylingual swearing. On one occasion he dealt with a raging—and hefty—diva by hoisting her up and dangling her by the heels out a window, finally pulling her back in and crying, "I know you're a vitch, but dun't forget I'm ze devil himself!"

If Handel's career sounds nicely rosy on paper, in practice it was rockier, both personally and professionally. Historians have retroactively diagnosed him as bipolar. He composed when he was manic, his mind racing beyond the scratching of his pen, but he had to endure the depressive interims.

For many years, Handel was primarily an opera composer, and in that respect he increasingly bucked the tide of fashion in England. His stage works were in the genre of Italian *opera seria*, meaning historical stories about royal clemency and charity, the music an alternation of mostly *da capo* (= ABA) arias and choruses during which the drama came to a halt, while the story was told in long stretches of *recitative secco*, "dry recitative," accompanied only by harpsichord. There was a great emphasis on vocal virtuosity—you had to keep your divas happy. Some leading roles were taken by *castrati*, men who had in youth been subjected to the eponymous barbaric operation to preserve their high voice. It all made for a dramatically static spectacle, and it took exceptional music to raise it beyond that.

On this increasingly obsolescent genre Handel lavished his extravagant gift for painting character, scene, and action. For a small sample of his operatic and oratorio style, try the sparkling **"The Arrival of the Queen of Sheba"** from the oratorio *Solomon*. With all the dry recitative, even the best recordings of his operas leave something to be desired; it is in live performance that they come more readily to life. Certainly they are full of marvelous stuff; several of them, including the *Giulio Cesare* of 1724, turn up now and then on the stage. Still, so far none has established itself in the modern repertoire that essentially begins with Mozart.

While vocal music was at the center of Handel's art, he was still a splendid composer of instrumental music. The most famous of his larger pieces are two that show off his genius for beguiling melody, vigorous rhythm, and variegated instrumental color: the *Water Music* and *Music for the Royal Fireworks*. Both are suites of short movements for outdoor occasions, so Handel wielded the loud stuff: brass, winds, and drums. *Water Music* was composed for a royal bash on the Thames in summer of 1717: George I's barge was followed by another with fifty musicians, then a gigantic flotilla, all of it cheered by crowds on the banks. The music is as winning as anything Handel produced, rich with trumpets and hunting horns and oboes. The king was so delighted with the music that it had to be repeated three times.

The *Royal Fireworks* was written in 1749 to accompany a regal pyrotechnic display. A rehearsal of the music at Vauxhall Gardens drew an audience of twelve thousand, showing the kind of popularity Handel enjoyed by that point. The music isn't fireworky, but rather a suite of vivacious and dancing movements, first performed by a band of sixty winds and drums. The premiere occasion ended in a magnificent fiasco: the fireworks set fire to a wooden pavilion, scattering the crowd in a panic. Both *Water Music* and the *Royal Fireworks* went on to be arranged in various collections for full orchestra with strings. I suggest going for one of the renditions of the complete suites with the original scoring and original instruments. They're great fun. Pick the rowdiest performance you can find.

Handel based his career on opera seria in Italian, but as the 1720s went on the style began to sag in popularity in England. The beginning of the end came in 1728 with John Gay's send-up of the genre, called *The Beggar's Opera*. This satirical potpourri of tunes was a runaway hit—hastening the decline of Italian opera. (A twentieth-century adaptation of *The Beggar's Opera* is Brecht and Weill's *Three-Penny Opera*, whose most famous tune is "Mack the Knife.") Handel obstinately continued to write operas for his own stage company until 1737, when the company went bust and he suffered some sort of breakdown.

Soon he was back, trying again with opera among other things. But the answer to his problems was already in his hands: the genre of oratorio, as noted before essentially an unstaged opera usually on a sacred subject. As the popularity of opera fell, oratorio rose. Handel had written oratorios in the 1730s; earlier, as a warm-up, in 1718 he premiered his pastoral masque **Acis and Galatea**. Have a listen to that; it's Handel in all his youthful vigor and wit, a delicious stretch of Arcadian charm.

In 1742 came his sixth and most ambitious oratorio, the one that secured his fortune in his time and his central place in Western music for all time: **Messiah**. It premiered at an overflowing concert in Dublin and quickly spread around England and Europe. On his first visit to London in the 1790s Franz Joseph Haydn was deeply moved by it; no less was *Messiah* the main reason Beethoven considered Handel the only composer to outrank him. (Beethoven knew little to none of Bach's choral works.) He admired Handel's ability to get huge effects with simple means. As Beethoven knew, simple is not easy.

Today as 250 years ago, *Messiah* is the most famous and beloved classical piece in the world. Handel wrote the gigantic composition in twenty-four days. Pious sorts call this a sign of divine inspiration, but in fact he often worked that quickly, manic and ecstatic, barely sleeping, sometimes sobbing, the progress of the work helped out by copious borrowings from his earlier music. The tremendous "Hallelujah" chorus, for example, began life as a hymn to Bacchus—that is, a drinking song—in one of his operas. The exquisite chorus "For unto us a Child is born" was originally a racy operatic duet for sopranos addressed to Cupid; after *Messiah* it turned up in an oboe concerto. Still, Handel is reported to have said that in reworking the music for "Hallelujah," he had a vision of the heavenly panoply before his eyes.

In *Messiah* Handel was on an exalted plane of inspiration few composers have ever reached. There are no dull patches, and so many moments of the most remarkable beauty. For one example, "For unto us a Child is born": it builds in a surging, almost childlike play of voices until it reaches the spine-chilling proclamations of "Wonderful! Councilor! The mighty God! The prince of peace!" the strings racing ecstatically above. Never has music driven home the meaning and emotion of words more powerfully. The music of *Messiah* ranges from the incomparable grandeur of "Hallelujah" to the tender intimacy of "Comfort ye my people." There is an old story that when King George II first heard "Hallelujah," he was so moved he rose to his feet. That could be true, but in any case from early on rose a tradition of standing for the "Hallelujah Chorus," and audiences still do. The chorus earns those centuries of reverence.

In 1751, working on the oratorio *Jephthe*, Handel wrote on the manuscript, "Reached here on 13 February 1751, unable to go on owing to weakening of the sight of my left eye." He finished the oratorio, but by the end of the next year he was effectively blind and his composing coasted to a halt. He kept supervising concerts, including an annual gala performance of *Messiah*, and played organ concertos in which he improvised the solo part. He died soon after a *Messiah* performance in April 1759 and was buried with great pomp in Westminster Abbey.

Handel's posthumous influence was—and continues to be—incalculable. For the first hundred-plus years he had virtually no competitors in choral music, because Bach was still being rediscovered. He established oratorio as the summit of choral music. Starting with Haydn, Mozart, and Beethoven, his style dominated nineteenth-century choral music. The century's amateur choir movement in Europe and America was founded largely on Handel; that includes Boston's Handel & Haydn Society, founded in 1814. He became inescapably woven into the conception of what it means to be British; it has been said that the empire was put together accompanied by Handel. The triumph of his music was also a triumph of musical art: never before had a composer lay so close to the center of a culture, and because of him composers of the future began to see themselves as part of a stream of music moving through history. Beethoven was virtually the first composer to aspire to immortality. And Beethoven called Handel the greatest of them all.

More Handel: *Coronation Anthems;* Concerti Grossi, Op. 6; the oratorio *Samson.*

Chapter 7

Further Baroque Listening

G iacomo Carissimi (1605–1674): In baroque religious
music, there are naturally many tragic pieces. One of
the most powerful I know comes from the relatively obscure
Italian Carissimi, the final chorus of his oratorio *Jephte*, from
around 1650. The story is of the biblical king who promises
God that if he wins a battle, he will sacrifice the first person he sees afterward. These kinds of vows don't tend to go
well. It turns out to be his beloved daughter Jephte, and God
doesn't come to her rescue. The tragic and beautiful final chorus, "Plorate, filii Israel," is a lamentation by her friends. The
music is a sustained wail of grief, building to a climax on a
chain of heartrending harmonies. Chorus singers report having trouble getting through the piece without choking up.

Giovanni Gabrieli (1553/6–1612): Much of his music took
shape around the interior of St. Mark's Cathedral in Venice,
which has balconies where he placed his singers and musicians to create intricate antiphonal effects—what we would
call surround sound. Thus flowered what we call the Venetian
polychoral style, which had wide influence on the next generation of composers, including Monteverdi, Schütz, and Bach.

Suggested works: *Canzon duodecimi toni* for brass; *In ecclesiis* for variegated voices, instruments, and organ.

Heinrich Schütz (1585–1672): While the Venetian style he studied was grand and effusive, the German Protestant Schütz had a more austere temperament, his work succinct and intensely spiritual. His harmonic style has an archaic cast that is nicely fresh to our ears. **Suggested works:** *Saul, Saul, was verfolgst du mich?*; *Ist nicht Ephraim mein teurer Sohn?*; *Danket dem Herren*; *Christmas Oratorio*.

Antonio Vivaldi (1678–1741): The insanely prolific Vivaldi—he wrote some five hundred concertos alone—had been largely forgotten when he was rediscovered by baroque buffs in the mid-twentieth century. In his time, as both composer and virtuoso violinist, he was a giant. Bach studied Vivaldi carefully, and I suspect learned from him a good deal about focus, directness, and rhythmic energy. **Suggested works:** *The Four Seasons*; *Gloria* in D Major.

Domenico Scarlatti (1685–1757): Having written his finest work for an audience of one, the queen of Spain, Scarlatti emerged after his death as sort of a cult figure. Quirky, endlessly diverse in tone, ranging from grandiose to violent to wry to busy little tempests-in-a-teacup, his 555 sonatas for the harpsichord explore everything the instrument is capable of. Scarlatti himself provided perhaps the best description of his music: "an ingenious jesting with art." The scope of Scarlatti's miniatures makes it hard to single out particular pieces to recommend, so I'd say find a recording by a celebrated harpsichordist or pianist and dive in. His champions have included pianist Vladimir Horowitz, whose lapidary playing was ideal for Scarlatti.

Part III

Classical

Chapter 8

The Classical Period (ca. 1750–1830)

The later part of the eighteenth century saw a flourishing of art and science that historians have dubbed the Enlightenment, or the Age of Reason. Politically, its fruits included the American and French Revolutions. Musically, the era is known as the classical period (a name that has caused generations of confusion between the classical period and the broad genre "classical music," which are two different things). The term "Enlightenment" tells us what the age thought about itself: that humanity had arrived at a historic turning point of higher wisdom and more equitable societies. And reason, as in "Age of Reason," was the force that was going to bring about this revolution in science, thought, government, and human happiness.

Why reason? Because the sixteenth and seventeenth centuries had produced what is known as the scientific revolution, in which the scientific method revealed that the laws of nature were universal and could be manipulated for our benefit. The new science produced astonishing results in physics, astronomy, and biology, new kinds of mathematics, and later ushered in the steam engine, the mastery of electricity, telephones, computers, and space flight (also, on the other side of the equation, the atomic bomb). During the Enlightenment, science provided a grasp of reality that promised to unveil all the secrets of nature. Wrote Alexander Pope about the genius who galvanized the scientific revolution: "NATURE and Nature's Laws lay hid in Night: / God said, 'Let Newton be!' and all was light."

The Enlightenment was an unprecedentedly hopeful era. It seemed that humanity was progressing by leaps and bounds, with no end in sight. Reason, applied to everything from governments to religion and the social and ethical development of human beings, could surely accomplish anything. That turned out not to be true, not by half, and our understanding of the universe remains incomplete. But that period still produced splendid and enduring things, among them modern science and the triumph (more or less) of representative democracy.

For many thinkers, even religion would now have to submit to reason. For many people, God receded beyond the stars in a kind of infinite retirement, letting the perfect mechanism of his universe run on its own. Emanuel Kant, the leading philosopher of the period, declared that the essence of Enlightenment was to think for yourself. Any religion that issued decrees with no room for discussion should be forbidden. No cosmic list of rules from God or from kings was acceptable. From here on, Kant said, we have to figure out for ourselves how to live. That was a simple idea, but it had gigantic consequences.

That was the attitude of the free-thinking humanists who forged the American constitution, based on the principle that people are born equal, that they have the right and the capacity to rule themselves, that the goal of life is not service to God or church or lord of the manor, but rather for each person to find his or her own way. The purpose of government, Thomas Jefferson wrote, is to foster "life, liberty, and the pursuit of happiness." The irreplaceable prerequisite for finding happiness is freedom: freedom from tyranny, from inherited power, from dogmas of all kinds.

What this led to in the arts was a new kind of directness and populism. Architecture turned away from the extravagance of the baroque to an elegant simplicity (though simplicity on the outside sometimes concealed extravagance within). Music followed suit. As befitted an optimistic age that prized reason, musical forms and harmonies were expected to be lucid to the ear. Tragic music receded in importance; Mozart's greatest operas are comedies. The orchestra became to a degree standardized into the familiar modern ensemble of strings, winds, and brass; musical forms became more rationalized.

The Age of Reason proclaimed nature, not religion, as the true scripture. Classical composers looked for what they called a *natural* style, popularistic and readily communicative, much of it laid out lucidly in dance rhythms and phrasing and style. Baroque music tends to sound big and extravagant, while the classical style sounds restrained, compact, and in many ways intentionally predictable. Haydn was a great master of setting up norms in his work and then surprisingly and wittily fracturing them. Artful sophistication was hidden behind a surface of artlessness. Haydn and his heirs aspired to write a music that was new and original yet seems to have written itself, sounds familiar the first time you hear it. Just as the universe followed consistent laws, musical style became to a degree international; there were regional accents, but everyone proceeded on similar assumptions, and the music of

Europe was more unified than ever before. For a beginner it's often hard to tell the difference in style among artists of this era, such as Haydn, Mozart, and J. C. Bach (the latter a son of J. S. and an important influence on Mozart).

The music of the classical period flowed from the developments of the baroque, which had created opera, challenged the primacy of counterpoint, focused more on accompanied melody as the basic texture of music, and gotten increasingly involved in abstract musical form. The baroque also came up with the three-part Italian *symphony*, which evolved into the classical symphony as practiced from the eighteenth century on. By Haydn's time the addition of a dance genre—minuet—expanded symphonies and quartets and the like from three to four movements. Counterpoint endured, with its canons and fugues, but was relegated mostly to episodes in larger pieces. Now the name of a genre—symphony, piano sonata, string quartet, and so on—meant something fairly specific, and the forms of the individual movements that filled out those genres were, while always flexible, still relatively rationalized and standardized.

String quartets—music written for four instruments—came to prominence for the first time in the eighteenth century. During the Enlightenment quartets were the most popular kind of chamber music, and the majority of amateurs played string instruments. (The piano took over that position in the nineteenth century.) Quartets were house music, done by amateurs in programs for friends in the parlor or music room, often part of enormous grab-bag programs that might have everything from quartets, to piano sonatas, to arias, to symphonies and concertos with a small, scraped-together orchestra. Private concerts in the homes of aristocrats and the well-to-do were the most important venue for most music in the eighteenth century and well into the nineteenth. Only once in his lifetime was one of Beethoven's piano sonatas played in public, and he was closely involved with the first professional quartet in Europe, who were the first to mount public subscription concerts. Music still thrived within the church, but in the classical period, secular music for the first time became more important than sacred. Music publishing burgeoned, catering to a growing class of amateur music lovers. Beethoven would be the first composer to be published steadily from the beginning of his career.

As specific formal outlines were applied to nearly every kind of music, there was a basic regularization of phrasing: two-bar semiphrases make up a four-bar phrase, two four-bar phrases make up an eight-bar period, sixteen bars are the next level, and so on. This is the phrasing of dance music. But like everything else, that was a norm made to be played with, to be inflected and bent in creative ways.

In terms of musical organization, the age produced the most sophisticated model in history: *sonata form*. Joseph Haydn put the finishing touches on it toward the end of the eighteenth century. From Haydn on, sonata form was the essential outline for first movements of nearly every multimovement instrumental work and sometimes last movements, and it invaded other forms such as concerto and rondo.

So, we need to examine sonata form. I call its basic outline "school sonata form," because it's one of those theories that in practice rarely happens according to the rules. The general idea—one of the few nearly invariable elements—is a three-section movement, the sections we call *exposition, development,* and *recapitulation.* (There may also be an *introduction,* usually slow, and a *coda* at the end.) The exposition puts forward a leading theme in the home key, then modulates to a related key for a contrasting second theme, then the whole exposition is repeated. The development section in sonata form is essentially a kind of on-paper improvisation on the themes of the exposition, often dramatic in tone and exploring a variety of keys. Then comes the recapitulation. The school version of the form says that the recapitulation brings back the themes of the exposition in their original guises and resolves everything into the home key.

Those are the rules in theory, but again, few pieces in sonata form happen just that way. In fact, both first and second themes are commonly full sections involving other subthemes and a variety of keys. But in the exposition there will usually be a clear sense of two theme sections, and always a modulation away from the home key, which creates a long-range tension in the harmony that eventually has to be resolved. Again, there may be a profusion of subthemes in the exposition. In any case, the first theme lays out the tone, the leading motifs, the general direction of the whole piece. Usually the exposition themes are contrasting; say, the opening theme bold and the second theme gentler. There may be a new theme or two in the development, and it may not treat all the themes of the exposition. The recapitulation usually has some modulations; to stay in the home key would be boring.

Sonata form was largely developed so as to rationalize and manage new intensities of *contrast* in material, and a broader variety of keys. While a baroque movement was founded on one basic musical idea and one expressive mood, the classical style was interested in a variety of ideas and moods within a single movement. Sonata form was able to keep those unprecedented contrasts under control. Connoisseurs were familiar with the basic formal model, so composers could play games with their expectations: say, a wrong-key false recap in the development, or an elided recap that sneaks in or starts on the second theme. Sometimes the recapitulation keeps on developing the themes. The way a composer handled a musical form became an expressive and distinctive element of the piece: a broken-up form might be part of an anguished or comic piece, and the like. In other words, the handling of form in a piece is as expressive as its melodies and harmonies and rhythms.

Meanwhile the model invaded other musical forms. The old simple tutti–solo–tutti–solo, etc. outline of baroque concertos was turned into *concerto sonata form*. Here the repeat of the exposition became a *double exposition*, where the orchestra first lays out the basic material, then the soloist enters on a second exposition. The old pattern called *rondo*, ABACADA, etc., became *sonata-rondo*, something like ABACABA, the A and B functioning like the two theme sections of sonata form, the C section standing in for the development. In the end, the power and flexibility of sonata form was one of the reasons instrumental music came to reign as the greatest of the arts in the nineteenth century, called "the art to which all other arts aspire." Instrumental music was pure expression, without words or story—though it could imply them, and so took on some of the qualities of drama and poetry and fiction.

A more consistent thematic logic also came to prominence during the latter part of this period. A theme is basically a tune of some sort, though classical ones tend to be open-ended so they can be manipulated and extended. Most often, either composers will build up a theme from motifs, which are a collection of two to four notes—a simple rhythm, a bit of scale, a turning figure, and the like; or the beginning lays out a main theme and the composer breaks off motifs from it with which to make further themes. A familiar example is Beethoven's Fifth Symphony, where the da-da-da-*dum* rhythm of the opening turns up in myriad forms in every theme of the piece right down to the last pages. A chord change or even a single strong-colored chord can be a motif. Often Beethoven uses single-note motifs, such as the out-of-key C-sharp on the first page of Symphony No. 3, "Eroica," which has implications for the key structure of the rest of the symphony. So the new contrast and profusion of themes in the classical style was held together partly by a rigorous formal logic, and also by thematic interrelationships that unified a whole piece.

It was often noted that sonata form echoed the literary arts, reflected in the titles of the sections: an exposition was like the thesis of an essay or a sermon; the development worked with the themes like the body of an essay, or like a drama with its conflicts among the characters. In the eighteenth century composers played and composed as a profession; their career was based on pleasing the public, and they wrote largely on commission. Individuality in artists was prized, but only up to a point. The idea of "expressing yourself" in art would be a symptom of the next century. Classical composers wanted to express universal emotions, not just their own. They therefore favored traditional forms because it gave listeners a starting point in following the music, but they also could play creative games with the norms and expectations of the form.

In the classical era a multimovement musical work—symphony, sonata, concerto, quartet, and so on—is a genre made up of smaller genres, each with its own history. The typical genres and tempos involved in a piece might run as follows: (1) fast first movement in sonata form; (2) slow movement in ABA; (3) stately minuet or racing scherzo, which have an outline close to sonata form, and with a central section called the *trio*; and (4) fast finale in sonata-rondo form. Other formal outlines that commonly turn up in movements are theme and variations or ABAB. Piano sonatas and concertos commonly have three movements, omitting the scherzo/minuet. Sometimes the scherzo precedes the slow movement. Sometimes, as in the finales of Beethoven's "Eroica" and Ninth Symphonies, the composer will create a unique, ad hoc form, but that's rare. Sonata form also turns up in freestanding pieces, such as concert overtures, in operatic numbers, and so on.

The coming romantic generation of the nineteenth century rejected what one poet called the Enlightenment's "cold light of reason" for a doctrine of individuality, innovation, the sublime, the godlike genius. But though romantics were less rigorous than classicists about form, composers still wrote fugues, often still used sonata form and the other classical patterns—forms so universal and useful they endure even today.

In many ways the illusions of the Enlightenment period—that we could forge a perfect science, a perfect society, an exalted humanity—fell to pieces like so many pipe dreams. But they were magnificent dreams, and achievements of the era, like the scientific method, sonata form, and the towering music of the classical period, live on undiminished.

Chapter 9

Joseph Haydn (1732–1809)

Joseph Haydn did not look or act like one of the most innovative and influential composers in our tradition. A lot
of his music sounds to our ears too genial and easygoing to be
anything earthshaking. In his person Haydn was homely, amiable, old-fashioned in clothes and wig, generally called "Papa"
by his employees and students. In adulthood he had few enemies other than his wife. They were childless and she had no
use for music; she cut up his manuscripts to roll her hair.

It is not strictly accurate to call Haydn a revolutionary; he
was too involved with tradition and too attentive to present
influences for that. All the same, nobody affected the history
of his art more profoundly than he did. He is remembered
today as the "father of the symphony" and "father of the string
quartet." He invented neither genre, but rather showed the future what could be done with them. Among the first to put
that wisdom to use was a younger friend of his named Mozart
and a student of his named Beethoven. The naturalness of his
music, its easy grace, its predictability here and boisterous un-
predictability there, were painstakingly mastered over many
years. If Haydn was no revolutionary, he left the future not
only marvelous music but a fund of ideas that proved virtually

inexhaustible. Long ago I learned that when encountering Beethoven's supposed innovations, you often find that Haydn got there first.

Franz Joseph Haydn was born in Rohrau, Austria, to a wheelwright's family. The child soon revealed a considerable talent for music. When he was five, a musical cousin offered to take him in and give him some training; from that point Haydn rarely saw his hometown again. He recalled the cousin as providing "more flogging than food." When he was eight, he was taken into the boys' choir of St. Stephen's Cathedral in Vienna—later known as the Vienna Boys Choir. (He narrowly escaped being made a castrato.) His younger brother Michael, destined to become an important composer of sacred music, joined the choir as well. Joseph spent nine years singing and studying the great choral literature, but when his voice changed at age seventeen, he was summarily booted out of the choir.

There followed years of intensive self-study and gnawing poverty. He lived in a garret and practiced on a worm-eaten harpsichord, taking what musical piecework he could find, including playing on the street. He pulled his way up the professional ladder slowly but with great resilience. In his early twenties he became a servant of the well-known Italian composer and teacher Nicola Porpora, who had Haydn accompany his singing students and gave him composing tips. At age twenty-six Haydn served briefly as the music director and composer for a Bohemian count, for whose orchestra he wrote his first symphony.

His music to that point was pleasant and conventional, as was expected of court composers. His next step up was a huge one: in 1761, aged twenty-nine, he became assistant orchestra conductor and composer for the glittering, rich, highly musical court of Hungarian prince Paul Antal Esterházy. If one was amenable to an existence as a uniformed servant composing and performing to order, a composer could not find a better position in those days. The prince had a palace in Vienna where he wintered and a castle 30 miles away at Eisenstadt. Haydn would appear before the prince for his orders in the morning, and spent his days rehearsing, conducting, and composing. After a few years he became court music director, which made him responsible for the palace orchestra, chamber music, operas, conducting, composing, teaching, hiring and firing.

Haydn lived and worked at the Esterházy court for thirty years. He did his assigned duties tirelessly and well, making the Esterházy instrumental and operatic forces into some of the finest in European courts. In the course of those decades he also made himself one of the most important and celebrated creators on the continent. As he later wrote, while he lived largely isolated from the world, with a prince who appreciated his music, and with a collection of first-rate musicians at his command, he could experiment, learn, and be as original as he liked.

Haydn worked away in the Esterházy palaces, watched princes come and go, and grew steadily in his art and his fame. Estranged from his wife, he took up with a married soprano at court, though she was likely more interested in his money than his charms. When Mozart arrived in Vienna, Haydn befriended him, telling his father, Leopold Mozart, that his son was the best composer he had ever known. Haydn was a generous man and a good friend, and the much younger Mozart reciprocated; the two traded composition tricks and musical ideas. Mozart said Haydn taught him how to write string quartets, and dedicated an important set of six to the older man. Haydn had written a number of operas for the court theater and for years considered himself mainly an opera composer. That illusion ended when Mozart's operas appeared in Vienna. The last time somebody offered Haydn a commission for an opera he responded, that would be a big risk for me— you should hire Mozart.

In the 1790s Haydn was more or less pensioned off by the current Esterházy prince, though he kept writing masses for the court. A letter to a friend shows he was relieved to see the end of his days as a court composer: "The knowledge that I am no longer a hired servant repays me for all my troubles." Shortly thereafter an entrepreneur showed up and promised him piles of gold and mountains of acclaim if he came to England. Haydn agreed, and the prophecy actually turned out: over two visits he found himself idolized by the British public, and ended up comfortably wealthy. If there had been any doubt that he was at the summit of living composers, there no longer was. The one sorrow of his London sojourns was when he learned of the death of Mozart. Haydn was staggered by the loss of "this indispensable man."

After his triumph in London he kept working, but with more and more difficulty. His last pieces were largely vocal, masses for the Esterházy court and the two oratorios *The Creation* and *The Seasons*. Both oratorios were inspired by his enthusiasm for Handel's oratorios, especially *Messiah*, which he heard in London. Meanwhile, inspired by the British anthem "God Save the King," he composed the exquisite "Gott erhalte Franz den Kaiser" (God Save Kaiser Franz), and was honored to find its becoming the unofficial Austrian anthem. It's surely the finest of national anthems, another Haydn melody that seems to have always been there.

By then he was slipping. He said composing *The Seasons* had been a struggle that "broke my back." His final years were melancholy; he was unable to compose and became increasingly frail, fearful, and forgetful. Every day he would sit down at the piano and play his Austrian anthem, the only musical effort he could still manage. His last public appearance was at a gala Vienna performance of *The Creation* in 1808, where he was extravagantly lauded and his one-time student Beethoven knelt to kiss his hands. But Haydn could not make it through the performance. The next year he died during Napoleon's assault on Vienna, shortly after a bomb exploded in his garden and terrified the household.

It was demanded of composers in those days that they be prolific. By the end of his life, Haydn's works included 108 symphonies, 68 string quartets, 52 piano sonatas, 20 operas, 14 masses, 6 oratorios, and a great deal of other chamber music. Some of those genres he changed once and for all.

Most of Haydn's concertos for various instruments have fallen by the wayside. He didn't give them that much time because while he played keyboard and violin, he admitted he was "no conjuror." The greatest concertos, from Bach to Beethoven and beyond, were mostly written by their composers for themselves. It's surprising, then, that a one-off concerto of Haydn's is among his most beloved works: the **Trumpet Concerto** that he wrote for a short-lived instrument that had keys like a saxophone. Trumpets and French horns in those days had no valves, so could only play a restricted range of notes. With its keys, this new trumpet could play all pitches. Clearly that excited Haydn. Here on display is his warmth, his melodies that are so inevitable they seem to have written themselves. Beyond that, for this oddball instrument Haydn wrote music that managed to suit it perfectly while at the same time had remarkably little to do with the traditions of trumpet writing, which tended toward the festive and fanfarish. Here perhaps for the first time, as in the lovely slow movement, the trumpet truly sings.

When it came to keyboard sonatas, not only did Haydn undergo a long artistic development over the course of his career, his instruments did likewise. He began writing for harpsichord, but in his later years the piano had edged out the older instrument. Meanwhile the piano itself was undergoing a rapid evolution from the near-harpsichord sound of the 1790s to bigger, richer, more robust models. In all cases, recall that keyboard sonatas in Haydn's day were house music, never played in public but rather for friends and family and one's own pleasure. I'll recommend two for a start. The **Piano Sonata No. 46 in A-flat Major** is a middle-period work that, despite its major key, manages to be poignant throughout. Its middle movement begins memorably with a single-line soliloquy. The finale is gay, charming, Haydn at his most winning. (I suggest listening to this and the next one both on a modern piano and on a period fortepiano.)

The **Piano Sonata No. 52 in E-flat Major** announces its eccentricity from the first bar: a rich, rolling E-flat chord and a quick and mystifying modulation to A-flat major. The grand opening phrase is followed by a sweetly tender interlude, which tells us that the movement and to a degree the whole sonata is going to be a dialogue of sharply contrasting characters. In the first movement we hear quick shifts from noble to puckish, warm to exhilarating. I taught this piece for years; my students were invariably boggled by how varied in material and keys it is, how unpredictable yet logical in form, how richly pianistic (Haydn wrote it in England, probably for the more robust British pianos). After a lyrical and affecting slow movement in the distant key of E major, the finale is racing, ironic, great fun.

When the young Haydn began writing string quartets they were extremely popular among amateur players but still a minor genre, usually what amounted to an accompanied first-violin solo. By his last quartets he had transformed them into the most important chamber genre, a dialogue of four largely equal instruments, though still aimed at music lovers who played them at home. Haydn also gave quartets the reputation of being a window into a composer's heart and soul, and the best demonstration of his craft. That's why history has named Haydn "father of the string quartet." His finest quartets are ageless, kaleidoscopic in variety, witty charming and poignant, one of those rare creative achievements that can help make life worth living.

Haydn published the six quartets of Op. 20 in 1772, when he was forty. They were dubbed the "Sun" quartets, from an engraving of the sun on the cover. They amount to the first modern string quartets, mainly because they have become a conversation of four roughly equal members, the cello liberated from its old role of just sawing away on the bass line. With his usual sense of logic, in **String Quartet, Op. 20, No. 2**, Haydn tells us that up front: it begins with a cello solo. This set also shows the impact of the decade's tumultuous, passionate, even anarchic "Sturm und Drang" (Storm and Stress) movement—a foreshadowing of the next century's romanticism. No. 2 is in C major, a key that in those days tended to be noble and uncomplicated in tone. But this is a C major touched by Sturm und Drang, with a quirky and pensive vein dogging the high spirits. After a rather ominous second movement in minor comes a folksy and delicate minuet. One of the ways Haydn lifted himself beyond the lightweight preciousness of the composers around him was to restore counterpoint to his music, as seen here in the fugal finale.

Haydn's Opus 33 quartets demonstrate a new depth and breadth of ideas and a delicious humor. He wrote that these pieces were composed "in an entirely new and particular manner," meaning that he stressed the equality of the four voices even more than before. They also unveil a brand new kind of movement: the *scherzo*, the word meaning "joke," created by speeding up the three-beat minuet to make a racing and usually exuberant movement.

The most famous quartet of **Op. 33 is No. 2 in E-flat Major**, itself dubbed **"The Joke."** The swagger of the first movement's opening theme is ironic, looking at itself with some amusement, and the rest is full of twists and little jokes. It's because of moments like this that some have called the whole of Op. 33 "music about music." (Another example of that kind of thing is the finale of Op. 76, No. 5, which starts off sounding like an ending and can't seem to get going because it keeps on ending.) The second-movement scherzo of "The Joke" has I think a tone of high irony, if you're listening carefully. The slow third movement begins with a tender duet and continues in kind. The finale sets off in a tone of impish fun, but the source of the quartet's nickname doesn't appear until the coda: the quartet ends; we start to applaud; it breaks out again and ends again; we applaud, a little tentatively this time; it starts again, teases us with silences as we sit there with hands suspended in air; and it finally concludes almost in midphrase, so we're still uncertain whether to clap. It's hilarious, one of many examples of Haydn playing his audience as a master psychologist, convincing us we know what he's doing while he sneaks around to administer a kick. The most famous example of that, of course, is the heart-stopping explosion in the middle of the slow movement of the **"Surprise" Symphony** (No. 94). Reportedly Haydn said it "will wake up the ladies." That joke, it's worth noting, is carefully set up earlier in a series of small pauses that we expect to mark the theme. The ability to be logical and surprising at the same time is one of the great achievements of the Classical period.

Not quite the last but the climax of Haydn's quartets are the magnificent four of Op. 76, published in 1799. **Op. 76, No. 2** in D Minor is known as the **"Quinten"** (Fifths) from the prevailing interval of the opening theme that dominates a movement a bit fierce and playful by turns. That fifth-motif turns up in the all the movements, including the canonic, mock-demonic "Witch's Round" of the scherzo.

Haydn was also called "Father of the Symphony." As he had done with quartets, he began writing symphonies in the style of the time, meaning pieces lightweight and short, for an orchestra of fourteen to twenty players. By the time he reached his last, No. 104, he had made the symphony the king of instrumental genres, at a level of weight and ambition that was ready for Mozart and then Beethoven to pick it up and carry it on.

With his massive body of symphonies it's hard to know where to begin. Try **Symphony No. 48 in C Major,** written around 1769 and dubbed **"Maria Theresia"** because it may have been composed for a visit of that Austrian empress. The tone justifies the title: from the pealing high horns of the first movement the music is the definition of grand and regal, but still vivacious. The second movement manages to be elegant and graceful without getting sentimental about it; much the same can be said of the minuet, though it strays into some stern territory. Both middle movements feature the horns again, as does the wry and chatty finale.

For Haydn on the other end of the spectrum, try **Symphony No. 80 in D Minor,** from around 1783. This is not one of his best-known symphonies, but it's one of his strangest. Biographers claim that he was past Sturm und Drang by this point, but to me this symphony says otherwise. It begins on a furiously driving figure enlivened by explosive accents. The movement is marked by sudden jolts of volume and shifts of direction: the intense and a bit scary exposition is finished by a tipsy little oom-pah-pah dance that emerges out of nowhere. The main theme of the second movement is a sighing, very beautiful melody, then the second theme arrives in a surge of passion and orchestral color. Some of the intensity of the first movement turns up in the minuet, which is far from the usual elegant and *galant* outing. The finale is one of Haydn's quirkiest. Much of its distinctive character has to do with rhythm: its main theme begins on an offbeat and is so syncopated that for some time we have no idea where the actual beat is. For the rest of an eccentric movement we are jerked back and forth between the real and the ersatz pulse.

The main fruit of his two British visits were twelve symphonies, the set collectively known as the "London." Haydn's last symphony from 1795, **Symphony No. 104 in D Major,** is individually called the **"London"** as well. Here he has left Sturm und Drang behind and as in the rest of the set is writing on a stately plane, partly because he had larger orchestras at his disposal. All the same, the symphony has its share of Haydnesque wit and folksiness. It begins with a stern introduction, but the amiable allegro that follows is folklike. The rustic finale quotes a Croatian folk song.

Haydn's virtues are ones that have fallen out of fashion: restraint, modesty, subtlety, the kind of art that hides its artfulness. He was one of the most sophisticated of musical thinkers, but he wasn't interested in showing it off. One of his favorite compliments was the word *natural*. If you're not paying attention, he can seem bland and slight. True, neither Haydn nor his contemporaries were much inclined to tragic expression; the Enlightenment was a period of tremendous hope for humanity and science and art. His music rose from that hope. Late in life Haydn said that if his music could lift us out of our cares for a little while, that was worth all his trouble. That's a modest ambition for an artist, but it's as worthy as any I know. If we let him, he can still do that.

More Haydn: the rest of the Op. 76 quartets and rest of the "London" Symphonies; *The Creation.*

Chapter 10

Wolfgang Amadé Mozart (1756–1791)

There is an aura around the name Wolfgang Amadé
Mozart. His name had that glow when he was six years
old and still has it today. Whenever the idea of prodigy comes
up, his is usually the first name evoked. When the notion was
promoted that classical music makes your kids smarter, it
was called the Mozart effect. A *New Yorker* cartoon showed
a blasted landscape with bits of trash blowing about, its cap-
tion: "Life without Mozart." The hit play and movie *Amadeus*
portrayed him as a virtual idiot savant, childish and dirty-
minded, an inexplicable vessel through whom music flowed
directly from God.

But an aura obscures more than it reveals. Wrote Jorge Luis
Borges: "Fame is a form of incomprehension, perhaps the worst."
Fame is a maker of myth, and from the day Mozart died the
myths proliferated until they became legend: neglect, financial
desperation, writing his Requiem for himself, a pauper's grave.

Here are some realities behind the aura. Mozart was a
born musical genius, but his gift for mimicry—as a child he
could breeze into a city and turn out imitations of the local
composers—was his worst enemy as an artist. He was reared
by his father, a noted pedagogue and mediocre composer, to

be a brilliant mediocrity. That Mozart turned out otherwise was a matter of painstaking work over years. At age twenty there was little to suggest what was to come: the incomparable melodies and social skewering of *The Marriage of Figaro*, the uncanny floating beauty of the nocturne of the Piano Concerto in C Major K. 467, the demonic drive of the Piano Concerto in D Minor and the Symphony in G Minor. In his glittering childhood, none of this was foretold.

Mozart was buried like most Viennese of his generation, not in the pauper's grave of legend. He died at a moment when his fortunes were on the upswing and he was paying off his debts. By then his operas were selling out all over Europe. Most important, he had escaped from the prison of his early fame. Most of his greatest music was written in his last five years. Finally, only a few times in his life did Mozart sign his middle name as the familiar "Amadeus," which means "beloved of God." Usually he signed with the German equivalent "Gottlieb" or the French "Amadé."

The stories of his youth are legendary, and some of these legends are actually true. His father, Leopold, was a court violinist in Salzburg, where Wolfgang was born. When he was five, the child began picking out at the harpsichord some of the tunes being studied by his older sister Nannerl, who was a budding keyboard prodigy. Leopold took his cue and tried teaching his son the pieces. To his astonishment he discovered that Wolfgang, not yet able to read notes and with no instruction in playing, could play and memorize whole keyboard pieces in a half hour. He began writing little compositions in a blotchy hand. Soon his father envisioned glittering possibilities of wealth and fame in showing the world "this miracle of God." Leopold was a sophisticated musician, author of a

celebrated violin method, a prolific composer, broadly edu-
cated in a number of directions. He would be Wolfgang's only
teacher.

In those days most artists lived largely as servants in
courts and palaces and churches, supplicants to the aristocracy who ran things at their whim. When Wolfgang was six
and Nannerl, at ten, a keyboard prodigy herself, Leopold decided to take his children to the courts and palaces and market
their skills for fame and fortune. A decade of touring all over
Europe and England began; stories proliferated of crowned
heads idolizing the tiny boy and scientists examining him as a
phenomenon of nature.

For Wolfgang and Nannerl it was a showbiz life. Leopold
handled every part of the tour, advertising Wolfgang like a cir-
cus act: the boy will name any pitch heard, play with a cloth
over the keyboard, improvise in any style, invent songs on the
spot. In London and Munich and Rome and Vienna the children met the most celebrated musicians and composers of the
day. The tours not only garnered cash and worldwide fame but
also for Wolfgang a comprehensive education in music. He
composed steadily during this time, with mounting maturity,
his main models the music he encountered en route.

By the time the three returned to Salzburg after the last
tour in late 1773, they were desperate to ride Wolfgang's fame
to a job somewhere bigger and better. Unfortunately for their
plans, the new ruler of Salzburg, Archbishop Hieronymus
von Colloredo, wanted his servants to stay home and serve
him. Grumbling, Wolfgang settled down to the work of producing sacred pieces to order, but spent much of his time writing music for local musicians to play in the private parlors that
were the main venue for music in those days.

In letters from his teen years we see the Mozart personality emerging: puckish, proud, cattily observant, endlessly imaginative, sometimes rabidly obscene. All this is epitomized in now notorious letters to his cousin Maria Anna. The two had engaged in some unspecified amount of fooling around. His letters to her show his style, using word games like music: "I must ask you, dearest dunce, why not?—if you happen to be writing . . . to send my regards to the two Misses Freysinger, why not?—Strange! Why not? And say that I beg the youngest one, Fräulein Josepha, to forgive me, why not?—Why should I not beg her to forgive me? Strange! Why should I not? Say that she must forgive me for having not yet sent her the sonata I promised . . . Why not?—What?—Why not?—Why should I not send it?—Why not?—Strange!"

Other letters to Maria Anna indulge in the kind of scatological humor common in the day—its fashion of being naughty. "Oui, by the love of my skin," Mozart poeticized to her, "I shit on your nose, so it runs down your chin." In another letter: "I kiss your hands, your face, your knees, and your ————, that is, whatever you let me kiss." In letters of his later life the rowdiness calmed down, but the vivacity did not.

It was in Mozart's last Salzburg years that he finally began to escape convention and wrote his first real masterworks. One of the most memorable of his Salzburg pieces is the **Sinfonia concertante** for orchestra and solo violin and viola, whose soaring first entrance sweeps you off your feet. He would write more searching instrumental works than this one, but none more enchanting.

At age twenty-one, his mother in tow, Mozart set out hoping to find a job at a court somewhere. His goal was

Paris, where he had triumphed in childhood. But he stopped in Mannheim on the way and there fell precipitously in love with a talented teenaged soprano, Aloysia Weber. Back in Salzburg, Leopold saw what was going on and was horrified. Finally at his father's insistence Wolfgang and his mother dutifully went on to Paris for what became a six-month disaster. He was no longer a prodigy but a young man in a crowded field of composers, who had never had to make his own way. He wrote little music, got little attention, and as a crowning misery his mother died. Defeated, he headed home, stopping in Munich where Aloysia was now working, her singing career going nicely without his help. As the crowning indignity of those months, Mozart found himself jilted. At a party he sat down at a piano and sang, "Those who don't want me can kiss my arse." Then he slunk back to Salzburg.

Finally came what Leopold called catastrophe, but what Wolfgang deemed liberation: in spring 1781, Mozart was summoned to Vienna by his ruler Colloredo as part of the archbishop's retinue. There he suffered more than his fill of indignities (among other things, he had to eat with the servants), made his disgust clear, and ended up literally booted out of the archbishop's service with a kick on the backside. Now he was free to make his career in Vienna. Austrian emperor Joseph II was progressive in his politics and a sophisticated musical connoisseur. History would go hard on his treatment of Mozart, but in fact Joseph knew genius when he saw it, and kept Mozart busy (though he never got a lucrative job at court and remained essentially a freelancer).

Here began Mozart's glory years. In Europe's capital of music he vaulted over the hundreds of other pianists and composers. A few years later, when Leopold visited Vienna, he was astounded at his son's relentless schedule of performing and composing, his income, his grand apartment, his extravagant wardrobe, his expensive pool table. Joseph Haydn, much older but by now a friend and mentor of Wolfgang, told Leopold that his son was the finest composer he knew.

In Vienna two things happened right away: from the court Mozart got a commission for a comic opera, in a genre called *Singspiel*, with spoken dialogue. He and his librettist picked an exotic yarn capitalizing on the Viennese fashion for quasi-Turkish music and stories. Called *The Abduction from the Seraglio*, it tells the story of an Englishwoman kidnapped for his harem by Pasha Selim. After the expected contretemps, most of them involving the cruel but bumbling servant Osmin, the lady is rescued by her lover, Belmonte. In a letter to Leopold, Mozart shows his minute attention to the emotional and physical life of his characters, and no less the qualities of his performers: "In working out [Osmin's] aria I've . . . allowed Fischer's beautiful deep notes to glow . . . As Osmin's rage gradually increases there comes the Allegro assai, which is in a totally different meter and key . . . For just as a man in such a towering rage oversteps all the bounds of order, moderation, and propriety and completely forgets himself, so must the music also forget itself."

The sparkle and charm that mark *Abduction* begins instantly with the overture, thrumming with the bass drum and cymbals and piccolo of the Turkish style. In the middle comes a preview of one of the arias, among the opera's row of knockout numbers. Tuneful, fashionable, funny, irresistible, *Abduction* was a gigantic hit in Vienna and soon found performances all over Europe. Here Mozart discovered that comedy was his real métier on the stage. Although he grew far beyond it as a musician, *Abduction* remained his most popular opera to the end of his life.

Meanwhile he married his lost love Aloysia's sister, also a singer though never a professional: Constanze Weber. Leopold gave grudging consent to the marriage; he and Nannerl never accepted Constanze as a worthy mate. But Mozart adored her, spiritually and physically, as shown in some lusty letters he wrote her on tour: Soon "I'll be sleeping with my dear little wife;—Spruce up your sweet little nest because my little rascal here really deserves it, he has been very well behaved but now he's itching to possess your sweet . . . [scratched out]."

For years he composed and played indefatigably, his servants trotting all over Vienna carrying his piano to performances. (By the 1780s the rapidly developing piano was edging out the harpsichord.) Home life was a lively uproar; Mozart liked having people around and was able to compose amidst the ruckus. He was a constant fidget, drumming his fingers, tapping his feet. His favored recreations were all physical: in Salzburg, air rifle competitions and the bowling game skittles; in Vienna, horseback riding and billiards at home. Constanze said he loved dancing, if anything, even more than music. Mozart was small and pale, often ill, nothing much to look at, but he possessed the tireless energy that also marks his music, along with the vibrant sense of drama and comedy and human psychology on display in his operas.

From his teens Mozart was one of the finest keyboard players alive, but though he thrived on applause, performing for him was a means to an end: he was a composer first. Still, much of his composing during the first Vienna years was geared toward furthering his career as a virtuoso, above all the series of spectacular piano concertos he wrote for himself. The history of the concerto from his time to ours rests on the foundation of those masterpieces. Late in the next century Brahms sighed in a letter: "The fact that people don't appreciate the best things in music, such as Mozart's concertos, is the reason people like me get famous."

Here we can only hint at the glories of the concertos. Have a listen to the celebrated **slow movement of the Concerto No. 21 in C Major, K. 467.** (The "K." is for numbers later assigned his pieces by a gentleman named Köchel.) This dreamlike nocturne is unique, not quite like anything else by Mozart or anybody else, but it's still absolutely him: drifting atmospheres, deceptive simplicity, a sense of languorous emotions washing through the music, the effect mysterious and unnameable. When you're in this movement you can't imagine anything more beautiful, more evocative of love sensuous and profound.

Here are two complete concertos in quite different directions. From its first page **Concerto No. 17 in G Major, K. 453** announces it will be one of the delightful ones, the style close to comic opera—delicately tuneful, lilting, a touch ironic. By this point Mozart had mastered the art of giving us lovely musical surfaces that point deeper and beyond. There is a whiff of poignancy lurking in the background of the first movement, and that flowers in the slow movement, one of those Mozart adagios that can bring tears with its first notes. In the last movement the imaginary opera takes a turn to dancing, joking delight.

Concerto No. 20 in D Minor, K. 466, is the kind of music that rather scared Mozart's contemporaries: dark, driven, overflowing with ideas. Its intensity prophesies the romantic generation of composers to come, who embraced the shadowed and demonic (later Beethoven played and admired this concerto). The driving intensity of the opening mounts steadily through the orchestral exposition, and the rest of the movement stays on that plane, relieved by lyrical moments. After a pensive and romantic second movement, the demon returns in an eruptive and searing finale that finally resolves to D major jollity. Mozart was able to convey sorrow and rage, but most of the time tragic endings were not his style.

He wrote a lot of pieces for everyday purposes, the kind of music played by small groups of amateurs in palaces and parlors while the audience browsed a buffet, played cards, chatted and flirted. The most familiar of these pieces is the exquisite *Eine kleine Nachtmusik* (A Little Night Music): Mozart relaxing at the top of his form, by turns vigorous, tender, joshing.

If opera was at the heart of his creativity, he was still a master of instrumental genres, what a later time would call "abstract music," making its point through the power of notes and form. Try one of his set dedicated to Haydn, the **String Quartet in C Major, K. 465**, nicknamed **"The Dissonant"** for its bizarre introduction that stretches his harmonic language almost to breaking. Surprisingly, this gnarly opening gives way to a lively and lovely outing in Mozart's high-C-major mood—a key that for him usually meant something sunny. The slow movement is a stretch of poignant feeling behind the mask of an elegant dance. After a folkish minuet the finale returns to the good humor of the first movement.

Mozart's G-minor mood was another matter, tending toward the dark and anguished. That is the key of one of the crowns of his chamber music, the **String Quintet No. 3 in G Minor, K. 516.** From its beginning note of surging nervous energy, the piece offers little consolation. The second-movement minuet is one of the most eruptive, almost troubling pieces imaginable for that traditionally elegant dance movement. The hymnlike third movement presages the deeply affecting slow movements that Beethoven would be writing in the next generation. The long introduction to the finale is some of the most tragic music Mozart ever wrote. It is followed by a G major allegro that seems to resolve the sorrow, but only on the surface: a cloud lingers over the gaiety.

When Mozart began writing symphonies in his childhood, the genre was popular but minor, something to enliven a program but nothing ambitious. By the time they were done, he and Haydn elevated it to the king of musical genres. One of the finest of the late-middle symphonies is **No. 38 in D Major, K. 504,** called the **"Prague"** from 1786, in three movements. For Mozart, the key of D major was usually bright and cheery, and he wrote this symphony in and for a city that adored him. After a solemn introduction a blithe and beautiful allegro appears, full of his dashing, darting rhythms. Second comes one of his dreamy romantic nocturnes. A buoyant finale shows that this symphony is mainly about delight.

Mozart wrote his last three and most ambitious symphonies in a scarcely believable six weeks of 1788. Legend says that he wrote them for himself and for posterity, and never heard them performed. That is more claptrap. Mozart always wrote for a reason and he never talked about posterity. He probably used them in some of his later concerts in Vienna and elsewhere. We can't confirm that these symphonies expressed his depression at a time when he was falling into debt and feeling desperate, but the idea is equally hard to dismiss. In Austria there was a war on with the Turks and not much money for art, Mozart was by then old news in Vienna, and he may have been gambling. During this period there were a number of pathetic letters to friends begging for loans. The depth of distress in the **Symphony No. 40 in G Minor, K. 550**, may have reflected his mood at the time. From its agitated beginning, as if in the middle of a thought, the piece lives on a plane of unrest. The main theme of the second movement is trancelike, the minuet a pounding G minor. The finale is the most agitated of all, its rocketing main theme like some threatful engine of fate.

For many of us Mozart is the greatest of opera composers. It certainly helps that he was one of our finest tunesmiths. Beyond that, he had a supreme understanding of the stage, of actors and singers, of the interaction between dramatic and musical pacing. And there was his understanding of people, their loves and lusts and yearnings and quirks, and how to turn these emotions into notes: brash and wily Figaro, girl-crazy Cherubino, Donna Anna searching for her father's murderer. In his later operas, he also had a brilliant partner in the poet Lorenzo da Ponte, who was a libertine in the mode of his friend Casanova, but also one of the most sophisticated and finest of librettists.

Mozart's greatest operas are all comedies, but he knew how to place comedy on top of deeper matters. As in all of them, *The Marriage of Figaro* unveils its tone and direction in its overture: skittering, whispering wit breaking out in laughter, perfect for a story of schemes and counterschemes. At the center of the story is sex. Figaro, barber for Count Almaviva, is about to marry the delicious Susanna, but it appears that the Count is planning to revive the ancient droit du seigneur, meaning the lord of the manor gets to sleep with the new bride on her wedding night. A jolly plot ensues. There's the knowing wit of Susanna, one of Mozart's collection of marvelous women: strong, sexy, smart, and as wily as the men they have to cope with. As for Figaro: "If you want to dance, little Count," he sings, "I'll play the tune!"

But beneath the scheming and laughter is something entirely serious. The original French play by Beaumarchais had been banned by Emperor Joseph II as too politically radical. The operative line from the original play, regarding the Count: "You went to the trouble of being born—nothing more! As for the rest—a rather ordinary man!" These years were the high Enlightenment, when the privileges and rule of the old regimes were coming under unprecedented scrutiny. Librettist da Ponte finagled Joseph into allowing *Marriage* by promising to take out the political stuff. Even so, it still remains a story of people at the bottom of the ladder fighting the depredations of the aristocracy with the only weapons they possess: their wits. The Count ends exposed and humiliated, apologizing pathetically to his wife.

Near the end of Mozart's life came another masterful comedy, the incomparable *Magic Flute*. More even than the earlier ones, this is a people's opera, full of tunes made to be whistled—and others far deeper than that. Prince Tamino is enlisted by the Queen of the Night to free her daughter Pamina from the clutches of the evil wizard Sarastro. There is a comic sidekick in Tamino's quest—the randy birdcatcher Papageno, who will find his destined Papagena. Tamino discovers that in fact Sarastro is a great and noble man, head of a band of spiritual brothers, and the Queen is the villain. (Sarastro is based in part on Shakespeare's wizard Prospero.) Of course, Tamino frees Pamina, and after trials of initiation both are inducted into the order.

Mozart was a passionate Mason, and *The Magic Flute* is a transparent allegory of Freemasonry, that international collection of lodges that were a kind of underground progressive force during the Enlightenment. I think, though, that the deeper subject of this opera is Mozart's favorite subject, love: the earthy love of Papageno and Papagena, the exalted love of Tamino and Pamina, the divine love of Sarastro for all humanity. At the end, with the betrothal of Tamino and Pamina, Sarastro hails the couple and the victory of light over darkness. For Mozart, love was that light, the highest wisdom we know.

In October 1791 Mozart wrote two letters to Constanze, who was ill and away in the spa at Baden. In the first he details his day for her: composing, a glorious pipe of tobacco, a delicious piece of fish, at night taking in *Magic Flute*, which had become an enormous hit. In the next letter he talks about seeing the opera again with his supposed rival, composer Antonio Salieri, who was boundless in his praise. He was writing the **Requiem**, which he loved doing—he had never written a Requiem before. He probably knew it was commissioned by a nobleman who liked to pass off such pieces, with a wink, as his own. The Requiem is the greatest of its genre, full of death and hope, lacerating sorrow and uncanny beauty.

But Mozart himself never finished the Requiem. A month after those letters to Constanze—full of the opera's triumph and of joie de vivre—Mozart lay in his deathbed. He died on December 5, 1791. Constanze commissioned a student of his to finish the Requiem, most of which was left in fragments, but the student did his job well. Then myth took over: that he was poisoned by Salieri, he was writing the Requiem for himself, he died in neglect and despair and was relegated to a pauper's grave. None of it true.

Still, there are all kinds of truths. Shakespeare wrote, "the truest poetry is the most feigning." Mozart was a man of the theater and had the temperament of an actor, who feigns for a living, who leaps nimbly from one emotion to another and in that can move us to the core. Mozart was a fierce craftsman, he studied and grew throughout his life, and he thought carefully about what he did. But what came out still flowed from a man who was made of music. He spoke sometimes in lace, sometimes from behind a mask, but all the same his spirit and soul and his joy and sorrow and love and lust emerged in sound: all at once, he was himself Papageno and Sarastro and Pamina and Tamino. When we connect with that, his works can illuminate our lives in a way unique to him. That is Mozart's true aura.

More Mozart: Symphony No. 41 and the "Linz" and "Paris" Symphonies (No. 36 and No. 31, respectively); *Don Giovanni*; the rest of the six Haydn Quartets.

Chapter 11

Ludwig van Beethoven (1770–1827)

Consider Beethoven's Fifth Symphony. It has long been the most famous symphony in the world, which means that it has gone beyond a cultural monument and become some kind of cultural cliché, like the *Mona Lisa* surrounded by an army of cell phones taking its picture. There have been disco and other pop versions of the Fifth. In World War II, since its opening dot-dot-dot-dash is Morse code for the letter *V*, it became an Allied victory mantra. Certainly anyone sensitive to music can see it's an electrifying piece, from its driving, explosive first movement, to its triumphant finale; the second movement is wonderfully beautiful (it was lifted for the teen hit song "Tammy" in the 1950s, something that in my youth it took me a while to get past). In its force-of-nature power, its boldness but also its songful lyricism, it is the essence of Beethoven.

Yet in its time the Fifth arrived as something between incomprehensible and dangerous: too strange, too sensational. A French composer recalled that after first hearing it he came out of the hall so excited and upset that when he tried to put on his hat, he could not find his head. It is the first movement that made the piece at first more notorious than celebrated. At the time, the idea that you could take a little scrap of rhythm and two pitches, G to E-flat, and fashion a whole movement with that as the theme, was absurd.

But Beethoven was always intensely focused and systematic in how he used his material. In myriad guises, the rhythmic tattoo of the opening will mark every theme in the symphony all the way to its last pages. The four pitches of that opening, G–E-flat–F–D, form a four-note pitch motif whose important element is simply the *shape* of those four pitches: down, up, down. That gesture, what I call "the Fifth Symphony S shape," is also heard throughout the symphony, fleshed out with various intervals, sometimes right side up and sometimes upside down.

After the first seconds of the Fifth, in which we hear the tattoo twice, what do we already know about the symphony? We know its basic rhythmic motif; we know the S shape that will dominate the themes; we know the forceful, dramatic expressive quality of the piece; we know its basically simple harmonic world; we know its sinewy orchestral sound. In the opening seconds, Beethoven conveys all the essential material in terms of rhythm, melody, harmony, color, and drama.

The trick to truly getting into Beethoven, beyond the cliché, is to put aside the hoopla and rediscover the passion, the humanity, the strangeness, the unceasing variety within his tireless pursuit of organic unity. Forget the myth. Listen to the *music*. You will find not "Beethoven," but instead a collection of unforgettable individuals that steadily reveal new territories of sound and emotion.

Beethoven's story begins in Bonn, Germany, where he was baptized on December 17, 1770. His father, Johann van Beethoven, was a tenor in the court choir, a respected music teacher in town, and an alcoholic. When Johann realized that this son was marvelously talented, he set out to beat music into him. Neighbors remembered the tiny boy standing on a bench to reach the keyboard, crying as he played, his father looming over him.

When Ludwig was ten, he came under the tutelage of his final mentor, having exhausted the resources of his father and other local teachers. This was Christian Neefe (pronounced *nay*-feh), a composer and writer and enthusiast for progressive ideas. The student Neefe took on was small, sullen, and grubby. Ludwig had two brothers, no friends, and very little schooling. Yet soon after their lessons began, in a magazine article Neefe declared that if this little boy kept going as he had, he could become the next Mozart. The child took this boggling prophecy in stride and from that point apparently never doubted his powers. Already Beethoven was equipped with iron tenacity, discipline, and pride. Once when their landlady's daughter scolded him for being so dirty all the time, Ludwig replied, "Someday I'll be a great man and nobody will care." He entered his teens already a remarkable pianist and a budding composer. Friends and mentors attempted to socialize him, but succeeded only to a degree.

If Beethoven had been born elsewhere than Bonn he might have been a great composer, but he would not have been the same one. His hometown was one of the most progressive of the hundreds of little German states, caught up in the tide of hope for scientific breakthroughs and human progress of the Enlightenment. While Beethoven was growing up in the 1780s, the hope of revolution was in the air, a sense that humanity was turning a corner into rational and humanistic governments, every individual free to pursue his or her own happiness. Beethoven was filled with these ideals by his teacher Neefe and by the intellectual atmosphere of Bonn in court and parlors and cafés. He was taught that it is everyone's right to pursue happiness, also every accomplished person's duty to serve humanity. Therefore, his talent was owed to the world. Even if Beethoven was too self-involved to much understand others, and in the end had contempt for most people in the flesh, he never deviated from his foundation in Bonn: his art was to be his gift to humanity.

When Beethoven left Bonn for Vienna at age twenty-two, he was already one of the finest pianists in the world, and he intended to be one of the finest composers as well. He was going to Vienna to study composition with Joseph Haydn, who on a stopover in Bonn on the way back from England had been mightily impressed with the young man's work.

During his first years in Europe's capital of music, Beethoven had a meteoric rise to fame as a virtuoso, celebrated for the unprecedented fire and imagination of his improvisations, which could leave audiences gasping and weeping. Improvisation was his main creative engine, the ideas flowing directly from his mind to his fingers, but on the page he worked out his ideas with relentless patience and perfectionism. Right away he made contact with some of the leading patrons in Vienna, and they stayed loyal to him despite his arrogance, his tantrums, his frequent boorishness. These were musical aristocrats who knew talent when they saw it. While often intransigent, Beethoven was ruthlessly self-critical, abjectly apologetic when he felt he had wronged someone. Always, human suffering moved him: he was capable of denouncing someone one day and the next, if he heard the person was in a bad way, emptying his pockets for him or her.

His lessons with Haydn lasted less than a year, and though Beethoven was respectful to the old master there was an undercurrent of friction between them. Beethoven wanted teachers but at the same time didn't like to be told what to do. Haydn knew exactly what kind of potential this budding genius had and was patient with him, but behind Beethoven's back he sardonically called him "the great Mogul"—in our terms, "the big shot."

Beethoven planned his early opuses with care, releasing works largely based on piano including sonatas and piano trios. His first string quartets, the six of Op. 18, were brilliant and accomplished but not particularly bold; Haydn had invented the modern quartet, and Beethoven was not yet ready to challenge the old man on his own turf. Likewise his First Symphony of 1800 is engaging enough, but not particularly ambitious or innovative.

Beethoven was already a master composer in the last years of the eighteenth century and the first of the nineteenth, but he experimented with voices; some of them say "Beethoven" to our ears and others don't. One of the first to leap out as a prophecy of what he would become, a work instantly famous and still among his most celebrated, is the **Piano Sonata Op. 13.** He named it the **"Pathétique,"** meaning it is a piece about pathos. It begins with a crashing C minor chord; the introduction that follows has an emotional nakedness never heard in music before—it seems not a portrayal of sorrow, but sorrow itself.

Beethoven already had a strong sense that an instrumental work could be, in its entirety, a single implied emotional and dramatic narrative, unified throughout by the motifs

presented in the beginning. For Beethoven a whole work, including an instrumental work, is one story, one collection of
ideas. As he put it: "It is my habit always to keep the whole in
view." So it is with the "Pathétique." The first response to the
sorrow and rage of the first movement is a second movement
of great peace and consolation, a kind of solemnly beautiful
hymn. Then the finale's answer: defiance, a driving, dramatic,
exultant movement building directly off a theme in the first
movement.

Beethoven was not often given to deliberate autobiograph-
ical echoes in his music, but the intensity of the "Pathétique"
may have had something to do with a devastating blow he received around the time he wrote it: he realized he was going
deaf. It was years before he could bring himself to tell anybody
about it, but finally he confessed to an old Bonn friend, "That
jealous demon, my wretched health, has put a nasty spoke in
my wheel; and it amounts to this, that for the last three years
my hearing has become weaker and weaker . . . I must confess
that I lead a miserable life."

At the same time, since his teens he had been afflicted
with chronic digestive miseries that bequeathed him violent
episodes of vomiting and diarrhea. In 1802 it all came down
on him at once. During a working vacation in the village of
Heiligenstadt, in an apparently unsent letter to his brothers,
he wrote,

> Oh you men who think or say that I am malevolent, stub-
> born or misanthropic, how greatly do you wrong me. You
> do not know the secret cause which makes me seem that
> way to you. From childhood on my heart and soul have
> been full of the tender feeling of goodwill, and I was ever

inclined to accomplish great things. But, think that for 6 years now I have been hopelessly afflicted . . . finally compelled to face the prospect of a lasting malady . . . for me there can be no relaxation with my fellow-men, no refined conversation . . . I must live almost alone like an exile.

History would know this letter as the "Heiligenstadt Testament." It is part suicide note, part defiance. He declares that he will be "the most wretched of men," and much of his life to come would bountifully live up to that prophecy. Unsaid in the letter is that his career as a virtuoso was doomed. But Beethoven had not only enormous talent and discipline, he also had about as much courage as a person can have. He understood what he would suffer, but he declared he would endure it for his work: "It was only my art that held me back [from suicide]. Oh, it seemed impossible to me to leave this world before I had produced all that I felt capable of producing, and so I prolonged this wretched existence."

Biographers have tended to see this crisis as the moment Beethoven girded his loins and by an act of will conceived the Third Symphony, which launched him into his glorious second, a.k.a. "Heroic," period of work. But in fact there is no blip at all in his music of that summer in Heiligenstadt—he was working at a white-hot pace the whole time, had already conceived the Third Symphony, would have written it in any case. So, did the crisis at Heiligenstadt change anything in the end? Yes. He had always seen himself as a composer/pianist, but now that was over. He understood now that he was a composer and, soon, nothing else. The end of performing also meant the loss of over half his income—you make more money playing music than writing it. To that terrible blow he responded with outsized defiance. In both quantity and quality, his productivity over the next six years would be staggering.

From first note to last, the **Third Symphony** was written as a piece named for, and concerned with, the most powerful man in the world: it was originally to be called "Bonaparte." So, it would be what we call a *program* piece (instrumental pieces that tell some kind of extra-musical story), shaped around the French conqueror who embodied the age. Like many liberals, Beethoven saw Napoleon as a liberator who would bring constitutional governments, better laws, an end to ancient tyrannies. With this work Beethoven joined his music once and for all to the ideals he grew up with in Bonn. In the process he intended to step beyond the role of musical entertainer and to place his work in the larger world, in history.

The Third begins with two massive chords introducing a kaleidoscopic movement that never flags in its energy, its driving momentum, its sense of constantly evolving toward something. It is not written in the style of military music at all; rather, it is a sweeping evocation of a battle or a campaign. The climax in the middle of the development is a shattering chord: a crux, the moment when the hero begins to come into his own.

If the first movement is a symbolic campaign or battle, the narrative point of the second movement is clear: it is a funeral march, based on a mournful and memorable theme. The silvery scherzo that follows, with its piping oboe and lusty hunting horns, suggests a return to life and joy after loss. After a militant introduction, the finale falls into dance music, in the form of variations over a repeating bass theme. Through the course of the movement that dance is transformed into heroic music, until a coda of overwhelming jubilation evokes a people celebrating the fruits not just of the hero's victory, but the new freedom he has bequeathed to everyone.

Beethoven knew the Third Symphony was the best, the most important thing he had done. But even he could not have predicted that it would stand as one of the great downbeats in the history of music. It changed the world's sense of what a symphony could be, and to a degree the sense of what *music* could be: more intense, more emotional, more complex, more individual, with more violent contrasts and unprecedented challenges to the listener. Haydn and Mozart had made the symphony the king of instrumental genres; the Third Symphony confirmed that, and carried the genre still further in ambition. All the same, it's important to remember that while the world has tended to paint Beethoven as a musical revolutionary, he never called himself one. Revolutionaries want to overthrow the past; Beethoven had no intention of that. Everything he did was grounded in models from the past, especially his prime idols: Mozart, Haydn, Handel, and J. S. Bach. Call him instead a *radical evolutionary*.

As it turned out, the Third would not go into the world with the name "Bonaparte." Soon after it was finished, Beethoven learned that Napoleon had crowned himself emperor of France, and realized instantly what that meant: his hero was not going to end the tyrannies of crowned heads but rather had made himself a crowned head. In a fit of rage he ripped up the title page. He finally published the Third with the title "Eroica" (Heroic), "in memory of a great man." That man was the hero Beethoven had once believed Napoleon to be.

The "Eroica" is a tall order for a listener—perhaps the first symphony to demand repeated listenings to get a handle on it. The piano sonatas are a quicker read, but no less impressive. Aside from the **"Pathétique"** I would suggest starting with **"Moonlight" Sonata** (No. 14 in C-sharp Minor, Op. 27), maybe the most famous of all piano works. It quickly became legendary, mainly because of its sui generis first movement, a quiet murmuring that conjures a haunting and poetic atmosphere—but the sonata's finale is unrelieved ferocity.

A few years later came the **"Waldstein" Sonata** (No. 21 in C, Op. 53), named for its dedication to a Bonn patron of Beethoven's. It begins *in medias res* with a sense of breathless, kinetic energy that will scarcely flag throughout. After a pensive slow interlude, the finale resolves the lingering tensions in an explosion of joy. Here Beethoven reveals his singular gift for taking an idea to a point of apparent maximum intensity, then topping it.

Like the thirty-two piano sonatas, his sixteen string quartets expressively, technically, and spiritually trace an epic journey from the eighteenth century into prophecies of the future of music. The best place to start is with the three quartets of **Op. 59**, from 1806, called the **Razumovsky Quartets** for the Russian aristocrat who commissioned them. They were Beethoven's first fully mature quartets, and they laid the path for the whole genre for a hundred years to come. As is usual with him, successive works even in one opus are radically divergent: Op. 59, No. 1 in F Major is expansive and grand, starting with its folklike, long-breathed opening theme; No. 2 in E Minor unfolds as more inward and esoteric, with a soulful and lamenting second movement; No. 3 in C Major has ebullient outer movements and a second movement like a folk song from some unknown country. (None of these quartets, like much of the second period, is really in Beethoven's heroic voice.)

In his later years Beethoven, now almost completely deaf, wretchedly ill and filled with sorrow, put away the heroic style and transparent emotional narratives of the middle period for a more mysterious and poetic world, some of it inward and intensely spiritual, some of it outward, comic, childlike. In effect he stretched his art in all directions: longer and shorter, more complex and more simple, more violent and more transcendent, more intense contrasts and more minimalistic concentration on one idea. The late music finds new colors and new kinds of continuity, finds places in the heart that music had never touched before. Much of this work took a century or more to be understood and accepted. Beethoven's last string quartets are supreme examples of this late style. Rather than a single narrative, each major work seems to enfold the whole of life, from light to dark, sorrow to joy. For a sample, try the **String Quartet in A Minor, Op. 132.** It begins like a mystical puzzle, then launches into a passionate song that keeps falling apart. A charmingly absurd scherzo is based on two simultaneous ideas that simply keep repeating in new configurations. Then the sublime "holy song of thanks from a convalescent to the deity." Its topic is taken directly from Beethoven's life; the music is a kind of sacred trance. A little march. A finale founded on one of the most beautiful, most touching melodies Beethoven or anyone ever wrote.

In his maturity Beethoven wrote seven concertos—five for piano, all but the fifth written for himself, one for violin, and one for piano trio and orchestra. **Piano Concerto No. 4 in G Major** begins with a brooding solo for piano alone, setting up an often conflicting dialogue between soloist and orchestra. In the first movement, the orchestra can never quite get the soloist's theme right; in the second, the strings answer the piano's introverted soliloquies with angry gestures; in the third, the divide is played as comedy, solo and orchestra bantering until they are cheerily united. The music is Beethoven at his most inspired.

Finally, back to the symphonies. By the time Beethoven finished the **Symphony No. 5 in C Minor** in 1808, he still had plenty of adversaries but was generally understood to be the peer of any composer who ever lived. The **"Eroica,"** which first met the inevitable incomprehension, was soon recognized as one of the greatest of symphonies. For Beethoven it could have been a delightful life if he were not so sick, so deaf, so steadily disappointed in love.

At last, the **Ninth Symphony.** Most of you know the theme of its finale because probably half the world knows it— which is just what Beethoven intended. It is a gigantic work barely containable by a concert hall, meant for great occasions and ceremonies. In its tumultuous first movement he returns to the heroic style only to bury it: on a sketch his word for the opening movement was *despair.* It ends with a funeral march. There is a dashing, mock-demonic scherzo, a drifting slow movement that has the exquisite, long-breathed melodies of his late style. Then the finale, a setting of stanzas from Friedrich Schiller's "Ode to Joy," a poem written in the revolutionary 1780s and filled with the hope and fervor of those years. It had been set many times; young revolutionaries sang it in the streets. Beethoven had been planning to compose the ode since he was a teenager. To set it in the Ninth, he created a little tune as simple as a drinking song, something anybody can sing, and on that mounted a towering theme-and-variations movement that stretches from East—in the form of a Turkish march—to West, from the private to the public, from the absurd to the sublime, to contain this message: heroes can't give us a better world, and neither will God; we have to do that for ourselves, as brothers and sisters and husbands and wives, in joy and freedom and brotherhood. That message, proclaimed in a time of repression when in Vienna you could be arrested for speaking the word *freedom,* was intended to keep alive some simple but timelessly important truths. His "Joy" theme was written in the spirit of the new national anthems, but it is an anthem for all humanity.

In his last years Beethoven was almost completely deaf, rumored to be insane, fatally ill with liver disease, drinking heavily, devastated by long struggles over the guardianship of his late brother's son (the nephew finally tried to kill himself). Yet he was still brilliantly productive and full of plans. He died in 1827 already a legend, sketches for a tenth symphony on his desk. As a towering, suffering genius he became the prime foundation of the romantic cult of genius as demigod, his art rising from the unknown and encompassing all. There are many legends around Beethoven, but in truth no composer, perhaps no artist of any kind, had a better grasp of the human heartstrings than Beethoven did. He had known life from wildest joy to deepest anguish, and he had the hardheaded discipline and skill to capture it all on the page—the whole of our lives in breadth and depth. That is his resplendent gift to the world.

More Beethoven: Symphonies Nos. 6 and 7; the Violin Concerto in D Major; the "Appassionata" Sonata (Piano Sonata No. 23 in F Minor); the *Coriolan* and *Egmont* Overtures; *Missa Solemnis* (Mass in D).

Part IV

Romantic

Chapter 12

THE ROMANTIC PERIOD (CA. 1830–1900)

Dates for all artistic periods are approximate and variable among sources—and each art tends to have its own dates. In music we begin the romantic period around the 1830s. Romantic painting and literature, on the other hand, developed well before musical romanticism.

A central philosophical element of romanticism across all the arts was a rejection of what one poet called "the cold light of reason" that had been the foundation of the eighteenth-century Enlightenment. The Enlightenment exalted science, reason, moderation, the universal, the hopeful future. Romanticism exalted emotion, excess, the uncanny, the unattainable, the individual, the hoary past. The Enlightenment loved formal gardens and elegant buildings; romantics loved mountains, nature in the wild, castles in ruins. A classic German romantic painting is Caspar David Friedrich's *Two Men Contemplating the Moon*, the moon being represented by a formless glow. It's the first painting in which the central focus is a void. The Enlightenment aspired to do away with myth and superstition; the romantics loved folktales, the exotic, the unexplainable, the ghostly and demonic: the *sublime*, defined as a mingling of awe and eternity and fear, like gazing at the stars.

In a remarkably short period of time there was a sea-change in the arts. In the eighteenth century genius was defined as a quality one possessed. The romantics founded a cult of the hero-genius that called it a sublime quality that possessed artists and exalted them to a kind of demonic demigod, roiled by the throes of inspiration. The model of the romantic genius was Beethoven: coarse, scowling, suffering, sublime. Classical-era composers hoped their listeners would be touched, moved, charmed, amused. Romantic composers hoped their listeners would be dazzled, overwhelmed, devastated. The classical period in music aspired to the formal logic of an essay; the romantics aspired to poetry in sound. For the first time in the arts there was an intense focus on artists as unique individuals "expressing themselves." Richard Wagner said artists were the crown of society, high priests in the religion of art, the true leaders and redeemers of a people.

The quintessential German romantic writer, E. T. A. Hoffmann, wrote stories about fluid identities, doppelgängers, automata, madness, nightmare. In his romantic youth Brahms identified intensely with Hoffmann's stories, and Hoffmann was fundamental to Robert Schumann's inspiration. This was the period of Mary Shelley's *Frankenstein* and of visionary German poets, including Novalis and Hölderlin—some of whom took the high-romantic path of suicide that had been laid out in Goethe's seminal *Sorrows of Young Werther*, about a youth who kills himself over an unattainable love. In France, Hector Berlioz's friend Eugène Delacroix painted harems, rapes, massacres. Berlioz's teacher advised him to aim for "Babylonian" effects; he wrote pieces for ensembles of hundreds and aspired to thousands. A half-dozen years after Beethoven died, Schumann issued piano works of loosely connected miniatures based on images: butterflies, a carnival, the music full of personal allusions. Schumann criticized most listeners as shallow philistines; his writing was a harbinger of a growing divide between artist and public that in the next century widened into a gulf.

Allied to all this was a new doctrine of nation, based on the romantic myth that folk music and art rise from the soil, that all true art comes from the spirit of a people. Thus the powerful influence of national folk song on such composers as Schubert and, later, Mahler. This was the era of fairy tale collections by the brothers Grimm, of the epochal collection of German folk poetry (much of it actually ersatz) in *Des Knaben Wunderhorn*. Artistic nationalism was closely allied to political nationalism, such as the struggle of fragmented Germany to become a unified country, of places like Hungary and Bohemia to be freed of foreign rule. As the century wore on the myth of *the people* turned more ominously to a myth of race, and finally to the horrors of racial ideology that lacerated the next century. Nationalism was an ideology and aesthetic that never really made sense, and much of which was delusion and fraud. At the same time, in the arts it galvanized a great deal of splendid work.

Around the middle of the nineteenth century Franz Liszt suggested the term *program music*, which describes instrumental pieces that tell some kind of extramusical story. Liszt invented the orchestral *symphonic poem*, a piece based on a dramatic, literary, or poetic idea. In **Richard Strauss's *Don Quixote*** you can't miss the windmills, the bleating sheep, and so on. His tone poems are as busy with incident as an opera. On the other side of the equation, while in his vocal works Brahms was concerned with expressing his texts emotionally, he did not want to be caught painting an image. But **Schubert** in his songs goes after every image in the text; the piano accompaniment of his **"Gretchen at the Spinning Wheel"** is a steady whirr that stops only at her memory of her lover's kiss.

Program works became a high-romantic genre that spilled into the next century, part of a larger goal of unifying the arts, bringing together music, literature, and visual media. The traditional opposite of program music is called "pure," or "abstract" music. This means a work by, say, Mozart or Brahms that has no stated or discernable story and expresses itself purely in notes. Tensions between these two schools of thought marked the period. On one hand, romantics thought of instrumental music as the supreme art, because it can move us in mysterious ways, speaking powerfully without words or story: pure expression. But Wagner and his followers rejected that idea, saying that music must be allied with words and ideas and images and stories in a great union, a total work of art. In the later nineteenth century there was a furious aesthetic "War of the Romantics" between the followers of Brahms who adhered to classical models, above all sonata form, and the Wagner-Liszt school that declared those forms dead.

Ultimately, the war between music that is pure, abstract, and other virginal adjectives, and music that is pictorial, visceral, capable of bracing vulgarity, has never been resolved and never will be. Over time the combatants in the War of the Romantics simply gave up the battle. Today both abstract and pictorial works by Liszt, Wagner, Strauss, Brahms, and Beethoven coexist happily in the repertoire, and music has been the better for it. If only all wars ended so well.

Helping to convey these grand musical programs was a new focus on orchestration. In the nineteenth century the modern orchestra as we know it came fully into form. In the Renaissance, what instruments played what parts was often ad hoc. If you were doing a madrigal for five voices and only had three singers in the house, a couple of instruments might fill in the other parts and that was fine. For Bach in the baroque period, there was no standard orchestra; you used the collection of instruments you wanted for a particular piece, and/or included a part for whatever virtuoso happened to be in town and/or you could afford. Then, as now, strings were the basis of most ensembles because they are considered the instruments most like the voice, don't tend to get tired, and don't need to breathe to make a sound.

By the classical period, in keeping with the period's habit of rationalizing everything, the orchestra became more consistent, though it still evolved. An early classical orchestra might have five to seven violins covering two parts, two or three violas, a cello or two, and a bass. Added to that were the primal classical wind section of two oboes, two horns (valveless hunting horns in this period), and one or two bassoons. For a festive piece, you'd add trumpets and drums. From there, things grew steadily. Composers added a flute, then two; this is the basic Haydn orchestra. Mozart loved the clarinet and used two in his later orchestral works. By then the mature classical orchestra was in place: pairs of flutes, oboes, clarinets, bassoons, and horns; two trumpets and timpani, if desired; and strings. The strings were divided into five parts: first and second violins, violas, cellos, and basses. (Most of the time in the classical period, the cellos and basses played the same bass line, in octaves.) Three trombones appeared in Beethoven's Fifth Symphony and turned up in many symphonies after. The standard romantic orchestra also included four French horns. The number of string players fluctuated with space and budget. Although our modern original-instrument ensembles—bands using historic instruments—tend to go with a small string section, in fact Haydn and Mozart felt that the more strings, the better. Beethoven's Ninth was premiered with a huge orchestra, all the winds doubled.

With the orchestra in place, the romantics of the nineteenth century, led by Hector Berlioz and Richard Wagner, began for the first time to look at orchestral color as a vital component in itself, and accordingly expanded and experimented with their ensembles so as to explore a richer and more varied palette. It helped that trumpets and horns had acquired valves, so for the first time they could play every note in every key. (Wagner's *Ring of the Nibelung* begins with an incredible prelude featuring twelve valve horns.) The full romantic orchestra might have twenty or more violins, ten or more violas and cellos, seven or more basses. The winds might include such instruments as the contrabassoon, high E-flat clarinet, or English horn (which is neither English nor a horn—it's an alto oboe). That is the essential makeup of the band to this day, to which is added a variety of percussion instruments as needed.

Which is to say that Haydn, Mozart, Beethoven, and other classicists looked at the orchestra first as a vehicle to present their music clearly, with coloristic effects as a secondary matter (though all of them had finely tuned ears for scoring). The romantics, however, loved orchestral color for its own sake. It's indicative that during this time Berlioz wrote the first orchestration textbook. Part of Wagner's genius was his gift for powerful and variegated orchestration. The romantic focus on instrumental color flowed into the twentieth century, until with Ligeti and others the orchestra can sound almost like electronic music. Yet on the whole it's the same old strings, winds, and brass playing it.

Romanticism was a boiling pot of contradictions, of ecstasy and madness, exaltation and despair, a doctrine of instinct and feeling over logic and form. What held it together was, perhaps, mainly the power and concentration of great creators, including Berlioz, Chopin, Schubert, and Schumann—all of whom had classical elements in their makeup. Brahms grew up a passionate young romantic, but in his maturity he was a loner, a singular blend of classical and romantic. At the end of the century and beginning of the next, Mahler expanded the ethos and the forces and the harmonic language of romanticism to the breaking point. The next generation, responding to that and to foreboding new social and political currents, had to find new paths. Yet in the end, with its exaltation of genius, of the messianic creator, and so on, modernism would in many ways be an extension of romanticism and its cult of genius into new technical and expressive territories.

Chapter 13

FRANZ SCHUBERT (1797–1828)

H istory amply demonstrates that the gods have no partiality to the arts. I'd go further and say that nature is indifferent to genius and loves the mediocre middle. Schubert is a case in point regarding my cosmic theories. Schubert died at age thirty-one, with a remarkable collection of work under his belt, much of the best of it the product of his wretched final years. As he took to his deathbed, his fame was just starting to take off. If he had managed to live another decade, he would have been the acknowledged inheritor of Beethoven's mantle. There is no question that he had that kind of gift. Unlike Mozart, in his teens Schubert was already composing historic pieces. Some have argued that he wrote a lifetime's worth of music in his short sojourn, so it's all fine. As far as I'm concerned, that's letting the gods off the hook.

Franz Peter Schubert was born to the family of a schoolmaster. The Schuberts were musical; from early on Franz played viola in the family string quartet. In 1808 he was accepted as a boy soprano into the choir of Austria's imperial court chapel—today's Vienna Boys Choir. Before long it became clear that this youth was some kind of phenomenon. He played violin in the student orchestra and sometimes took the baton. One of his instructors ran out of things to teach him and declared, "He's learned it all from God himself!" For years he studied with Antonio Salieri, whom history remembers, wrongly, as the supposed bête noire of Mozart.

When Schubert's voice broke, he was retired from the choir and was thereafter on his own. Here his limitations set in: he didn't push himself with people, was at once shy and rough in manners, and generally enigmatic. To be attracted to Schubert, and he was to have friends who did a great deal for him, was mainly to be attracted to his art.

With nothing else turning up to make his way, in 1814 Schubert reluctantly went to work in his father's school. As much as possible in the classroom, it is said, he composed and expected the students to leave him alone. Those who bothered him got a hiding. By that point he had written a great deal of music, including pieces for orchestra or piano as well as chamber music, and part of an operetta. In 1813 he finished a full-length opera, but more important than that big effort was a small one: a little *lied*—the German word for "art song"—on a lyric from Goethe's play *Faust*: **"Gretchen am Spinnrade"** (Gretchen at the Spinning Wheel).

In the play Gretchen is a young girl seduced and abandoned by Faust, who falls into despair: "My peace is gone, my heart is heavy. I'll find it never and nevermore! Where I don't have him, that is the grave." In its intensity of longing it is among Goethe's most powerful lyrics. Schubert set it to music in one day, October 19, 1814. It lasts just over three minutes. He was seventeen years old. It is hardly believable that a teen-aged boy with no known romantic experience could sound the depths of longing and erotic passion in that poem, but the music shows that Schubert did exactly that. In its seamless joining of great poetry and great music, and in its depth of passion "Gretchen" did not only herald the arrival of a new genius, but marked the beginning of a change in the history of music in the nineteenth century. Now a little thing, a fragment, a song, could enfold big themes, big emotions.

This three-minute revolution tells us a lot about Schubert's instincts. Already his singular style and approach are in place, his gift for painting every aspect of a lyric. In "Gretchen" the right hand of the piano is a turning figure that implies both the spinning wheel and the whirl of the girl's feelings. As her feelings change, the music follows them in vigorous harmonies and changes of key—all his life Schubert would be a virtuoso of quick, expressive key changes. The spinning wheel comes to a halt with the girl's "Ah, his kiss!"—it is almost a shriek. The wheel begins again, the emotions in the last part of the song still more torn, the tension rising until a breathtaking climax at "On his kisses, I could die!" The music fades out on the spinning wheel, which has become an image of churning heartache. The other Schubert trademark in "Gretchen" is the beauty of the melody, both in the voice and in the swirling line the piano spins. Already in his teens he was one of the greatest of tunesmiths.

Over six hundred Schubert lieder followed "Gretchen." They are the foundation of the romantic lied tradition, in which for the first time art song became an important genre. As he worked in a trance they poured out of him, thrown onto the page, jotted on a napkin at dinner, sometimes several lieder completed in a day. At eighteen he wrote another electrifying outing on Goethe's quasi–folk poem **"Erlkönig"** (Elf King). A father is galloping with his little child on a stormy night when the enchanting voice of the Elf King begins to sing to the boy, coaxing him to come play and enjoy endless delights. The father cannot hear the spirit. Schubert makes the story into a four-minute cantata of competing voices: the fevered and frightened boy, the dismissive then terrified father, the silken and insinuating voice of the Elf King, plus a narrator, all over the pounding hooves of the horse. Schubert characterizes each voice with its own style, at the same time building a rising line of tension that reaches a shattering point before the blunt ending: "In his arms, the child was dead." His first publication years later, "Erlkönig" would do as much as anything to establish Schubert's fame.

In 1816 Schubert took leave from teaching and, living at the house of a friend—more or less his lifestyle from then on— he plunged into composition full-time. He sat writing all day; when he finished one piece, he said, he simply started another. Some pieces were ambitious, some not; he loved writing and playing dances. Nights he spent with friends or sat alone in a tavern, smoking a pipe and staring into space and getting sozzled, like a boxer between bouts. Often by the end of the night he'd be smashing something, a plate, a glass.

As for Schubert's romantic life, we have only rumors and legends. There was a singer he had a crush on as a teenager, a countess who was a student. There are testimonials from people who knew Schubert saying that he had a sexually excessive side, but they did not provide details. In recent years some have theorized that he was gay, but that is speculation without solid evidence. In any case he probably frequented prostitutes, because that is what most bachelors did in those days. In Vienna there were thousands of ladies offering their services. Eventually, tragically, somebody gave him syphilis.

Schubert's career, such as it was, took shape in a singular way, centered on intimate parlors more than grand halls. A bohemian collection of friends gathered around him. Most of them were creative sorts; they included painter Moritz von Schwind, poet Johann Mayrhofer, the musical Hüttenbrenner brothers, and artistic dilettante Franz von Schober—the latter an extravagant character, a cross-dresser and probably gay.

The friends threw parties involving dancing, wine, food, and games. Schubert and his music were at the center of these occasions, so they were called "Schubertiads." There are drawings and paintings and stories commemorating the parties. One series of sketches recounts a rowdy wagon trip to the Vienna woods and the group's comic despair over a broken wine bottle. On another occasion Schubert had a go at his virtuosic "Wanderer" Fantasy at the piano but soon gave up, crying, "Oh, the hell with it. Let's eat!" Schubertiads spread through the well-to-do parlors of Vienna, some of them held without the composer present, but all featuring his lieder. Meanwhile in 1819 Schubert and his champion, celebrated singer Johann Michael Vogl, mounted a tour of upper Austria and found the songs receiving tremendous acclaim. There is a wry drawing by Schober of bespectacled Schubert clutching sheet music and dwarfed by the tall, commanding figure of Vogl.

Schubert wrote a number of piano sonatas, but some of his major contributions to the canon were small character pieces in loose collections, which had an outsize influence on the coming generations of romantic piano composers. The set of four **Impromptus, Op. 90** starts with a solemn movement, then come a breathless one, a lovely song without words, and a whirling final movement. For a sample of his middle-period chamber works—which are just as powerful as the piano pieces—the obvious choice is the **"Trout" Quintet** (Piano Quintet in A), a delightful piece written during the 1819 tour with Vogl. As is typical with Schubert, this quintet written at age twenty-two was not published until after he died. From the first movement onward the piece is full of joie de vivre and overflowing with melody. Its fourth movement is a theme and variations based on his song "The Trout."

Schubert and his friends made efforts to get his music published without success until 1821, with a private printing of "Erlkönig." That turned out well, "Gretchen" followed, and from that point a steady trickle of pieces began to emerge in print.

The main effort from 1822 was a symphony Schubert planned to write as thanks to the Graz Music Society, who had given him an honorary degree. Schubert completed two movements in score and sent them to his composer friend Anselm Hüttenbrenner. Then, nothing. He never completed the symphony. There was no performance, and Hüttenbrenner never released the score—it was only discovered forty years later. The mystery has never been explained, including the question of whether Schubert realized how potent and important his first movement was. From early on the piece (No. 8) has been called the **"Unfinished" Symphony.** Starting with an ominous bass line answered by whispering strings, it finds a quite new voice in music. The movement continues in kind, a sweet second theme crushed by fateful declamations, a development section full of anguish. The second movement is a delicately lyrical stretch. History calls the "Unfinished" the first romantic symphony. The question of whether Schubert was more classicist or romantic has been long debated. He certainly had a romantic temperament, scornful of Enlightenment reason and exalting individual feeling and instinct. His music reflects that attitude. But he also stayed true to sonata form and other classical patterns, over the years tightening his form by trimming back his tendency to long-windedness. His more ambitious pieces were carefully sketched and revised.

It was late 1822 when Schubert contracted syphilis. For him the next years were miserable; he endured rashes, chancres in the mouth, the loss of his hair, weeks prostrate in the hospital. In 1823 he penned a devastated poem: "See, annihilated I lay in the dust, / Scorched by agonizing fire, / My life's martyr path, / Approaching eternal oblivion."

Yet his productivity never faltered. In 1823 he wrote what became the most beloved of song cycles, *Die schöne Müllerin* (The Beautiful Miller's Daughter). Years earlier Beethoven had pioneered the idea of a series of songs telling a story. Schubert picked up that idea and expanded it, unifying German folk music with classical style. His accompaniments exploit the new, more colorful and robust pianos that were appearing. The story of *Schöne Müllerin*, from faux-naive poems by Wilhelm Müller, is a simple one of love, loss, and death. A young miller is on the move: "To wander is the miller's joy! He must be a wretched miller, who never wants to wander!" He comes on a stream, follows it to a mill, falls helplessly in love with the miller's daughter. But after a moment of hope she takes up with a handsome hunter, and in his anguish he hurls himself into the brook.

What Schubert made of these twenty slight poems, in music of sophisticated ingenuousness, is one of the miracles of music. Every song has a melody that sounds timeless, inevitable, unforgettable. No less are the accompaniments striking in their colors and in their pianistic imagination, painting the emotions and the setting of each lyric: the babbling of the brook, the heady rush of impatience, the trance of love, the streaming of tears. The final song is a gentle lullaby sung by the brook to the drowned miller, and I don't know of any stranger and more touching moments anywhere in music—one of the few comparable examples being the last song of another Schubert cycle, *Winterreise.*

In early 1824 Schubert was feeling overwhelmed by illness and poverty and his failure to find a wider audience. He was clearly a master—why was his fame so slow in coming? The traditional explanation is that "genius is never recognized in its own time." In fact, that's rarely the case; artists who are giants in history were usually giants in their own time. Some of his slow rise surely had to do with Schubert's personality: diffident, in some degree oblivious, and, crucially, not all that motivated by money or glory.

William Faulkner said that he produced his first novels because he was driven to write them and it hardly occurred to him that anybody would read them. Schubert seems to have been something like that. By and large, to become famous you need to have a burning desire to be famous. Schubert lacked the steely resolve required to claw to the top of a viciously competitive music scene in Vienna. He could accompany his songs but was not enough of a virtuoso to put his piano works across, and he was short and plump (his nickname was "Tubby") and generally goofy looking. He spent much of his time and energy writing operas, which were the fastest way to gain prestige and fame as a composer. The trouble was, opera was the one genre Schubert seemed to lack much instinct for.

Of his nine completed operas, only a couple were produced. They failed to catch on and have rarely been heard since.

When Schubert's name finally acquired some luster in the last years of his life, most likely it was the cumulative effect of many private performances and the impact of his publications. Composers in those days made their reputations mainly with sheet music, which was purchased by a growing middle-class audience. Schubert's songs and piano miniatures were ideal material for amateurs to sing and play in their parlors. Much of his work is light, its tone what Germans call *gemütlich*, meaning "comfortable"—the kind of feelings you enjoy from cozy, wine-enhanced hanging out with friends.

Later in 1824 Schubert's health and spirits improved, though he still felt little hope of recovery. He had some months of continuing good work and good spirits, his songs gaining a larger audience in the concert programs and the parlors of Vienna. In those days private performances of lieder, piano music, and chamber music were far more frequent than public concerts. (As noted before, only one of Beethoven's piano sonatas was performed publicly during his life.) That reality has contributed to the partly mythical tradition that Schubert was neglected his lifetime. More accurately, he was a cult figure emerging into the limelight when he died.

In his earlier work Schubert was most influenced by Mozart; he skirted the daunting peaks of Beethoven. In his later ambitious works he embraced the model of Beethoven and became his first great heir. The work of Schubert's last two years was tremendous. His health failed again and he probably understood how little time he had left. He put everything he had into everything he did, knowing any piece could be his last. Four masterpieces represent this period. *Winterreise* (Winter Journey), is another song cycle, the twenty-four lyrics again by Wilhelm Müller. But these are not in the folksy vein of *Schöne Müllerin*, and neither are Schubert's settings. "A stranger I arrived, a stranger I depart," it begins. A poet is fleeing a lost love, setting out in that despairing direction Kafka called "anywhere but here." Winter lies not only outside the narrator, but in his soul. He finds his tears freezing on his cheek, he has a passing memory of a rustling linden tree, he carves the name of his beloved on the ice of a frozen brook, he dreams of spring, he is shadowed by a crow. The last song, "The Hurdy-Gurdy Man," is an uncanny evocation of finding yourself at the end of your rope. He comes across a shabby old man cranking his instrument, barefoot in the snow, surrounded by snarling dogs, his plate empty, nobody listening. The piano part involves a weird twisting melody over a drone, everything done with the simplest possible means. "Strange old man," the poet concludes, "shall I go with you? / Will you play your organ / To my songs?"

Schubert was correcting the publishing proofs of *Winterreise* on his deathbed. The old hurdy-gurdy player is an image of obliteration, and the speaker, really, is Schubert himself—dying and feeling as if he has been singing for no one. Another example of his state of mind is **"Der Doppelgänger,"** one of the most unsettling of songs—likewise its lyric by Heinrich Heine. A man is drawn to the house of an old love and in the distance sees a figure standing before the house wringing his hands in anguish. Coming nearer, he finds with cold terror that the man is himself. "You pale comrade!" he cries. "Why do you ape the pain of my love / that tormented me here/ so many nights, / so long ago?" Beginning with a bleak and ominous bass line, the lied is a crescendo of horror. It ends quietly, but with spine-chilling harmonies.

Schubert's two last large instrumental works are both his greatest and among the greatest of any in their genres. Both of them are far-reaching emotional journeys from deep darkness to shadowed joy. The **Piano Sonata in B-flat Major, D. 960** begins with a broad, beautiful, affecting melody that is suddenly interrupted by a low rumble in the bass. In that foreboding gesture we find a key to Schubert's late music. Now for him beauty is fraught, shadowed. He is like a man who loves parties but can no longer go to the party, only watch it from outside. The beauty of music has become a symbol of life itself, receding away. The second movement of the sonata is a trance of desolation, singing ceaselessly through its pain. After a delicate, almost fairylike scherzo, the finale paints a joy halting and uncertain, clouded to the end.

For me this sonata is among the most powerful of piano works, and when it comes to chamber music, I say the same about Schubert's incomparable **String Quintet in C Major.** It begins like a groan of pain, in a mingling of major and minor. Good old C major has never been as apprehensive as this first movement. The slow movement is a sighing, exquisite song of lamentation. Then leaps up a stupendous scherzo of dancing, shouting gaiety that gains much of its breathtaking effect from the shadows of the previous music. The finale is another kind of dance, its tone strangely stern and ambiguous: a dance as if from end of dancing.

Weakened by syphilis, Schubert was finally felled by typhoid fever. Staying with his brother in November 1828, after weeks in bed he turned his face to the wall and murmured, "Here, here is my end." Wrote a friend, "Schubert is dead, and with him all that was brightest and most beautiful in our life." In March of that year he had finally found public acclaim in an overflowing concert in Vienna. Before that, he had been given the honor of carrying a torch in Beethoven's funeral procession, and he was laid to rest next to Beethoven. His gravestone read, "Here music has buried a treasure, but even fairer hopes." True, the world did not yet know many of his greatest works, and some have deplored that inscription. I don't. What Schubert could have achieved with more years is dismal to contemplate, and we should not forgive the gods for their indifference.

More Schubert: Symphony No. 9 in C Major (The Great); recorded collections of single lieder; Piano Sonatas No. 20 in A Major and No. 14 in A Minor; String Quartet in D Minor (whose second movement includes variations on his song "Death and the Maiden").

Chapter 14

HECTOR BERLIOZ (1803–1869)

The first great work of Hector Berlioz, the *Symphonie fantastique*, has as its backstory a drug trip that ends with a hallucinated witches' sabbath. *Harold in Italy*, perhaps his finest symphony, ends with an orgy of brigands, something Berlioz had observed firsthand. His teacher had encouraged him to pursue "Babylonian" effects in his music, and Berlioz took the instructions to heart. His gift for excess flowed from his own hyperbolic responses to music. No decorous little emotions for Berlioz: "I feel a delicious pleasure in which the reasoning faculty has no share . . . emotion, increasing proportionately with the energy and loftiness of the composer's inspiration, soon produces a strange commotion in my circulation . . . there are spasmodic muscular contractions, a trembling of all the limbs a *total numbness of feet and hands* . . . vertigo . . . a half swoon." If that suggests other, more intimate experiences, it is supposed to.

Berlioz had an unpoetic background. He was born to a physician's family in La Côte-Saint-André, France. His father was agnostic, his mother fanatically Catholic. In childhood he gravitated to music and by age twelve, self-taught, he was writing pieces for local musicians. By his teens he had learned to play the flute and had become a virtuoso on guitar. Because of his family's indifference to music, he never really learned piano. Sent by his father to study medicine in Paris in 1821, he was dutiful in his studies for a year, but spent most of his free hours at the Paris Opéra. He soon left medicine behind and got himself into the Conservatoire, determined to be a composer despite the disapproval of his father and the hysterical protests of his mother, who considered artists to be more or less automatically damned.

Sitting in a theater in 1827, two new passions overcame Berlioz at once. At a performance of *Romeo and Juliet* he was thunderstruck by Shakespeare, who became a lifelong obsession, and no less by the comely Juliet of the production, the Irish-born Harriet Smithson. For the actress he conceived on the spot a helpless passion. But she did not respond to his maddened letters, which frightened more than attracted her.

His *amour fou* going nowhere, in 1830, at age twenty-seven, Berlioz conceived a programmatic symphony based on his unrequited love: a young artist, tormented by love, decides to kill himself with opium. Instead of dying he falls into a series of hallucinations, each represented by a movement of the symphony. In all the movements the beloved is represented by a recurring theme Berlioz called the *idée fixe*. Thereby the inception of one of the most celebrated and symptomatic works of the romantic age: *Symphonie fantastique*. In fact, the future development of romantic program music to come was founded above all on two pieces: Beethoven's "Pastoral" Symphony (No. 6) and the *fantastique*. Its movements are wide-ranging: "Reveries, Passions," a pensive but troubled introduction followed by a turbulent allegro in which the beloved theme is introduced; "A Ball," a luscious waltz with delicate harp writing, in which the idée fixe turns up in middle and end; "Scene in the Country," a remarkable stretch of musical painting—we hear shepherd's pipes, distant thunder, then things get passionate again.

The last two movements are surely the most frenzied music heard in the era. In "March to the Scaffold," the artist imagines he has killed his beloved and is going to the guillotine. After the rising excitement of the march, in his last seconds on the scaffold the condemned recalls his beloved by way of the idée fixe, then we hear the crash of the blade. From there it gets wilder: "Witches' Sabbath," a kind of après-execution nightmare full of howling demons and what all, in which the beloved's theme is transformed into a shrieking witch's song. In the end, though, at least for modern listeners the finale is more a matter of delighted guffaws than shivers—literally, a hell of a good time.

In 1830 Berlioz wrote a cantata proper enough to win him the Conservatoire's Prix de Rome, which involved two years of residence in the city. By then, not one to rest on his heartbreak, he was engaged to a beautiful and flighty pianist named Camille Moke. Reluctantly he said his farewells to Camille and headed for Italy.

As it turned out, Berlioz hated Rome and found it creatively stifling. Still, he garnered experiences of a lifetime. He hiked around the countryside with his guitar and gun, shooting game and accompanying brigands at their revels. Life was pleasant until bad news arrived: his fiancée had ditched him for a piano maker. In a transport of rage Berlioz decided that what needed to be done was to murder the lot: Camille, her mother, her new boyfriend. He somehow decided that his best bet to get into her house was to disguise himself as a woman. To this end he secured a dress, wig, veiled lady's hat, and two double-barreled pistols—the fourth bullet intended for himself. Thus equipped, he set out to sea on his mission. By the time he landed in Nice, however, he had come to realize its ridiculousness. (We know this story because he told it himself, in his *Memoirs*.) Instead he composed a couple of overtures and headed back to Rome. After only a year he was back in Paris, where began his most fertile period.

Berlioz's career from that point can be summarized as occasional moments of glory and years of frustration. For starters, Harriet Smithson finally heard the *Symphonie fantastique* and really liked it, they got together, they actually got married—and discovered they could not stand living together. Musically, his style and sympathies were really more German than French, and his countrymen never quite forgave him for that. He championed Beethoven, whom the French had never much warmed to. He longed to write opera, but his efforts, including the gigantic *Trojans*, were received indifferently in Paris and cost him terrific financial losses. He made most of his living writing musical critiques, hundreds of articles over the years, all of it marked by his wry and impassioned voice. Despite it all, Berlioz could be quite funny, as in the beginning of his *Memoirs*: "I was reared in the Catholic and Apostolic Church of Rome. This charming religion (so attractive since it gave up burning people) was for seven whole years the joy of my life . . . although we have long since fallen out."

Disgusted with the way other conductors mangled his work, he picked up the baton and before long became one of the leading conductors of his time. Never very popular in

Paris, Berlioz spent much of his performing life on the road, including lucrative tours to England and Russia. He mounted concerts involving hundreds of performers, over whom he presided like some great bird, with his hawklike nose and what poet Heinrich Heine called his "monstrous antediluvian hair." (Heine also wrote that Berlioz's music "makes me dream of fabulous empires filled with fabulous sins.")

Besides *Symphonie fantastique*, perhaps the best introductions to him are his two most famous overtures. *Le Corsaire* concerns pirates, a high-Berlioz subject. Just how strange and original it was for its time is apparent in an early review: "It torments you like a bad dream, and fills your imagination with strange and terrible images." The **Roman Carnival** Overture is based on material from his opera *Benvenuto Cellini*. Both pieces are orchestral tours de force from the man who wrote the first important treatise on instrumentation; the book has been in print ever since.

His *Harold in Italy*—based on Lord Byron's romantic hero, but in a new landscape—was commissioned by a living legend, violin/viola virtuoso Niccolò Paganini. But when the score was done Paganini took a look and politely declined to premiere it—he had expected a normal concerto, and this was really a symphony with solo viola. When Paganini heard the premiere, though, he fell on his knees before Berlioz and declared him the heir of Beethoven, and for good measure added a handsome check. *Harold* is a work of refined beauties, lively adventure, tenderness, and glowing orchestration, all of it based on his old rambles in the Abruzzi. Even the finale's "Orgy of Brigands" is more romping than licentious.

Berlioz's personal favorite of his works was the **Requiem**, from 1837. This is no work of piety; he was agnostic from early on. It is rather a humanistic work using the Catholic Mass for the dead as a foundation on which to explore every part of his creative temperament, from tender lyricism to his most Babylonian imaginings. The instrumental forces include twelve horns, eight tubas, twenty trumpets and cornets, sixteen trombones, ten timpanists belaboring sixteen drums, and a huge chorus. The opening "Requiem aeternam" movement is quiet and poignant, the choir entering with broken figures like sobs. Then the second movement, "Tuba mirum," evokes the Last Trumpet with a vengeance: four brass choirs at the corners of the hall break out in hair-raising proclamations. The brass choirs are handled tactfully after that, but always to grand, climactic effect. The "Lacrimosa" movement, naturally tending to lachrymose in other requiems, is here founded on a series of orchestral eruptions like giant hiccups. Although there is much music of gentle poignancy in the Requiem, it is entirely like Berlioz to portray the occasion of death at least in part as an epic thriller.

The last piece I'll recommend is one of his lesser-known but most beautiful, the song cycle for mezzo-soprano and orchestra, **Les Nuits d'été** (Summer Nights). No grandiloquence or bombast here, rather a story of love and loss in six songs of exquisite grace. I think the lucidity and heartfelt expression of these songs cast a glow over the rest of Berlioz, for all his love of the demonic, of revels and massacres. Much like Shakespeare, whom he worshipped, Berlioz also understood the human spectrum from tenderness to violence, love to hate.

Meanwhile his effect on his century, including as a conductor and orchestral colorist, can be seen on composers as varied as Wagner, Liszt, Mussorgsky, Richard Strauss, and Mahler. Berlioz may have been a maverick, but he was no eccentric. He could be over the top, he could be banal, but he was always authentic. He is one of the great originals of our tradition.

More Berlioz: *The Damnation of Faust;* the opera *Béatrice et Bénédict.*

Chapter 15

Robert Schumann (1810–1856)

Robert Schumann grew up with two forces dominating his life: a manic creativity that from his early years manifested in poems, plays, novels, and music; and the threat of madness that harried him throughout his life until it finally claimed him. He stands as one of the defining figures of the romantic age, an era which gave rise to his creative voice, and which in turn he marked with his own personality as composer and critic. Even his madness was part of the atmosphere of his time, and his fragmented personality was woven indelibly into his work.

Schumann was the son of a bookseller and writer in Zwickau. He began playing piano at six and composing soon after. Besides music he was fervid about literature and imbibed literary romanticism directly from the sources. He was attached above all to the wild fictions of Jean Paul, with his doppelgängers and faked suicides, and to the fantasist E. T. A. Hoffmann.

After the death of his father he entered law school at his mother's insistence, but spent his time there either at the piano, composing, or carousing. Finally his mother gave him permission to leave school and study piano with the celebrated teacher Friedrich Wieck, whose most famous pupil was his eight-year-old daughter Clara, a keyboard prodigy. Schumann hoped Wieck would lead him to a career as a piano virtuoso, but that dream was ended by a hand injury. Instead, Wieck led him to Clara.

Schumann turned to composing with a vengeance. In short order he produced some of the most brilliant piano works of his time, one of them the Jean Paul–inspired *Papillons* (Butterflies), finished in 1831. It is startling to realize that this revolutionary collection of boisterous miniatures appeared only four years after Beethoven died, yet is utterly distinctive in voice.

Part of Schumann's innovative pianistic style had to do with the instrument itself, which had evolved far from the harpsichordish instruments of Beethoven's youth. Pianos were now more robust and resonant, offering new kinds of figuration and pedal effects that Schumann and his contemporary Chopin exploited in historic ways.

In that heady period came another force that rocked Schumann's life: by the time Clara Wieck was sixteen, now a celebrated piano virtuoso, she and Robert had fallen desperately in love. Her father, outraged at the presumption of a penniless composer known to be a drinker and womanizer and generally unstable, did everything in his power to keep them apart. The couple resorted to secret notes and codes and anxious rendezvous that went on for years. From this point on, Clara would be an intimate part of Robert's music as well as his life.

But everything in Schumann's life went into his art. Most of his finest early works have evocative titles, with secret games and personal symbols imbedded in the notes. *Carnaval*, finished four years after *Papillons*, is a more extensive assemblage of short movements evoking the yearly costumed bacchanal on the streets. The movements range from grand to tender to wild gaiety, all of them singular in their handling of the piano and their harmonic voice—Schumann is one of those composers usually recognizable in seconds. Each segment has a title, ranging from "Pierrot" and "Arlequin," the clowns of carnival season that precedes Lent, to "Chiarina," a secret name for Clara. Holding the movement together is a cabala of four notes: A–S–C–H (in German parlance the notes A–E-flat–C–and B). In that order the letters form "Asch," birthplace of an old girlfriend of Robert's; they are contained in the German word *Fasching* (Carnival); and *Sch* are the first three letters of his name. Later, he turned the musical letters of Clara's name into a theme: C–B–A–G-sharp–A. It became the leading motif of his Fourth Symphony.

Another echt-Schumann work is **Kreisleriana**, based on the half-mad poet-composer Johannes Kreisler invented by fantasist E. T. A. Hoffmann. The piece is a kind of portrait of madness, beginning with an explosion of energy like two pianos at once, then it sinks to a quiet lyrical interlude. The rest of the piece explores that bipolar temperament. The century romanticized madness and suicide, and Schumann was marked by both in his art and in his life.

Two of the movements of *Carnaval* are "Florestan" and "Eusebius." These were names Schumann gave to his own conflicting alter-egos: brash, impulsive Florestan and quiet, introspective Eusebius. It was often in the guise of those characters that Schumann wrote criticism in a music journal he cofounded. These personas formed the basis of the imaginary "Davidsbund," a little band of Davids fighting the Goliath of

philistinism in music—shallow composers and empty virtuosos and the audiences who idolized them. (Here we see the
beginnings of a divide between composers and audiences that
would only grow throughout the century.) In his years as critic
Schumann spread the word about a number of composers
whom he deemed worthy, including Mendelssohn, Berlioz,
and Chopin (in the Chopin article, Florestan bounds into the
room crying, "Hats off, gentlemen: a genius!").

After a long and mutually humiliating court battle with
Friedrich Wieck, Robert and Clara finally married in 1840.
They became one of the great creative teams of the age. Their
love was hugely fulfilling, but it was no easy business: Clara
was often pregnant (they had seven surviving offspring), and
she had to deal with children and her performing career while
still holding Robert together through his advancing afflictions.
Few could have managed all that, but Clara was made of steel.

Schumann composed in a fury, very fast, with long fallow periods sometimes filled with mental breakdowns. To say that
his way of working was manic is not a figure of speech; today
he would probably be diagnosed as bipolar. Another symptom was a fanatical concentration on one medium at a time.
In his "song year," 1840, he wrote 138 lieder. With these songs
Schumann stands alongside Schubert as a founder of the German lied tradition that lasted into the next century.

Many of the songs are joined into cycles telling a story or
circling around a theme. To get acquainted with Schumann's
songs, perhaps start with two from *Liederkreis* (Song Cycle),
Op. 39. **"Mondnacht"** (Night of the Moon), by Joseph von
Eichendorff, is one of the quintessential romantic poems,

a vision of a moonlit night that ends with the poet almost merging into the landscape: "as if my soul were flying home." Schumann's piano part sets the scene in soft drifting and twining lines. The always defining role of the piano in his songs is seen in a different way in **"Auf einer Burg"** (On a Hilltop), also by Eichendorff. It pictures an ancient stone knight in a ruined castle above the Rhine, watching a wedding party on the river; it ends with the stunning last line: "and the beautiful bride, who weeps." Here Schumann with the simplest means paints a scene of refined weirdness—the weird and uncanny being high-romantic territory.

Dichterliebe (Poet's Love), is one of the most beloved of song cycles, based on the wistfully and bitterly ironic poems of Heinrich Heine: "I'll not complain!" is the refrain of one poem that is a litany of complaints. With his literary background Schumann had a particular sensitivity to Heine's exquisite ambiguities. The first song, "In the beautiful month of May," is from the piano's first weaving lines a romantic landscape both interior and exterior. In "I hear a fluting and fiddling," Schumann's piano part paints a wedding ball and the singer watching from the side; it is his love's wedding to somebody else.

After their marriage Clara pressed Robert to put aside piano miniatures and lieder and take up the big, traditional genres: symphony, opera, string quartet. Robert obeyed, the results were mixed. He was a brilliant miniaturist, but had a limited ability to shape large-scale forms in an organic way; still less did he possess an innate orchestral imagination. All the same, he produced some fine and much-loved major works.

The best known of his chamber music is the **Piano Quintet in E-flat**—more piano than quintet, which in Schumann's case is a good thing. Its success has much to do with its string of yearning, surging themes with his signature poetic quality. The second movement is a haunting funeral march. The **Piano Concerto in A Minor**, written for Clara, is also full of lyrical beauties. It has long reigned as one of the most popular of all concertos. The piece has a universal quality, attaching itself to your own yearnings and sorrows as truly great music can do.

Schumann wrote four symphonies, all of them flawed, none entirely sure-handed with the orchestra, yet still often moving and powerful. In the end he brought a new kind of intimacy to the traditionally epic genre of symphony. He also helped establish the idea of "cyclic" instrumental works, in which the same themes are developed throughout a piece.

In 1853, in Düsseldorf where Schumann had faltered in a conducting job, a twenty-year-old music student named Johannes Brahms knocked on their door. After he had played them a few pieces and left, Schumann wrote in his journal: "Visit from Brahms (a genius)." Soon after, he published an article called "New Paths" that proclaimed this young unknown the coming messiah of German music. With that he placed a sword over Brahms's head that remained for the rest of his life—but even if being a messiah was not his style, Brahms entirely lived up to the prophecy.

Schumann would not be around to see his prophecy fulfilled. By the time he and Clara met Brahms, Robert was becoming suicidal, beset by angelic and demonic choruses in his head, terrified he might hurt Clara or the children. Finally, in the middle of carnival festivities he made his way through the grotesque crowds of masked revelers and threw himself into the Rhine. He was pulled out, but at his own request committed to an asylum, where he died two and a half years later, in

1856. Clara was not allowed to see him until the end, when he could hardly speak and could only lick wine from her fingertips. It may have been syphilis contracted long before, or some other brain disorder on top of his bipolar personality.

Schumann's music made its way into the world slowly, and in his lifetime he was never as celebrated as Clara. But by the latter half of the century he had been enshrined not only as an irreplaceable composer but as one of the central avatars of the romantic spirit, and no less a model of the romantic genius-hero, his art soaring above the gnawing afflictions fate hurled at him.

More Schumann: Symphonies 2 and 3, collections of lieder on recordings.

Chapter 16

Frédéric Chopin (1810–1849)

Frédéric Chopin was a prodigy as both pianist and composer, marked from childhood for a brilliant career. When he came of age he was expected to give concerts and to write in the familiar genres—concertos for himself, chamber music, symphonies. Very little of that came to pass. He got no pleasure from public performances, and while he wrote a couple of early concertos and a few other instrumental works, in his maturity he composed primarily for the piano, drawing colors from the instrument no one had ever imagined before. His keyboard style he largely discovered for himself, likewise his bold harmonies that to some ears of his time sounded like chaos. He mostly wrote small to medium-length pieces, yet he had an outsize influence on the romantic century and beyond. He knew how to make small things loom large.

Chopin was born near Warsaw, his mother Polish and his father French-born. He started piano lessons at six, made his public debut at eight, at eleven played before the tsar of Russia. By the time he entered the Warsaw Conservatory at sixteen he was writing little piano pieces, many of them based on Polish dances: polonaise, mazurka, and the like, plus variations, rondos, and other traditional forms. He would write the same kinds of pieces for the rest of his life, exploring each of them with mounting originality and ambition—he did not so much invent new forms and genres as expand them from within. For inspiration, as performer and composer he shied away from Beethoven and immersed himself in Bach, Mozart, and Italian opera. Meanwhile the piano was developing fast; now there were pedals and richer resonances that made new colors possible.

In Warsaw in 1829 and 1830, after making his formal debut as a soloist in Vienna, Chopin wrote two piano concertos to show off his singular approach to the instrument. They were his first and only large orchestral pieces. The Polish revolt against Russia broke out in 1831, and he made his way to Paris, full of regret at leaving his homeland. He never recovered from his homesickness, and never saw Poland again. In Paris he was taken up in a brilliant group of young composers who included Hector Berlioz and Franz Liszt. Liszt produced a book about Chopin's music, much of it examining how his use of dance forms reflected the nature of each dance. At the same time the two men had a testy relationship, full of jealousies regarding women and still more regarding music: Liszt, the extrovert showman on a grand scale; Chopin, the introvert who recoiled from the public and wrote mostly small pieces. He only gave some thirty public recitals in his life.

It wasn't long before Chopin found his natural milieu: the parlors of wealthy Parisian music lovers, among whom he became a cult figure. From private playing and teaching, plus publications, he began to make a handsome living. His personality suited this scene: he was fastidious, dandyish in dress, a snob, fashionably anti-Semitic. Among friends he was charming and loyal.

A good place to start with Chopin's music is his book of twenty-four **Preludes for piano, Op. 28**. These miniatures in all the major and minor keys show the enormous variety in his treatment of the piano, from fine tracery to roaring cataracts. They were inspired by Bach's *Well-Tempered Clavier*, which likewise covers the keys; also by the romantic devotion to fragments, and by the poetic idea of preludes to nothing or anything. Robert Schumann called them "sketches, beginnings of études, or, so to speak, ruins, individual eagle pinions, all disorder and wild confusion." To Schumann, those were terms of high praise. Listen to **the first two Preludes: the C Major**, which is like an explosion on the piano, an epic that lasts half a minute; then the eerie, moaning song of **No. 2 in A Minor**. The set finishes with the nearly berserk **D Minor Prelude**.

Chopin wrote the Preludes in Majorca. He had gone there with his new mistress, the prolific and notorious author who called herself George Sand, who wore men's clothes and smoked cigars but was vigorously heterosexual. To get him, she ditched her current lover and disengaged one from Chopin. Beginning in 1838, their liaison was passionate, stormy, and so forth, in spades. Sand left a memorable description of Chopin at work, breaking pencils and weeping and reworking passages for weeks. The wet, cold winter in Majorca was a disaster for his fragile health and sensibility. One stormy night Sand returned to find Chopin sitting rigid at the piano, paralyzed with fear. Luckily, later summers on the island of Nohant turned out idyllic and productive. He was relatively healthy and prosperous from teaching, and his music was spreading gratifyingly in publication.

His music became steadily more ambitious and more daring, though still in the same genres and in works rarely going beyond ten minutes. For a tour of his handling of genres, start with the most famous of his pieces, the **"Military" Polonaise** (in A Major, Op. 40, No. 1). This is dance music on a majestic scale, commanding and aristocratic, steeped in the Polish nationalism from which he never departed. He also wrote many nocturnes (night-pieces). The leading theme of **Nocturne in D-flat Major, Op. 27, No. 2**, shows off the melodic influence of opera, also his rhapsodic, dreamy keyboard tracery. He was the first to write what became the high-Romantic genre of the ballade, meaning an instrumental work telling an implied story rather than the specific narratives of program pieces. The **Ballade in G Minor, Op. 23** is a dark-toned piece that wanders in a passionate emotional landscape. Like so much Chopin, it is full of elegant and exquisite melody.

The **Scherzo in B-flat Minor, Op. 31** takes the old idea of a racing, usually cheery piece and makes it into a kaleidoscopic meditation on the idea of a scherzo, from sparkling filigree to solemn and magisterial moments. He takes that idea further in the **Polonaise Fantasy in A-flat Major, Op. 61**, which is like a dream of a polonaise. Here he combines genres: his old favorite Polish dance the polonaise with the idea of the *fantasy*, meaning a piece that sidesteps predictable forms for a feeling of improvisatory immediacy, the kind of freedom Chopin could evoke while maintaining meticulous control. A solemn proclamation begins a far-ranging journey, tender and ecstatic, in just over twelve minutes.

Chopin's last years saw a steady decline as tuberculosis killed him by inches. George Sand took to calling him "my dear corpse." They parted in 1848. Exhausted and depressed, running out of money, no longer able to compose, he hastened his decline with a tour of London and Scotland. His last concert was a benefit for Polish refugees. He died shortly thereafter in Paris in 1849. Most appropriately, his body was buried in Paris, his heart in Warsaw. By then Chopin's place in the history of his art was secure. In a century of outsize ambition his was a victory of imagination over grandiloquence. In music of modest scale and ambition he made himself irreplaceable to the future of romantic music and to the future of the piano.

More Chopin: Nocturne in C-sharp Minor; Waltz in A-flat Major, Op. 69, No. 1.

Chapter 17

RICHARD WAGNER (1813–1883)

R ichard Wagner was a colossus not only in the music of the nineteenth century but in its drama, literature, visual art, and culture in general—and he achieved this level of fame and influence partly because he set out to. It can be argued that it was necessary for Wagner to be that kind of figure to do the work he was born to do: write gigantic music dramas, including the four-evening, seventeen-hour *Ring of the Nibelung*. A piano sonata or a string quartet were simply not grand enough for Wagner's gift, nor his ego. To find his métier as an artist, he had to invent a new kind of art. As pervasive myth and sacred monster, Wagner looms large over the Western tradition not only in music but in all the arts.

The *Ring* took him twenty-six years to complete. Bringing it to fruition and then marshaling the forces to mount it was a project of unprecedented ambition in the history of music. At the same time, Wagner was one of the most innovative composers who ever lived, and in his work he had the tenacity and courage to make the world accept whatever he chose to do. The effects of his achievements reverberated throughout the rest of Western music; the next generation including Brahms and Verdi show the impact of his genius. His *Ring* meanwhile is a wellspring of epics and satires of epics ever since, from superhero comic books to Tolkien's *Lord of the Rings* to *Monty Python and the Holy Grail.*

Given that this book is not concerned with opera—that would be a book in itself—I won't go into Wagner's full operas. Rather, I'll concentrate on his orchestral music, all of it excerpted from the operas. Together with Franz Liszt, Wagner headed a movement calling itself "The Music of the Future." By way of a mountain of polemical prose the two men put forward the idea of leaving traditional classical forms behind and basing both vocal and instrumental music on stories and literature. Liszt invented the orchestral *symphonic poem,* essentially a program piece for orchestra; this new genre began the great age of romantic program music. Beyond that, Liszt and Wagner maintained an image of the artist as a kind of hero-priest, the spiritual leader of society, his work changing and renewing society. The new artist was to be not merely a genius, but a "world-historical" one.

The opposing faction lined up behind Brahms, though led not by the composer but largely by Viennese critic Eduard Hanslick. For years the critic mounted a relentless resistance to Wagner, not only fulminating against his music but the "Dalai Lama cult" around him. Elsewhere whole books were written against Wagner. Deploring program music, the Brahmsians proclaimed allegiance to the old abstract classical forms and genres: sonata form, theme and variation, symphony, string quartet, piano sonata, and so on.

As I've noted, the bitter struggle of the two factions, which included critical diatribes on both sides and gangs trying to break up the other side's performances, is remembered as the War of the Romantics. It raged well past the deaths of Wagner, Liszt, and Brahms. For himself, Wagner not only survived but thrived in this atmosphere. He prospered partly because he was a tougher and meaner son of a bitch than any of his critics. And some of the most bitter denunciations from the deep wells of his vituperation were directed against Jews. Whether Wagner contributed to the horrors of the next century, whether he can be blamed for being Hitler's favorite composer, is a question that will be debated forever, without resolution. It will, in any case, not affect Wagner's importance.

Wagner was born into a theatrical family in Leipzig. In his youth he became passionate about music, but he had no patience with teachers or schools. He did spend a short interlude at the University of Leipzig, studying mainly wine, women, and song. He taught himself piano (he would remain a terrible pianist throughout his life) and studied scores to learn how to compose. He took up conducting early on, and married Minna Planer, a successful actress. Minna earned most of the wages in their first years as he worked his way up in theaters.

Wagner's first opera was never produced, the second one enough of a fiasco on its single performance to bring the company down. He decided to try his luck in Paris; he and Minna spent three years more or less starving there. All the same, in Paris he composed his farewell to traditional opera, *Rienzi*, and his first truly Wagnerian work, *The Flying Dutchman*, an opera based on an old legend of a ghost ship. Listen to the *Dutchman* **overture**. It marks the first emergence of a bold new voice in music, with a gift for spine-tingling orchestral moments and brilliant tone-painting. After his return to

Germany at age twenty-nine, *Rienzi* was mounted to acclaim and the *Dutchman* found a modest success.

In 1842 Wagner was appointed conductor of the court opera in Dresden. With two big premieres under his belt and his new professional position, he seemed on his way to a comfortable career. But his progressive politics, his radical music, his operatic reforms, his ego, his excesses and fractiousness would allow him little peace in the next decades. Already Wagner had a talent for setting everything and everybody around him ablaze. In 1848 revolutions against a repressive status quo flared all over Europe. Wagner, who was a fierce socialist, took a leading role in the Dresden uprising, which among other things led to the burning of his own opera house. When the uprisings failed, he fled over the border with an arrest warrant behind him. While he was in exile, in 1850 Liszt premiered Wagner's opera *Lohengrin*, a story of a mysterious knight who cannot reveal his name, to great success in Weimar. Wagner would not hear the opera until he returned to German lands, fifteen years later.

In Zurich and other cities around Europe during his exile, Wagner wrote as much polemic as music, and premiered no new work. In the treatises—the prose in his trademark turgid and obscure style—he laid out his conception of what came to be called *music drama*. As its thematic material this new kind of opera uses *leitmotifs* (leading motifs) that represent characters and images. (For example in the *Ring* Siegfried has his personal leitmotif; his horn and his sword have their own.) Besides tone-painting, these motifs were to function like themes in a gigantic symphony. Moreover, this new kind of theater would be a *Gesamtkunstwerk*, total work of art, unifying music, drama, poetry, and the visual arts. The music would be continuous, not divided into numbers like traditional opera. The orchestra in this new art form was to function like the ancient Greek chorus, commenting on and amplifying the story; the characters would move and act within the orchestral fabric. The stories would be drawn from myth, fairytale, nationalistic legend, epic poetry. The goal, in short, was to ravish audiences in all their senses, and in the process renew not only opera but society as a whole. The ultimate goal of the artist-hero was to change the world.

Meanwhile, over in Vienna, Johannes Brahms, who had no use for Wagner's politics or his personality but deeply respected his music, did not believe art could change history. For his part, Wagner had nothing but contempt for his rival and everything he represented. He declared Brahms "a Jewish czardas-player," referring to Brahms's Hungarian Dances, which Wagner considered trivial. Brahms, of course, was not Jewish; the slur was thrown in for effect.

In Zurich during his exile Wagner began a heated affair with Mathilde Wesendonck, lamentable poet and wife of a rich patron of his. The ensuing *amour fou* sparked a new epic stage work, an exploration of helpless love embodied in the medieval story *Tristan und Isolde*. Here, to represent the restlessness of desire, Wagner at times suspended tonality, writing unresolved, keyless stretches. When he finished the libretto, he assembled his wife and Mathilde and her husband for a reading, plus his conductor champion Hans von Bülow and his wife. Thus, as Victor Borge once summarized: "He read it aloud to his wife, his mistress, his mistress's husband, his future mistress, and his future mistress's husband. They all said they liked it."

The *Tristan* score was not only revolutionary, it was apparently unperformable; the first attempt, in Vienna, was abandoned after seventy rehearsals over two years. Here we see one of Wagner's great virtues: he had a steely courage of conviction. He refused to simplify the score or admit that it was unplayable—and he was right; it is performed regularly today.

The affair with Mathilde petered out, but did relieve him of his fractious marriage. Minna wrote Mathilde with bitter irony: "I must tell you with a bleeding heart that you have succeeded in separating my husband from me after nearly twenty-two years of marriage. May this noble deed contribute to your peace of mind, to your happiness."

In 1861 Wagner finally received amnesty from Germany and was able to return. He lived in Vienna, Austria, for a year, where he first heard *Lohengrin*, and began what was intended as a relatively practical and popular little opera, which became instead the massive comedy *Die Meistersinger von Nürnberg*. In Vienna Wagner was quite broke but still spent extravagantly, writing his milliner to order expensive silks and satins and oriental slippers and wall hangings. (The letters eventually got into the hands of Brahms, who gave hilarious readings of them to friends.) Wagner had to flee Vienna to escape debtor's prison.

He arrived penniless in Stuttgart. But salvation was at hand. By this point the Wagner cult was in full bloom, with fanatics all over Europe. Chief among them was a youth who had the resources to pursue his obsession: King Ludwig II, a.k.a. the "mad king of Bavaria." He came to the throne in 1864 and invited his hero to live in Munich. Wagner played the young king as the prize catch he was, and never mind his own socialist politics. The next years saw acclaimed performances in Munich, including *Tristan, Meistersinger,* and the first two installments of the *Ring.* Ludwig came close to emptying his royal coffers by bankrolling Wagner; meanwhile the king spent huge sums erecting fantastical castles based on the operas. Eventually Wagner was forced out of Munich, but Ludwig continued his support. (Having finally been declared insane and deposed, Ludwig would die in 1886 under mysterious circumstances.)

For his part, under the king's extravagant patronage Wagner still managed to spend beyond his means. He meanwhile attempted to use his position to influence the government. His enemies mounted. To complete the trifecta, he stole the wife of his most loyal conductor. This was the aforementioned Hans von Bülow, one of the founders of the virtuoso conducting tradition that began in the nineteenth century. The lady was Cosima, daughter of Franz Liszt. For a while Hans played along, pretending Cosima's latest child was his, before decamping to the other side—he became a champion of Brahms. "If it had been anybody but Wagner," Hans declared, "I would have shot him."

No doubt you've gotten the idea by now: Wagner was a piece of work on a monumental scale, a monomaniac, a cad, a user, a virulent anti-Semite—and a brilliant, revolutionary, overwhelming artist who believed the world owed him a living. Perhaps the world did, but still. His infamous 1850 essay "Judaism in Music," which branded Jews an alien race in Germany, contributed to a rising tide of anti-Semitism in Germany. In the article Wagner laid out a *cultural* anti-Semitism: Jews, he said, must renounce their religion and become fully German, or else. In person, though, Wagner was a gut-level racial anti-Semite. Cosima, if anything, was worse. Perhaps nowhere else has an artist of his caliber had such irrational malevolence woven into his character.

But none of this was simple. Many of Wagner's supporters were wealthy Jews, who prospered in what in fact was a liberal atmosphere for them in Germany at that time. Meanwhile there was a good chance that Wagner himself was born illegitimate, his actual father a possibly Jewish actor named Geyer. Wagner suspected as much, and kept Geyer's portrait in the house. Cosima would tease him about it, saying how Semitic the man's features were and how much Richard looked like him. Wagner's was a house full of both genius and madness.

The rest of Wagner's story is more or less of triumph: with support from Ludwig II and admirers around the world, he built his own theater in Bayreuth, Germany, and began to mount productions of the completed *Ring* series and his other operas, to wild acclaim. Bayreuth is still going strong—and still run by the Wagner family, which inherited a streak of the brilliance and the craziness of its forebear. Wagner died of heart failure in February 1883, in the middle of an argument with Cosima about a singer Wagner was paying too much attention to. His last words were among the truest and most to the point of his life: "I feel lousy." Brahms was told in the middle of a choral rehearsal that his greatest enemy had passed. He put down his baton and said, "The rehearsal is over. A master has died." When Hans von Bülow heard the news, he fell down in a fit, clawing and gnawing the carpet.

For a sample of Wagner's music I'll suggest some of the familiar orchestral excerpts. If you don't know them, give yourself a treat and put on **"Siegfried's Funeral March"** from *Götterdämmerung* (Twilight of the Gods), and turn up the volume.

It's Wagner's elegy for his great, flawed, murdered operatic hero. It mounts steadily, interweaving various leitmotifs to a hair-raising climax of cinematic vividness. If this piece doesn't give you goosebumps and visions of a solemn procession in a dark forest, maybe Wagner is not for you. Nearly everybody knows the soaring **"Ride of the Valkyries,"** which was blasted from an attacking helicopter in the movie *Apocalypse Now* and now has become one of those cultural clichés that are both regrettable and inevitable. (Recall *2001: A Space Odyssey* and Strauss's *Also sprach Zarathustra*.) In *Die Walküre* the "Ride" depicts the Valkyries galloping across the sky to gather the souls of fallen heroes and bring them to Valhalla.

Other excerpts show how remarkably far-reaching Wagner's instrumental imagination was. **"Forest Murmurs"** from *Siegfried* is an unprecedented and astonishing piece, as if made from wind in the trees and the songs of birds. I believe that the exquisite end of Brahms's Third Symphony is indebted to it. And for all Debussy's eventual hatred of Wagner, his innovations with the orchestra are unimaginable without that model. For another look at music from the *Ring*, there's the apparently triumphant, resounding **"Entry of the Gods into Valhalla."** Except in the opera it encloses a brutal irony: as Wotan leads the gods over a rainbow bridge into his shiny new palace, he knows Valhalla was built with the proceeds of a crime, gold stolen from the Rhine Maidens, and he already knows that someday that crime will bring down the gods and their palace together. In the opera the triumphant music is interrupted by the Rhine Maidens below, crying for their gold. Seeing those moments at the end of *Das Rheingold* in Vienna was one of the most transcendent, hair-raising moments I've ever experienced in the theater.

Two more remarkable pieces. The **Prelude to Act I of Lohengrin** begins with a sublime texture of high strings that depicts the descent of the Holy Grail from heaven to earth. Finally, try the **Prelude and "Love-Death" from *Tristan und Isolde*,** which is about hopeless love and helpless desire, which is to say about sex at its most supreme. As noted earlier, this is essentially atonal music, here wielded to express the sense of an endless yearning that can only be consummated in death. If you want to take on a full opera, I'd suggest *Lohengrin*, because it's gorgeous, and *Die Meistersinger*, because it's great fun. Brahms agreed—in one year he went to see *Meistersinger* over forty times. (The early *Tannhäuser* has some fine music, but I find Wagner's libretto . . . how to put it . . . pretty silly.)

Wagner lived in a century where music was the king of the arts, largely because German music had seen a series of towering geniuses from Bach and Handel and through the romantic period that was perhaps the most remarkable such streak since the visual artists of the Renaissance. In the nineteenth century, music was closer to the center of Western culture than it has been before or since, and Wagner placed himself at the center of music. That there was corruption at the core of Wagner's personality, which rose from and contributed to a corruption in his culture, is something that will forever be debated and never resolved. In any case, Wagner will not be forgotten, for well and for ill. He saw to that.

More Wagner: Complete operas: start with *Lohengrin* and *Die Meistersinger*, then try the whole *Ring*.

Chapter 18

Franz Liszt (1811–1886)

W hat Franz Liszt did in the concert hall was analogous to what Wagner did in the theater. It's not surprising then that the two were colleagues and considerable influences on each other's work (although there was a rupture between them for a while, after Wagner took up with Liszt's married daughter).

Liszt was born in Raiding, Hungary. He began playing piano at age five and revealed a spectacular talent. He began composing at eight and made his public debut the next year. From there he went to Vienna and studied with Carl Czerny, who was a pupil of Beethoven's and the author of books of keyboard finger exercises still in use. Then came Paris, more studies, and a sensational debut. But en route to this glorious career, Liszt faltered; there was a failed love, depression, religious yearnings, a years-long separation from the piano. Luckily, after 1830, he pulled himself together. Part of his resurrection came after hearing the demon fiddler Niccolò Paganini, who provided Liszt with a vision of supreme virtuosity. He made himself into a Paganini of the keyboard, the greatest pianist of his time and perhaps of all time. Even Brahms, who was not well treated by Liszt and who loathed his music, still

said: "If you haven't heard Liszt, you haven't heard piano playing. There's him, a long space, and then everybody else."

Liszt's way of building pieces out of single short motifs
influenced Wagner's invention of leitmotifs. As a keyboard
innovator he along with Chopin redefined the instrument
in ways still being explored a century later. He and Chopin
were friends, the first extravagant and extroverted, the latter
introverted as a person and restrained as a player. With their
music, Liszt brought brilliance and color to the piano, Chopin
subtlety and a quieter but no less original palette. The later
history of piano music is unthinkable without both of them.
Meanwhile with a series of arrangements for keyboard, Liszt
helped spread the neglected orchestral music of Bach, Beethoven, Berlioz, and Schumann. He maintained his allegiance to
Wagner and the Music of the Future while generously helping
many young talents on the opposing side, including Grieg and
Debussy.

Besides his supremacy as a virtuoso in an age that worshipped virtuosos, Liszt also happened to be devastatingly
handsome. He invented the idea of the solo piano recital. Female fans would flock to his recitals to be transported in ways
that resembled something between the screaming rock-star
concerts of the twentieth century and a shark feeding frenzy.
Liszt fed the frenzy with James Brown–like antics onstage:
fake fainting fits, being carried offstage and staggering back,
and so on. Like his friend Wagner, Liszt was a mad mixture
of qualities, his mastery mixed inextricably with charlatan-
ism. But he embodied what the age craved: the artist as hero,
as showman, as semi-divine genius and superhuman virtuoso.
He was a tireless womanizer, his conquests including famous

women of the time, such as notorious dancer and actress Lola Montez. Mixed with his sexual profligacy was an abiding yen for religion, for purification and absolution. In 1848 Liszt settled in Weimar with his longtime mistress, the cigar-puffing Princess Carolyne von Sayn-Wittgenstein. She ghost-wrote much of his tracts and books, including one on Chopin. Amid a collection of students and devotees, Liszt wrote a great deal of music including symphonic poems, such as the *Faust* **Symphony**, after Goethe's drama. In Weimar he produced perhaps his greatest work, the one-movement **Piano Sonata in B Minor,** and revised his wickedly difficult *Transcendental Studies After Paganini* for piano. His best-known music was and remains the visceral, deep-purple piano works, such as the four **Mephisto Waltzes,** exercises in the romantic-demonic. His **Hungarian Dances** are longtime popular favorites. Everywhere you look at Liszt as composer and man, you find ambiguity. His music can be strong, innovative, and splendiferous in color; at other times, flaccid, overwrought, and cloying. Brahms more or less forgave Wagner his personality and his bigotry, but he could not forgive Liszt his lapses in taste.

In later life, by now fat and warty, he took minor religious orders and called himself Abbé Liszt. During that period came eight years in Rome, attempts at holiness, a break with the princess, a return to Weimar, a reconciliation with Wagner, and a more experimental approach to music that was to have a great influence on later composers including Debussy and Bartók. There is a short *Bagatelle Without Tonality* from 1885 that is truly startling, on the way to Scriabin, reminding you that the modernist Schoenberg and his school were about to emerge. Much the same can be said about the atmospheric and hypnotic *Nuages gris* (Gray Clouds). Liszt died in July 1886 in the most appropriate way: in Bayreuth, where he had gone to take in Wagner's *Ring*.

More Liszt: The complete *Années de pèlerinage* (Years of Pilgrimage); oratorio *Christus*.

Chapter 19

JOHANNES BRAHMS (1833–1897)

In our age when celebrity is often viewed as the ultimate accomplishment, the life of Johannes Brahms is a study of what a burden it can be. He was made famous at age twenty, virtually declared the heir of Beethoven when he knew he had not earned such a prophecy. He spent the rest of his life trying to measure up to the reputation that had been thrust on him. By his own accounting, he would never measure up. But Brahms was a man of immense talent, likewise immense patience and courage and hard-headed common sense. While he had to cope with the usual obstacles to making a career as an artist, plus the resentment of his enemies and his own self-doubts, when all was said and done, he had about as good a career in his lifetime as any composer ever did. He did not have to die to be named one of the "three great Bs" of music, alongside Bach and Beethoven.

His fame was no accident. For one thing, he wrote a good many light pieces, among them the irresistible *Hungarian Dances* and the ubiquitous **"Lullaby,"** all of which flew off the shelves. Even if he never admitted it, he knew he was some kind of genius, but he also knew that genius is not enough to make a name. He maintained an air of indifference toward money and glory while managing his career deftly and making lots of money. His efforts included cultivating a stable of powerful friends and champions. If he had been capable of satisfaction at what he had accomplished, which he was not, he would have had a largely pleasant career.

Brahms was born in Hamburg, his father a workaday musician and his mother a seamstress. The family was of peasant stock, as shown by his name, which in German means "Johnny Broom." His father wanted the boy to learn cello and horn so someday he could play in the Hamburg Philharmonic. But with a strange obstinacy tiny Johannes insisted on playing the piano. By the time he was ten it had become clear that he was a tremendous talent. But now he insisted that he wanted to compose. His teacher reluctantly agreed to look at some pieces the boy had written, and found himself astonished. "I was bound to recognize," he recalled, "that an exceptional, great, and peculiarly profound talent was dormant in him." When Felix Mendelssohn died, the teacher declared, "A great master of the musical art has gone hence, but an even greater one will bloom for us in Brahms." Johannes was fourteen at the time. He would inspire that kind of respect for the rest of his life.

But Brahms's teens were hardly as pleasant as they sound. The family finances were perennially dicey, and his father declared that if the boy could play piano he had to bring in some money. Johannes was sent to play in waterfront dives that catered to sailors. A longtime Hamburg institution in the St. Pauli district, these pubs conveniently joined the functions of restaurant, bar, dancehall, and brothel. The waitresses, in short, were versatile. (If you want to get some idea of what they looked like, see the label of St. Pauli Girl beer.) The thirteen-year-old was paid to play dance music at the piano. But, as he described with anguish for the rest of his life, he was also abused by the women for the amusement of the sailors. In describing it later, Brahms said that the bars had been terrible but he would not have missed the experience, because it steeled him. Perhaps he believed that. At the time, when it became clear to the family that the boy was in bad shape physically and mentally, he was taken out of the pubs and sent to the country to recover. There Brahms started a lifetime of robust health.

In 1853 a historic career began with an unassuming concert tour. Brahms went on the road with Hungarian violinist Eduard Reményi; they drifted from town to town playing violin sonatas plus popular pieces in a style called "Hungarian" or "Gypsy." This exotic, rhythmically exhilarating music was the jazz of its time, and Brahms was involved with it from then on. Meanwhile he had composed some piano music and songs—brilliant work for his age, if not that much of it. For a sample of his early music, try the lied **"Liebestreu," Op. 3, No. 1.** In a dark-toned and agitated piece of remarkable musical and psychological maturity for a composer barely twenty, Brahms sets a text of love's anguish that is a prophecy of his own bachelor life: a mother sings to her son, "Oh sink your sorrow, my child, in the sea, in the deep sea! . . . And the love that you carry in your heart, break it off, my child!"

When Brahms and the violinist reached Weimar, they visited Reményi's mentor Franz Liszt. The famous man was welcoming, played through Brahms's luscious, faux-demonic **Scherzo in E-flat Minor** brilliantly at sight. As Liszt went on to play his own B-Minor Sonata, however, Brahms was observed dozing off. Soon began a musical feud that would simmer for decades, Brahms on one side and Liszt and his colleague Richard Wagner on the other.

On the same tour Brahms met violinist Joseph Joachim, a celebrated prodigy who when he was twelve years old had established the Beethoven Violin Concerto in the repertoire. Here began a long friendship and collaboration. Already Brahms had a gift for sitting down at the piano, playing his music, and finding instant and lifelong admirers. That at age twenty he was stunningly handsome, wiry and athletic, with blue eyes and long blond hair, did not hurt. (He did not grow the famous beard until his forties.)

Joachim was close to composer Robert Schumann and his wife, Clara, who was perhaps second only to Liszt among piano virtuosos. The violinist insisted Brahms visit the couple in Düsseldorf. In October 1853, with a pack on his back and walking staff in hand, Brahms knocked on the Schumanns' door. After he played a few pieces for them, Robert patted him on the shoulder and said vaguely, "We understand each other." That night Schumann wrote in his journal, "Visit from Brahms (a genius)." From that point the couple more or less adopted Johannes, adding him to their noisy houseful of children. A few months later, Schumann wrote a journal article that essentially declared this twenty-year-old student the heir of Beethoven and the coming savior of German music—by implication, saving it from what Schumann saw as the depredations of Liszt and Wagner, who had turned away from classical forms toward music based on ideas and stories.

With the article's publication, the European musical world erupted in gossip and scandal. Some were curious to hear this new phenomenon; others—especially the followers of Liszt and Wagner—despised the intruder already. Wagner sarcastically dubbed him "Saint Johannes." Brahms was appropriately grateful to Schumann, but at the same time horrified by the burden that had been thrown on him. As he was staying with Joachim and trying to come to terms with this unwanted notoriety, the terrible news arrived of Robert's attempted suicide and commitment to an asylum.

Schumann's wife, Clara, was devastated, alone with their seven children, and pregnant. Brahms rushed to her side, took up residence in a downstairs bedroom, helped out with the children and household chores. Over the next months, as they spent their days talking and making music, Brahms began to fall for this tremendous musician fourteen years his senior. So began a miserable two-year odyssey of longing and sorrow and guilt between them. Whether their love was spoken or unspoken, consummated or not, we don't know. But when Schumann died in 1856, their connection was common knowledge and many, including Clara, expected Brahms to propose. Instead he went back to Hamburg and stayed a bachelor. Yet Clara remained the love of his life; their relationship lasted to the end.

After Schumann's infamous article, Brahms was knocked off his stride for years. Among the relatively few products of that period is the **Piano Trio No. 1 in B Major**, from 1854. It begins with an exquisite cello melody of a kind that Brahms would produce for the rest of his career. It is mostly known in a much-revised version he did in 1889, though the revision retained its youthful passion.

The **Piano Concerto No. 1 in D Minor** cost Brahms four excruciating years of work before he finished it in 1854. It started as a two-piano sonata he drafted just after Robert's collapse. The concerto begins on a note of high drama, with an ominous low D in the basses and snarling horns, with wild shivering trills above. That opening is the most turbulent in the concerto repertoire to that time, with an expressive urgency that Brahms rarely attempted again. Surely the impetus for the work came from his years of turmoil with the Schumanns. If the vertiginous opening is applied to the image of a suicidal man leaping into the water, they are almost cinematically apt. The enormous movement continues with a wealth of contrasting themes, the piano writing massive, the soloist given little rest. After a slow movement that Brahms told Clara was "a tender portrait" of her, the finale turns to youthful high spirits and a driving Hungarian/Gypsy voice. Audiences of the time, though, were not ready for huge concertos sometimes tragic in tone. When Brahms soloed in the second performance in Leipzig, he was hissed off the stage. But by his last years he had the satisfaction of hearing this product of his youth applauded everywhere.

After the chaotic years with Robert and Clara, Brahms wanted no more drama in his life. He pulled himself out of his anxieties, found his voice, and settled into a busy life of composing, performing, frequenting brothels, and fighting with his friends. An exemplary composer's career, really. He gave up any ambitions as a pianist, though kept playing his own music in concerts. In 1863 he moved to Vienna, and before long had the city's leading critic, the Wagner-bashing Eduard Hanslick, as a friend and champion. Brahms stayed away from overt politicking; Hanslick was the real leader of the Brahms faction in its decades-long struggles with Liszt and Wagner and their Music of the Future followers. As their figurehead however, he was constantly under attack. Given his allegiance to sonata form and other traditional models, Brahms belonged, Liszt declared, to "the posthumous school" of composers.

Of Brahms's early masterpieces the best-known is *Ein deutsches Requiem* (A German Requiem), finished after years of work in 1868. A skeptic and agnostic, Brahms assembled his own text from scripture and pointedly avoided mention of the eponymous founder of the Christian religion. This is a requiem with no smell of incense or bowing to the altar; it is directed to all humanity. "*Selig*" (blessed), the chorus begins. At the end of its journey, the music comes to rest again on the word *selig*. The gentleness and limpid twilight beauty of the opening sets the tone of the whole work. It was an unequivocal success from its premiere, and since then has lived in the heart and soul of the choral repertoire. Singers sometimes speak of performing it as a life-changing experience.

Brahms came to maturity mainly writing chamber music. For a sample, I'll propose two pieces in quite different directions. The **Piano Quintet in F Minor** is a work of piercing tragic intensity, from its relentlessly driving opening to its spine-tingling non-scherzo to its finale that begins with a bleak landscape and ends in fury. The relief is the lilting nocturne of its slow movement, where Brahms's lyricism—partly learned from Schubert, but essentially his own—is on tender display.

Since Brahms never wrote program pieces and rarely left overtly personal elements in his music, his followers have always tended to view him as an abstractionist, his music free of autobiography. He was indeed an intensely guarded and private man, but he never made any such claims, and periodically admitted to friends that his music had been drawn from his life. The exquisite **String Sextet in G Major** is another work suffused with beautiful lyricism, much of it wonderfully warm, music of love, but woven into it is a vein of piercing regret. The climactic theme of the first movement is made from notes that spell out "Agathe," the name of a woman Brahms was once engaged to, and jilted. "Here," he said of the piece, "I have freed myself from my last love."

From the early years of his fame, everybody was expecting a symphony from Brahms. He could only fulfill Schumann's prophecy and officially take up the mantle of Beethoven if he attempted that king of musical forms. Partly for that reason, Brahms took decades to allow a symphony out of the house. What became **Symphony No. 1 in C Minor** began with a draft of a first movement that he sent to Clara Schumann in 1862. Then, fourteen years passed. "I'll never write a symphony!" he anguished. "You have no idea how the likes of me feels with the tramp of a giant like him behind you!" The giant, of course, was Beethoven.

Yet over the years Brahms kept hammering away at the piece. The First was finally finished in 1876. It begins on a note of searing drama: keening, searching melodies spreading outward, under them the pounding timpani Brahms always associated with fate. The introduction gives way to an allegro that never flags in its driving, churning energy. Next is a slow movement marked by melting, heart-tugging themes. Then comes a new kind of symphonic movement, an intermezzo that begins with a blithe clarinet theme, developed at length. All the movements lead to the finale, when the tensions of the first movement and the shadowed lyricism of the middle ones find their resolution. The music reaches a breathless climax, then as if with a burst of sunlight through clouds, by way of a French horn we hear the call of an alphorn. It brings us to the main theme, an unforgettable chorale melody. There in a moment of heart-filling C-major beauty the First Symphony turns toward solace, fulfillment, and finally triumph.

After the over fifteen years of struggle on the First, the next two symphonies took Brahms a summer each. (Mostly he composed at various summer resorts and spent the winters revising, copying, performing.) The **Third Symphony in F Minor**, from 1883, is his most tightly knit, with questions posed in the craggy opening that are finally resolved only in the superb final pages. It begins with two pealing chords in the winds and brass, then a great string proclamation starting in F major; in the next measure the basses rise to an A-flat, violently wrenching the harmony into minor. There is the central musical and expressive drama of the Third: a struggle between major and minor, between anguish and a fine but fraught lyricism. The second movement begins gently in the winds. After a lovely flowering of the theme, the second section is a somber chorale in strange, complex harmonies. In a wash of strings the first theme returns, but not the chorale. Its moment is later. Then the extraordinary third movement, with its soaring cello melody set in a fluttering texture of strings. This movement is like some distilled essence of passion and yearning. I think you never forget the first time you hear it.

The last movement of the Third begins with a murmuring string line, then a more measured theme appears—it is the mysterious chorale theme of the second movement, which finds its climax here. It leads to a powerful, almost desperately surging theme. In the coda of the finale Brahms achieves something remarkable: this tumultuous symphony ends with a long gentle coda that gradually returns, in a magical shimmer of strings, to a gentle falling line in pure F major that is the opening theme of the symphony, stripped of struggle and uncertainty and grief, resolved at last into a whispered farewell.

By his forties Brahms had become the plump, bearded bear that history would remember. He was sunk into his old-bachelor life: private, melancholy, and pessimistic. But he was still sociable enough, with an entourage who doted on him. It doesn't often show in his music, but Brahms had a subtle and finely tuned sense of humor—usually at somebody's expense, often at his own expense. A few samples. At a dinner his host tried to play up to him, flourishing a bottle with, "I call this the Brahms of my wines!" Said Brahms: "Let's have a bottle of Bach, then." He was rehearsing a string quartet when the violist asked, "How do you like our tempos?" "They're good," Brahms said. "Especially yours." When somebody asked him what he had done that summer, he described his monumental Fourth Symphony thus: "Oh, once again I've just thrown together a bunch of waltzes and polkas." He hated facile compliments, and those who attempted one usually got them back in the face. "How do you write such divine adagios?" cooed one lady at a party. "My publisher orders 'em that way," Brahms deadpanned.

Brahms died in April 1897. In his last years he was celebrated wherever he went, and it would seem that he could have had no doubts about his place in the history of his art. Being who he was, he doubted it anyway. He was more troubled about his beloved Austro-German culture, which he saw tumbling downhill toward—his word—catastrophe. Unlike many, he understood what lay at the center of it: "Anti-Semitism is madness!" he cried to friends. He could not have imagined what shape the catastrophe would take, but his late works, including the Fourth Symphony, reflect his sense of his culture rushing to destroy itself.

History would paint Brahms as the great abstractionist, but he never saw himself that way. He was intensely connected to the world, and his art rose from and reflected life. Only it was not his style to proclaim epochal agendas, as Wagner and his followers did. Brahms didn't believe art could change the world, no matter how much the world needed changing. For him music was a private matter, from the heart of the composer to the heart of each listener. He had his own version of Beethoven's heroic voice, but perhaps his greatest moments are the ones of songful tenderness. In the way those moments reach the heart, he is unsurpassed.

More Brahms: String Sextet in B-flat Major; *Schicksalslied*; Piano Concerto No. 2; Symphonies 2 and 4; Violin Concerto; Clarinet Quintet in B Minor.

Chapter 20

PYOTR ILICH TCHAIKOVSKY (1840–1893)

From his lifetime to the present, Tchaikovsky has been a go-to composer for people who like their music with heart on sleeve. His lapses in judgment are to a large extent made up for by the wallop of his emotions, the brilliance of his orchestration, his gift for grabby tunes. I'm one of the many who more or less started in classical music with Tchaikovsky. He was easier to digest than my other early passions, among them Brahms. Most of my descriptions here, including the lapses of taste, Tchaikovsky himself knew perfectly well. He wasn't a self-doubting artist so much as a self-loathing one, and the often poisonous reviews of his critics didn't help. All the same, he was terrifically productive, he found a huge audience, and in the end he went out with perhaps his greatest piece.

Pyotr Ilich Tchaikovsky was born to a factory manager's family in Votkinsk, Russia. He gravitated to music in toddlerhood and began composing at four; by his school days he was an able pianist. At age twenty-two he became one of the first students at the new Saint Petersburg Conservatory, where he studied composition with the celebrated composer and pianist Anton Rubenstein. Three years later he joined the faculty of the Moscow Conservatory.

At the conservatory he reached his first maturity, producing pieces such as Symphony No. 1. His first big success was the 1875 **Piano Concerto No. 1**, though from the beginning there have been about as many people who hate it as love it. Have a listen; in seconds you'll understand its overheated expressive world and its perfervid tunes. Those tunes had a considerable influence on popular music in the next century. For one example, in the 1940s the opening theme became the hit "Tonight We Love."

The first of Tchaikovsky's classic ballet scores, *Swan Lake*, premiered in 1877. To counteract this brilliant success, the low point of his life also came that year, when he allowed himself to be conned into marriage by a music student who idolized him. After a few weeks with her, he fled in a state of collapse. The woman spent her last years in an asylum for the insane. For Tchaikovsky, though, this disaster perhaps helped him for the first time to come to terms with his homosexuality, which was then a capital crime in Russia. Struggling with his orientation and with the fear of exposure wore miserably on him. But after the marriage he wrote his brother, "I have finally begun to understand that there is nothing more fruitless than not wanting to be that which I am by nature." With that Tchaikovsky came to about as much peace with himself as he was going to.

By that point his artistic salvation had already turned up in the figure of a wealthy widow named Nadezhda von Meck. She adored his music and offered him a generous stipend so he could devote all his time to composing. To keep their relationship on an ideal plane they agreed that they would never meet. However, they constantly exchanged letters, which form an invaluable record of Tchaikovsky's creative life. By the later

1870s he was enjoying a rising tide of fame and his production was voluminous: symphonies, ballets, operas, tone poems, overtures. But the bad reviews never stopped. Many Russian composers felt he was not nationalistic enough, too much involved with German, French, and Italian influences. Others simply didn't respond to his brand of emotionalism. Leading Viennese critic (and Brahms enthusiast) Eduard Hanslick concluded his minute thrashing of the Violin Concerto by declaring that the piece "stinks to the ear." Tchaikovsky could recite that review word for word.

To get to know Tchaikovsky one obvious route is through a piece most of you know already: the **1812 Overture**, from 1880. With its pealing chimes and live cannons and jubilant conclusion it has become an indispensable accompaniment to Fourth of July fireworks shows around America. It was commissioned to commemorate the Russian defeat of Napoleon in 1812, and follows the story of the campaign as literally as possible. It's one of Tchaikovsky's richest scores, beginning with a lovely full-throated Russian hymn. The climax is sort of a battle of the bands, with French and Russian marches contending until the homeland wins the day.

Among the ballets there's another clear choice: the perennial holiday favorite *The Nutcracker*, from 1891. Tchaikovsky has only one real rival as a composer for ballet, Stravinsky, and both of them created music ideal for dance that works equally well in the concert hall. You'll want to start with the *Nutcracker* Suite rather than the whole ballet. The charm is incessant in the music, which is also marvelously nimble in rhythm. Most famous and most original is the "Dance of the

Sugar-Plum Fairy," with its tinkling celesta. There seems to be some innate Russian genius for orchestration, and, again, one of the few who outdoes Tchaikovsky in that respect is his fellow Russian Stravinsky. Who, by the way, loved Tchaikovsky.

Perhaps the quintessential Tchaikovsky piece that might please people who don't like Tchaikovsky is the **Serenade for Strings in C Major.** He was a great lover of Mozart and here for a change it shows, in music that is as melodically compelling as he usually is, but is also more objective, less hothouse in expression than much of his music.

Of the symphonies I'll recommend the last two, both of them among the most beloved in the repertoire. **Symphony No. 5** (1888) begins with a shadowed and somber theme that sets the tone of the movement. The slow movement has another of his familiar and soulful tunes, highly influential on movie love scenes in the next century. In place of the usual scherzo there is an elegant waltz. A recall of the symphony's opening theme serves as introduction to the finale, leading to a grand and a bit edgy allegro that concludes on a note of triumph.

In 1893 came **Symphony No. 6** (the "Pathétique"). Despite a dicey reception at its premiere Tchaikovsky considered it his best, and the world has largely agreed. In begins with a moaning theme in low bassoons, creating an atmosphere of inwardness and shadow. This is his most personal symphony, all his sorrows on display. The graceful and waltzlike second movement is not what it seems: it's in, for the time, a highly unusual five-beat meter. After a skittering and good-humored scherzo comes a finale that is a sustained and unforgettable song of anguish. The grieving and the moments of fraught hope in the Sixth are not responses to a particular tragedy; they are what the romantics called *Weltschmerz*, world-pain, the innate sorrow of living itself.

There were many honors at the end of Tchaikovsky's life, including a triumphant American tour that began at the inauguration of Carnegie Hall. Tchaikovsky could scarcely believe his fame in America. In 1893 Cambridge University awarded him an honorary doctorate. In October of that year he was so unwise as to drink unboiled water, something all Russians knew not to do. Whether it was carelessness or suicide has never been settled. He came down with cholera, the wretched disease that had killed his mother, and quickly died. For all the complaints that can be lodged about his music, generations of composers after him, including Mahler, Sibelius, Rachmaninoff, and Shostakovich, would not have been the same without him.

More Tchaikovsky: Symphony No. 4; *Marche slave; Capriccio italien.*

Chapter 21

Antonín Dvořák (1841–1904)

As much as anyone it was Johannes Brahms who championed Antonín Dvořák in his belated rise to fame. The older master, who composed with considerable self-consciousness and labor, admired the way the younger man appeared to spin out his pieces effortlessly. "A more lovely, refreshing impression of real, rich and charming creative talent you can't easily find," Brahms raved. Brahms also enjoyed the unmistakable Bohemian accent of the music. Dvořák seemed to be made of music, though in practice his maturity was late and hard-won. In the end he was viewed as the model of a nineteenth-century nationalistic artist, his work rising from the rich folk tradition of his native land, which he placed into his chamber and orchestral music.

Antonín Leopold Dvořák was born in Nelahozeves, Bohemia (now part of Czech Republic). His innkeeper father was an amateur zither player; the boy took up violin in childhood and by twelve was studying music intensely. By the time he reached the Institute for Church Music in Prague he was composing and for his keep playing viola in low-rent bands. He later said that this period was one of more studying than eating. In the 1860s, barely getting by, he accumulated stacks of unperformed pieces.

In 1875, when he was thirty-four, Dvořák was awarded an Austrian government grant. As a result he met Brahms, who had been one of the competition judges. Brahms took the younger man under his wing and introduced him to his own publisher, for whom Dvořák wrote his *Slavonic Dances* in imitation of Brahms's *Hungarian Dances*. The pieces made a sensation, and Dvořák's name was on the map. He also absorbed Brahms's symphonic style and adapted it to his own personality and background. Soon he began a steady regime of appearances around Europe and as far as Moscow in one direction and the United States in the other.

In 1892 Dvořák was brought over to join the new National Conservatory of Music in New York. The intention was for him to show American composers how to be nationalists like himself. He went about the task dutifully, but it is said that what really drew him to America was the chance to see Grand Central Station: Dvořák was a train fanatic who was often taken for an employee of the terminals, because he was on the platforms so much and knew the schedules by heart. He was charming, but how much of his apparent humbleness and naïveté was real and how much studied has long been pondered. He was also agoraphobic, meaning he had a neurotic fear of open spaces, surprising given his love of nature and his wide travels.

Having been introduced to Native American and African American songs in New York, Dvořák proclaimed them to be the true voice of the nation—which in some circles provoked a chorus of racist outrage. At Carnegie Hall in 1893 he premiered what is still his most famous work and one of the most popular of all symphonies, **Symphony No. 9 in E Minor** ("From the New World"). He claimed that it had been inspired by American native music, including a slow movement in the style of a black spiritual. To what extent that declaration is true has been much debated, but whatever its mingling of Bohemian and American elements the piece is individual and irresistible, so a good introduction to Dvořák's temperament and style. In tone it ranges from nervous to poignant to, in the finale, a bracing stretch of trombonic banality. The symphony also shows off Dvořák's rich and glowing voice with the orchestra, in the orbit of Brahms but unmistakably his own.

Dvořák lasted only three years in the States, but he left an indelible impression on contemporary American composers, who at that time were struggling to find an authentic voice in the concert hall. Charles Ives's Second Symphony, the first of its kind with a true American voice, has echoes of Dvořák all over it. In America Dvořák spent his summers in a Bohemian community in Spillville, Iowa, playing organ at the local church and composing. One piece that came out of those sojourns is the **String Quartet No. 12 in F Major** ("American"). It begins with a delightfully garrulous tune in viola and keeps that folksy tone—call it Bohemian Yankee—to the end. There is an especially moving and songful slow movement. Dvořák was hardly all fun and games; his soulful side is strong and unique.

I'll recommend two more symphonies. **Symphony No. 8** is full of Bohemian echoes on a grand canvas, showing off Dvořák's genius for captivating melody. The Eighth begins with a touching and expansive theme, but most of the symphony is joyous. That opening returns transformed as the main theme of a romping finale. I remember the first time I heard the Eighth, played by the Boston Symphony while I was in college; when, in the finale after a luscious tune in cellos, the wild horn trills erupted, and I had a moment of delighted disbelief that anybody could have thought of that.

Symphony No. 7 is quite another matter. This is Dvořák's most nearly Brahmsian symphony, where I think he set out to write a tragic work and succeeded splendidly. The deeper regions of sorrow were not Dvořák's style, but as he demonstrates in the Seventh he could write music of penetrating and fateful passion. The delicately darting scherzo is one of his finer inspirations. As here, he has the immediate appeal of Tchaikovsky without being too heart on sleeve about it. In his way he was a classicist, disciplined in his forms and devoted to traditional genres, which he filled with dazzlingly fresh material.

Dvořák died in Prague in May 1904. For a long time many twentieth-century critics did not take him all that seriously because he appeared too popular, too pretty, too much fun to be really profound. True, his facility sometimes led him down frivolous paths, but in the end he mastered every genre he took up and wrote masterpieces in most of them. Dvořák came into his own in the late twentieth century partly because, like Brahms, audiences came to value exactly the charm and communicativeness that were unique to him.

More Dvořák: Cello Concerto, *Dumky* Trio, Piano Quintet in A Major.

Chapter 22

Gustav Mahler (1860–1911)

I n his person Gustav Mahler was one of the most tormented of composers, feeling from beginning to end like a stranger in the world, and his music was made in his own image. But sorrow is only one of the notes in the rich fabric of his art, which ranges from the childlike to the despairing, the earnest to the sardonic. His symphonies signal the end of romanticism, reaching a level of giganticism in forces and ambition that could hardly be carried further in the concert hall. In the freedom of his harmony and form and in his mingling of popular and exalted elements, he was equally a prophet of the music of the coming twentieth century.

Mahler was born in a small Bohemian village, son of an Austrian-Jewish tavern keeper. He spent his youth in Iglau, a German-speaking Czech town, where as Austrians the family were outsiders and as Jews doubly so. His father was distant and abusive, his mother frail but loving. Gustav inherited her weak heart and in adulthood seemed to affect her limp. There were a total of twelve children, variously afflicted, half of whom died in infancy; other siblings died later, from illness and suicide. From early on Gustav was obsessed with music, especially Czech folk music and the military marches he heard in the street. For him this music seemed to resonate with his feelings and his sorrows, and he never lost that sense of it. He began composing at four. His talent was prodigious; he made his piano debut at ten and at fifteen entered the Vienna Conservatory.

From the beginning Mahler intended to be a composer, but after his early efforts caused little stir he took up conducting and relegated composing to summer vacations. That pattern would last for the rest of his life. If his reputation as a composer was sketchy in his lifetime, as a conductor his success was spectacular. In seventeen years he rose from provincial opera houses to perhaps the most important podium in Europe: at age thirty-seven, likely with the backstage influence of Brahms, he became artistic director of the Vienna Opera. To secure the job he was more or less required to convert to Christianity. Mahler was not raised religiously, and in the next years his music was full of Christian imagery, partly born of his gnawing obsession with death and his desperate hope of resurrection. But the anti-Semitic press in Vienna never let the public forget his origins. In Vienna in those days, born a Jew, always a Jew. For Mahler, it cemented his position as an outsider.

In musical terms his regime at the opera was triumphant, historic. But if his performances earned him admirers, the fierce and relentless way he pursued his goals earned him enemies. His most celebrated performances were of Wagner and Mozart. In 1902 he married Alma Maria Schindler, called the most beautiful woman in Vienna. Mahler was not made for contentment, but in the next years he was among the most prominent conductors of the time and massively productive in his work. Despite his shaky health, he was an indefatigable swimmer and alpine hiker. He and Alma had two daughters, whom he doted on. This was the period of Symphonies 4 through 8.

In 1907 everything seemed to fall in on him at once. He was hounded out of the Opera by his critics, his three-year-old daughter died, and he was found to have a heart condition that he was not likely to survive for long. He declared that he had prophesied those three disasters in his tragic Symphony No. 6, which had three massive hammerblows of fate, the last of which he said felled the hero of the work. In despair, he went back to the score and took out the last blow. Meanwhile his marriage was increasingly troubled; eventually Alma took a lover.

At forty-seven, having lost probably the best job he could hope for in Europe, Mahler turned to the United States. In early 1908 he began conducting at the Metropolitan Opera and then took the podium of the New York Philharmonic. Once again his performances were hailed but his enemies proliferated. Alma later said the machinations of the board of the Philharmonic destroyed his position and hastened his death. Exhausted, Mahler returned to Vienna in 1911 and died there in May. At the end he seemed to be conducting, whispered the word "Mozart . . ." and was gone.

Along with much critical lambasting, Mahler had some successes with his music, but it never really triumphed in his lifetime. It was some fifty years after his death before his work was really embraced by the world. As he said prophetically near the end: "My time is yet to come." His eventual triumph was largely due to the efforts of later champions, above all Leonard Bernstein. To many in his time, Mahler's music was simply incomprehensible. Its temper ranges from the naive and childlike to towering proclamations. His harmonies are searching; sometimes a piece ends in a different key than its beginning; sometimes tonality all but disappears. His joining of little marches, shopworn popular tunes, simple folk melodies, military marches, and stretches of Beethovenian grandeur was bewildering to listeners who had grown up on Beethoven and Brahms. "The symphony must be like the world," Mahler said; "it must embrace everything."

Brahms was a friend to Mahler and admired him greatly as a conductor, but Mahler's first two symphonies scared the old master, though he could not have missed Mahler's extraordinary gift with the orchestra. For me there are four supreme masters of the art of orchestration: Stravinsky, Debussy, Ravel, and Mahler. All of them worked in the twentieth century, when orchestral color had become more important than ever before.

Mahler wrote little but symphonies and song cycles. For those new to him I suggest starting with one of the cycles for orchestra: **Des Knaben Wunderhorn** (The Youth's Magic Horn). (If you can find it, listen to the classic recording by George Szell and the London Symphony Orchestra.) The texts are from a collection of German folk poetry published in the early nineteenth century, from which generations of German song composers drew. The subjects are all over the place, from the spooky ghost-march "Reveille" to the childlike naïveté of "Who made up this little song?" to the sweet goofiness of "St. Anthony of Padua preaches to the fish." Every number is a delightful and individual gem. His love of folk music, naive and sentimental tunes, and military music are all over the settings. In each of them—performances range in number and order, but there are around a dozen—you hear Mahler's wonderfully colored and vibrant orchestration. He usually required a large orchestra, but picked out constantly changing combinations within the band. The *Wunderhorn* is a teaser for his later symphonies, because he used some of his song themes in them.

For the symphonies, his worlds in sound, naturally start with the five-movement **Symphony No. 2** (1888–1895). Its nickname is **"Resurrection,"** because its subject is nothing less than Mahler's life, death, and resurrection. There's a gigantic and portentous first movement, a slow movement based on the Austrian folk dance called a *Ländler*, a deliriously demonic scherzo based on the St. Anthony song in *Wunderhorn* (for me this exquisitely scored and utterly original scherzo is the glory of the symphony). The fourth movement features an alto singing a *Wunderhorn* poem, "Urlicht" (Primal Light), about longing to return to God; much of it is hymnlike in tone. The mammoth finale brings in a choir singing a lyric of Klopstock's about resurrection, followed by a poem of Mahler's own whose operative line is "I will die to be alive." The tone of the opening is magical, radiant; when Mahler wants to conjure paradise, he can do it as well as anybody. The choral conclusion is either monumentally grand or monumentally tacky, depending on taste. Many would agree that in the symphonies Mahler falls into banality sometimes, and does so on the same epic scale as nearly everything else he does.

The **Fourth Symphony**, finished in 1900, is unique in his output, small-scale, good-humored, delicious from its jangling introduction and folklike first theme. After a wry scherzo and expansive and gorgeous slow movement, the finale features a soprano on another *Wunderhorn* song, a child's vision of heaven that mainly involves lots of good things to eat. Mahler makes it at once ironic and touching. By this point his scoring sounds as if somehow a light had been turned on inside the orchestra, giving it a singular glow.

Finally, his penultimate completed (more or less) symphony, **Das Lied von der Erde** (Song of the Earth), in six movements. Sung alternately by a tenor and alto, the poems are German translations of Chinese verses. Mahler finished it in 1909 and didn't live to hear it. He probably didn't expect to. The music is a farewell to life, in tone everything from grotesque and anguished to nostalgic. It begins with music that will later paint a bizarre image in the text: a howling ape crouching on a gravestone. It goes on to a drinking song: "The wine beckons in golden goblets . . . first I'll sing you a song. The song of sorrow shall ring laughingly in your soul." The middle movements are enchanting pastels evoking the joy of life: "Young girls picking flowers, / Picking lotus flowers at the riverbank. /Amid bushes and leaves they sit, / gathering flowers in their laps and calling / one another in raillery." The finale builds to a hair-raising dance of death. The coda, ending on the word *evig* (forever), is heartbreakingly beautiful. This is a work from a man who no longer believes in immortality staring into his grave, but singing to the end.

If Mahler was virtually the last gasp of the romantic era, he also prophesied a great deal of the century to come, in its music and in its tragedy. Leonard Bernstein said, "Ours is the century of death, and Mahler is its spiritual prophet." He saw it through the lens of his own joy and suffering, but he was singing of universal themes that will never lose their resonance.

More Mahler: The orchestral song cycles *Kindertotenlieder* (Songs on the Death of Children) and *Rückert Lieder*; Symphonies Nos. 5, 6, and 7.

Chapter 23

FURTHER ROMANTIC LISTENING

The following figures get short takes only because I have to stop somewhere, but none of them are minor composers, and all of them wrote music that is widely loved and can be transformative. In my case, for example, I could not imagine a musical world that did not include Bruckner, Mussorgsky, and Sibelius.

Felix Mendelssohn (1809–1847): Mendelssohn was perhaps the most spectacular of all musical prodigies: by the end of his teens he had already written some of his finest, most important, most original music (the same could not be said of Mozart). In 1826, at age seventeen, Mendelssohn brought off one of the most remarkable feats in the history of music: his overture for Shakespeare's *A Midsummer Night's Dream*, which remains in the repertoire as one of the most original and enchanting works of its kind. Written while Beethoven was still alive, it announced a brilliant new voice. **Suggested listening:** Octet for Strings; *The Hebrides*, also known as *Fingal's Cave*; "Italian" Symphony (No. 4); Violin Concerto in E Minor.

César Franck (1822–1890): Franck was a child prodigy who entered the Liège Conservatory at age eight to study piano and at twelve won a prize at the Paris Conservatoire.

Most of Franck's best work as a composer comes from the last ten years of his long life. He is celebrated for his creative fastidiousness, for his lyricism and quiet originality, for bringing a helping of German tone and seriousness to French music. **Suggested listening:** Symphony in D Minor; Sonata for Violin and Piano in A.

Giuseppe Verdi (1813–1901). Verdi was the greatest of Italian opera masters. As a composer he began roughly; over the years of his enormous production he raised his sights and his craft step by step until the climactic masterpieces of his seventies, *Otello* and *Falstaff*, the finest operatic versions of Shakespeare ever written, both of them showing his assimilation of Wagner. **Suggested listening:** his massive and operatic Requiem, from 1874.

Anton Bruckner (1824–1896): With the background (and personality) of a pious peasant, Bruckner was an unlikely creator of epic symphonies. He grew up in the school of the abbey of St. Florian and served as a teacher and organist there while he started to compose. In 1866, at age forty-two, he finished his First Symphony in Vienna. From that point Bruckner was primarily a symphonist, spending years laboriously fashioning each one. In a way, he transferred his hero Wagner's orchestration and scope to the concert hall, though Bruckner has an unmistakable voice of his own: massive, surging, brassy, passionately lyrical, with huge folksy scherzos. It is the art of a man for whom music is more or less equivalent to God. **Suggested listening:** Symphonies Nos. 7 and 8.

Edvard Grieg (1843–1907): The nationalism of the nineteenth and twentieth centuries got the world in a great deal of trouble, but it was very good for music. Grieg is a model of how a place can flavor a composer like a pungent herb. The country in question was Norway, for whose national concert music Grieg was basically the founder. After starting on piano with his mother, he studied in Leipzig. When he returned to Norway, he discovered his native folk music, grounded his music in it, and reached maturity as one of the more engaging composers of any nationality. Among his biggest fans was Brahms. **Suggested listening:** *Peer Gynt; From Holberg's Time;* Piano Concerto in A Minor.

Nikolay Rimsky-Korsakov (1844–1908): Rimsky is another echt-nationalist, one of the Russian Five of the late nineteenth century that also included Mussorgsky. He is the distillation of what seems to be some innate Russian genius for brilliant orchestration. In the end, though, maybe the best thing Rimsky did for music was teaching the young Igor Stravinsky how to make magic with an orchestra. **Suggested listening:** *Capriccio espagnole; Scheherazade.*

Modest Mussorgsky (1839–1881): Mussorgsky came from a more or less peasant family in Russia, and as a young man was considered a bit of a fop, a ladies' man, a bit of a fool. Under all that was an astonishingly original genius, who on the way to drinking himself to death created one of the greatest, most electrifying of all operas, **Boris Godunov.** **Suggested listening:** *A Night on Bald Mountain; Pictures at an Exhibition* (written for piano, but start with Ravel's orchestral arrangement of it).

Aleksandr Scriabin (1872–1915): Of our three Russian composers in a row, Scriabin is the least nationalist in his music. The main inspiration for his early piano pieces was Chopin—many are charming and even euphoric salon items, but with a distinctive personality. Two forces intertwined in his mature works: a determination to forge a new harmonic

language, and a mystical obsession that grew out of an esoteric philosophy called Theosophy—a fascinating if a mite
loopy movement that influenced a number of artists in the
early twentieth century. In his later years Scriabin conceived
a hyper-Wagnerian, multiday transcendent work called *Mysterium*, a cosmic union of all the arts to be mounted beneath
the Himalayas, which was to raise its worshippers to "a supreme, final ecstasy." The show would be followed by the end
of humanity as we know it, to be replaced by transcendent
beings. Whew. Before *Mysterium* properly got going Scriabin
died, embarrassingly, from an infected pimple on his lip. Not
surprisingly, he started as a cult figure. While he's now more
or less standard repertoire, many of his followers still have a
touch of the old fanaticism. **Suggested listening:** *Poem of Ecstasy*; Piano Sonata No. 5.

Sir Edward Elgar (1857–1934): As you can tell from the
Sir, Elgar was very much an establishment figure in Britain,
and a certain amount of his work has the expected straight
laces. One familiar example is the **"Pomp and Circumstance"
March No. 1**, which has graduated millions from school. At
his best, Elgar is a finely tender and expressive composer, with
a distinctive blend of the plummy and the lyrically intimate.
Suggested listening: *Enigma Variations*; Cello Concerto
(preferably the classic recording by Jacqueline du Pré).

Jean Sibelius (1865–1957): I scratched my head about
where to put Sibelius, given that he died in 1957. But his orbit
as a composer was late-romantic, musically grounded in the
likes of Brahms and Tchaikovsky (with a dash of Debussy),
and no less in the forests and skies and language of his native Finland. After leaving the law for music, he concentrated
on violin and began to compose. In Vienna and Berlin he

studied with Brahms disciples, but on his return to Finland he announced himself as a thoroughgoing nationalist with the symphonic poem *Kullervo*. After a further series of works based on epic and folklore, the hyperbolic *Finlandia* of 1899 cemented his place as the country's leading composer. (I once loved this piece, now find it unbearable.) Over the years Sibelius's reputation has ebbed and flowed, and there have always been people who can't stand him, but his star has maybe never been higher than it is as of this writing. Sibelius has his sins of judgment and technique, but he has a voice soulful like none other, and in that he is irreplaceable. **Suggested listening:** *The Swan of Tuonela*; Violin Concerto; Second Symphony; Fifth Symphony.

PART V

MODERNISM AND BEYOND

Chapter 24

THE 20TH AND 21ST CENTURIES
(CA. 1900–PRESENT)

I'll introduce this section with a flyover of music from roughly 1900, more or less the beginning of modernism, to roughly the present, more or less the postmodern and/or post-postmodern period. It's a gigantic and daunting territory. The hope is to give some context to the varicolored work on display during the most democratic, most innovative, most hopeful, also most bloody, tragic, and perilous period in human history.

Musical modernism began in Europe around the turn of the twentieth century, rising from the lingering death of romanticism, which succumbed to excesses of ambition and ego and the decay of old forms and assumptions. By that point traditional systems of tonal scales and harmony had been so bent out of shape that they needed either to be rethought or discarded entirely. Culturally, the term for this period is *fin de siècle*—end of the century, end of an era. But it was more than a simple ending; it was a falling apart. Much of that disintegration was social: the first two decades of the twentieth century saw the rise of nationalism and anti-Semitism in Germany that produced the Nazis; in Russia came the Russian Revolution. Both movements would move the world inexorably toward war and to mass murder on an unprecedented scale.

So, modernism in all the arts came in part from a time of cultural malaise, decadence, and despair in Europe—in creative terms, though, a highly productive malaise. But there was a good deal more at play. A useful date for the arrival of modernism in music was the appearance of Debussy's *L'après-midi d'un faune* in 1894 (while Brahms was still alive, by the way). As we'll see, Debussy was arguably the most revolutionary composer of all time. Part of his inspiration came from an early encounter with a Javanese gamelan ensemble. This exotic music galvanized Debussy, in the same way that the young Picasso was galvanized by the stylized distortions of African masks, which led him to conceive cubism.

Beyond the broadening of horizons provided by quicker travel and communication, there was a general restlessness among artists. They strove to find new languages, new freedoms and new disciplines, new visions of the human. In music, after Debussy there was a rage for fresh instrumental colors and harmonies—which was partly stimulated by the increasing variety and sophistication of modern orchestration. In the past originality had been prized but innovation less so, at least by audiences. Now among modernist artists innovation became the coin of the realm. Thus the old modernist manifesto: "Make it good or make it bad, but make it *new*."

Modernism, for all its revolutionary ambitions, was really a continuation, expansion, and intensification of trends that had been growing in the arts through the nineteenth century. Part of that was a Wagnerian vision of the artist as a visionary genius, a demigod, and so on. In many ways, the romantic cult of genius went on to fuel modernism. Added to that was a growing divide between artists and audiences, which also began in the nineteenth century. Artists cared less and less what audiences thought of them. For modernist composers this meant that, while the pay had never been lavish or predictable, there was steadily less chance to make a living from their art. Once they embraced this fact composers felt even less beholden to their listeners—art would be for art's sake only. By the twentieth century, most composers made their living teaching or in nonmusical jobs. Many works of the twentieth century, the good and bad alike, depended on courageous performers who sometimes mounted pieces over the protests of the audience.

Two historic premieres of 1912–1913 represent the full emergence of modernism, in the persons of two composers who seemed to embody the movement in virtually opposite ways. The year 1912 saw the premiere of Arnold Schoenberg's *Pierrot lunaire*, a setting of unsettling fin-de-siècle poems in a style that amplified their strangeness. *Pierrot* is a small-scale chamber piece, but its effect in history was that of a bombshell. The other bombshell was even grander: Stravinsky's *Le sacre du printemps*, a work of dazzling, highly sophisticated primitivism.

For the rest of the century those two composers seemed to embody the two sides of musical modernism: Schoenberg the more austere, theoretical, and audience-defying, Stravinsky the more voluptuous and eventually more audience-pleasing. In the early years of modernism audience riots became familiar in premieres of new pieces. The biggest riots of all were at the notorious 1913 premiere of *Sacre*, and at a concert that same year in Vienna with premieres of Schoenberg and Berg.

In both concerts there were screams and fistfights in the audience; in Vienna the police had to be called and the orchestra played ashen with fear. (Why do riots no longer happen in the concert hall? Most likely it was because people in 1912 cared more about music than audiences do now. In those days, if audiences hated your piece, they wanted to do you harm.)

Modernism as it unfolded in the rest of the century is harder to summarize. In their explorations artists were going in every direction at once: primitivism and futurism and post-impressionism, serialists and minimalists and neoclassicists, extremes of complexity and of simplicity. Alongside these movements were late-romantic holdouts, such as Rachmaninoff; Americanists, such as Aaron Copland; and more or less unclassifiables, such as Charles Ives and Samuel Barber. If this sounds something like chaos, so it was and so it remains. But it's an often fruitful chaos.

War played its part in all of it. The aftershocks of cultural movements, wars, and other historic events reverberate through the generations, and that process affects music as much as any other human endeavor. A postwar period is a frame of mind, something on the order of culture-wide posttraumatic stress. What often follows war is a retreat, a need to find new rhymes and reasons because the old ones proved catastrophic. The First World War had been followed by the Jazz Age, the economic crash, and the grueling Depression of the 1930s. In the aftershock of World War I, composers including Schoenberg and Stravinsky turned in their own way to a more formal, more rationalized, less freely intuitive direction: Schoenberg to the twelve-tone method, Stravinsky to neoclassicism.

After World War II the response of music and the other arts to the postwar zeitgeist was varied and contradictory. As always, some of the leading ideas came from Europe, especially since some of the most influential European artists were now working in the United States. Before and during World War II, many leading figures in music and the other arts had emigrated there. Schoenberg and Stravinsky each had legions of American disciples.

One of the wellsprings of modernism was *impressionism.* The movement began in France, where starting in the 1860s painters began hauling their canvases outdoors and trying to capture light and rippling water. The studio-bound gloom of nineteenth-century academic painting was replaced by pastel canvases glowing with sunlight that dissolved hard edges and shapes. The style of Claude Monet, Jean Renoir, and others came to be called impressionist because it proposed to capture an impression rooted in an instant of perception.

When Claude Debussy burst onto the scene with music based as much on tone color and rhythm as on form or melody, it was soon dubbed impressionist. Like the painters, Debussy wanted to capture the sea, clouds, festivals in sensuous washes of color. Also like them, Debussy was more interested in atmosphere than in traditional form and logic. As had the painters, he used the discipline he had learned in the academy to throw out much of what the academy taught him. When the younger Maurice Ravel came along with his pastel harmonies and luscious instrumental textures, critics joined him to Debussy as a co-impressionist. (Really Ravel, who hung on to the old formal patterns, was as much a neoclassicist as anything.) In art and music impressionism was a revolution quickly and widely embraced. It influenced composers as diverse as Charles Ives,

George Gershwin, and Béla Bartók. At the same time impressionist harmony became an indispensable element of the great period of twentieth-century American popular song from the 1920s to the 1950s.

Expressionism was a gnarlier founding element of modernism. While impressionism was fundamentally French, expressionism was fundamentally Austro-German. In those countries political reaction, militarism, and anti-Semitism were more belligerent than in France. Artists embraced Freud's new science of psychoanalysis, which created an image of the human mind as a fragile crust of rationality over an unconscious tide of urges, violence, sexuality, and pain. As much as anything, that joining of inner and outer turbulence created this distinctly Germanic creative revolution. In painting, expressionism took shape as an art whose tortured forms and sometimes clotted colors rose from a willful primitivism. Much of the style took off from Vincent van Gogh, Edvard Munch, and James Ensor, painters of nightmare, terror, and ecstasy. The later echt-expressionist painters included Ernst Ludwig Kirchner, Emil Nolde, and Egon Schiele with his disconcerting self-portraits. The first expressionist film was the legendary *Cabinet of Dr. Caligari*, in which the nightmare distortions of the sets echo the mind of a violently insane man.

There had always been a certain objectivity about impressionism. It was concerned with feeling, but more with trying to catch the tangibility of nature: Monet's water lilies, Debussy's sea wind. For the expressionists, it was about the interior regions of the mind, the irrational, madness and dream. Whereas the impressionists reveled in the perfumed, vaporous, and sensuous, expressionists reached for the convulsive, raw, and dissonant. Beauty and lyricism were not forbidden, but they had to be fraught, shapes and colors filtered through the conscious and unconscious mind of the artist.

The prophetic writer and social critic Karl Kraus called fin-de-siècle Vienna "an isolation cell in which one was allowed to scream," and beyond that, "the research laboratory for world destruction." To cite one example, virulently anti-Semitic Vienna provided historic inspiration for an Austrian corporal and would-be painter named Adolf Hitler. It's no surprise then that Vienna was the wellspring of musical expressionism, seen above all in the music of Arnold Schoenberg and his pupils Anton Webern and Alban Berg.

Schoenberg and his disciples turned away from traditional tonality and toward steady dissonance and what came to be called *atonality*, their melodies rejecting the smooth lines of the past in favor of lines jagged and sometimes shrieking. Much of the early period of their art dealt with extremes of anguish and tragedy. Defining works include Schoenberg's *Erwartung*, in which a crazed woman stumbles over the body of her lover, whom she may have murdered. Webern's stunning Six Pieces for Orchestra, written in a tumult of feelings after the death of his mother, is a landscape of pain. Berg in his opera *Wozzeck* created with heartbreaking honesty and compassion the story of a soldier doomed by inner and outer forces beyond his control.

After the convulsion of World War I both impressionism and expressionism receded, the first moving toward irrelevance and cliché, the second toward exhaustion. Schoenberg, Webern, and Berg turned to the new twelve-tone method of composition, which searched for a new order and a more spiritual vision. But the reverberations of both impressionism and expressionism are still with us, for well and for ill. Both were powerful, fertile, and fertilizing modes of thought and expression that gave new languages to art.

After World War I, a formidable train of thought flowed outward from Europe in Schoenberg's twelve-tone, eventually dubbed *serial*, method, in which a whole work is based on a single arrangement of the twelve notes of the chromatic scale. In the work of Schoenberg and his disciples Anton Webern and Alban Berg, the twelve-tone method was a theoretical rationalization of their earlier *free-atonal* music.

What we call *tonal* music has been around more or less since the beginning of music, each culture inflecting it in its own way. Tonal music is based on *scales*. What is a scale? If you know *The Sound of Music*, sing the end of its song about the scale, on the traditional syllables: do–re–mi–fa–so–la–ti–do. There you have a seven-note *major scale*, the most common scale in Western music for the last 500 years or so. A *minor scale* lowers the *mi*, *la*, and sometimes the *ti*. In the past five hundred years nearly all Western music has been based on major and minor scales in the various keys. We tend to think of major keys as "brighter" and "happier" than minor ones, and minor ones more given to sadness and poignancy. Those scales tend to work that way expressively, except when they don't: there are minorish majors and majorish minors.

When you sang the scale, did you notice that the first and last notes, *do* to *do*, sounded like the main notes in the scale? In all cultures, a given scale has a keynote, a tone that is considered its home base. That tone is why we call the music *tonal*: it is based on that idea of a home tone in each key, with its associated scales. That home tone is called the *tonic*, or *tonal center.* Every key is named for its tonal center: C major, D minor, A-flat major, and so on. The other notes of the scale function in a hierarchy of relationships to the tonic. The fifth degree of the scale, *so*, is the second in command and is called the *dominant.* In effect, you can say that in a given scale only the tonic is the true home; the other notes in the major or minor scale yearn for it, each in its own way.

On each note of the scale you can build a *chord.* The most common kind of chord in tonal music is a three-note one called a *triad.* The lowest note in a triad is its *root.* You make a triad by going up two notes from the root, then two again. Each triad in a key is named for the scale degree that is its root. The *tonic triad* in the key of C major, for example, is spelled C–E–G, the *dominant triad* G–B–D.

Like scales, triads come in various flavors, mainly *major* and *minor.* D–F-sharp–A is a D major triad; D–F–A is a D minor triad. A *chord* is defined as any three or more notes played together. There are many kinds of chords besides a major or minor triad, some of them traditional and some of them first explored in the twentieth century. Here's a traditional four-note chord: if you take a triad and add a note a third from the top note, say, G–B–D–F, you've created a *seventh chord*, because the F is the interval of a seventh from the G.

In Western classical tonality a seventh chord is defined as a *dissonance.* In tonal music dissonance means two things. First, it is an acoustically busier, more complicated sound than a consonance, so is considered less restful. Second, a dissonance is expected eventually to resolve into something more restful or acoustically more smooth. That smoother sound is called a *consonance.* So, in traditional tonal music, *dissonance is expected to resolve to consonance*; that is, tension to resolution.

Some people think of dissonance in music as something ugly and say it should be banished. That's nuts. Dissonance is absolutely necessary, in music as in life. All Western music is an ebb and flow of dissonance and consonance, moving away from rest and back to it, putting off cadences, deflecting expected resolutions, and generally playing subtle and expressive games with the creation and resolution of tension. In his late music Beethoven put off cadences achingly long, sometimes to create tension, sometimes a sense of suspension and reverie. The skilled manipulation of tension and release, consonance and dissonance, is what separates a master from a hack.

Whereas Mozart and Haydn in the classical period largely wanted to keep their tonality and harmony and form fairly clear, Beethoven got increasingly interested in more distant key relationships, more prolonged harmonic periods, less overt forms. By the romantic century composers were exploring deliberate harmonic ambiguity, rising levels of dissonance, long delays of resolution. The first song in Robert Schumann's cycle *Dichterliebe* ends exquisitely on an unresolved seventh chord.

Over the nineteenth century composers poked and prodded at the diatonic tonal system, added more dissonance to the mix, more complex and nimble key changes, explorations of sustained tonal ambiguity that left the sense of key suspended. By the early years of the twentieth century some composers, mainly Arnold Schoenberg and his pupils Webern and Berg, came to the conclusion that the tonal system was exhausted. For reasons as much expressive as technical, they began writing music with free harmony, meaning no triads, no hierarchy of consonance and dissonance, little or no sense of a tonal center. Keys, in other words, were banished. Tonality was dead. Any harmony was allowed. Now we've arrived at *atonality*, meaning music without tonal centers. (Not that all music with free harmony is atonal—some composers, including Bartók, wrote quite freely but retained a sense of a central note.)

The best way to compare tonal and atonal music is by listening to some examples. First listen to **the first movement of Mozart's *Eine kleine Nachtmusik*** (A Little Night Music). Here harmony and key are straightforward. Now listen to **the opening of Brahms's String Quintet in F Major, Op. 88.** Both pieces are tonal, but Brahms is interested in more colorful, out-of-the-way modulations (changes of key) and harmonies than Mozart. Next, try **Wagner's Prelude to *Tristan und Isolde*.** He's using chords that existed in tonal music, but mainly the more dissonant ones, and he's putting them together so freely that the music has little to no sense of a tonal center. Now listen to one of the pioneering modernist atonal pieces, **the first of Schoenberg's *Drei Klavierstücke*, Op. 11** (preferably Glenn Gould's recording). What you hear is dreamlike music, wandering, unpredictable, but with an intense personality of its own. The harmonies are steadily dissonant by traditional standards, though there is still some ebb and flow of *relative* consonance and dissonance. So, in an atonal piece there is not a scale in sight except for one: the *chromatic scale*, which includes all the notes within an octave—if you count them on the piano, they add up to twelve.

Part of what marks tonal music is its large-scale predictability. You know that dissonance will resolve to consonance, and however far the music has ranged among the keys, it will usually return to the tonic key at the end. That's why pieces are labeled by their tonic key, as in Symphony in D Major: no matter how far it ranges in keys, it will return to the D tonic at the end. (Sometimes pieces begin in a minor key and end in a major, but the tonic will be the same: say, F minor to F major.) In atonal music, however, there is no tonal resolution and you can't predict much of anything. You have to live in the moment. For some, that's a limitation; for others, a freedom. I find it simply a characteristic, and enjoy it for what it is. (Atonal music does not *have* to be constantly dissonant, though it often is.) Meanwhile atonality opened up, for the first time, the fullest possible palette of harmony.

One further point needs to be made about atonal music. In my musical education I was taught that atonality and tonality were purely a technical matter, products of ongoing innovation in history and methods that can be learned. They are those things, but music is equally an *expressive* matter. To get at the emotional territories they were after, some of them dark and scary territories, composers needed to write music like this. In my student years I found many American composers writing in ways that mimicked early twentieth-century Austro-German expressionism in technique and style, which I regarded as puzzling. Those composers ignored the fact that the style was connected to a place, a culture, a zeitgeist, and stemmed from particular artistic personalities writing out of particular needs and concerns and ecstasies and madnesses. Whatever a composer's technique, one needs to write out of who one is and when and where one came from.

We're getting to twelve tone now. At first, Schoenberg and his followers to a degree experimented freely in terms of harmony and such; each piece had its particular motifs and material, but there was no overall procedure. This phase, the first years of all their mature work, is called *free atonality*. No tonal center, no overriding method, dissonance and consonance considered equal—that is, dissonance liberated from the need to resolve. A number of tremendous pieces were written in free atonality: Schoenberg's *Pierrot lunaire*, Webern's Five Pieces for String Quartet, Berg's opera *Wozzeck*.

But after World War I Schoenberg wanted a more disciplined direction—in other words, a *method*. I think there were a number of reasons for it, some emotional, some historical, some technical. After the irrational chaos and disruption of war there is often a yen for things more calm, more reasonable, more under control. (And/or more fun—consider the Jazz Age of the 1920s.)

After the war, Stravinsky turned to his more focused, backward-looking neoclassic style. Schoenberg came up with a new way of writing, which he called the *twelve-tone method*. Like traditional tonal music it had its rules and regulations. As will be examined in the Schoenberg essay, a twelve-tone piece is based throughout on what amounts to a single chromatic melody: a particular arrangement of the twelve notes of the chromatic scale called a *row*, which can then be handled in a great variety of ways. To a large extent the idea of a row came from the nineteenth century's increasing focus on thematic relationships, such as Liszt's basing a whole piece on a single small theme or motif.

Think of twelve tone as Schoenberg's version of Stravinskian neoclassicism—after all that winging it, a return to law and order. (Stravinsky had winged it in *Le sacre du printemps*, with surpassing brilliance.) After World War II there was a turn to the kind of intensified concentration on rows pioneered by Webern; this postwar, post-Webern music came to be called *serial* because it is founded on a series—a row, more relentlessly applied than ever. Among the apostles of "total serialism" were Pierre Boulez and Karlheinz Stockhausen, but neither of them necessarily conformed to its rules in the long run.

If the neoclassic faction in some degree resonated with the postwar yearning for peace and normality, the intellectual rigor of serialism arose in part from a drive for rationality after the catastrophic irrationalities of World War II. In Europe and soon in America, composers, including Boulez, took up post-Webern serialism as a holy cause, proclaiming its historical necessity as a new common practice. Meanwhile Boulez's colleague Stockhausen, who in his German youth saw the remains of his fellow townspeople hanging in trees after Allied bombings, declared that every composer must pursue an endless revolution.

In the United States the serial idea settled in as an endeavor largely associated with composers in academe. There the dichotomy rested for a while: the often academic atonalists and serialists in one camp, the more popularistic neoclassicists in the other. Then something remarkable happened. After the death of Schoenberg in 1951, Stravinsky turned away from his decades of neoclassic works and took up serialism, starting with his ballet *Agon*. The shock waves reverberated around the Western musical world. It was as if the commanding general of an army had gone over to the enemy. Stravinsky's historic turn certified the triumph of serialism and the avant-garde in the forefront of new music. The revolutionists took over the shop. Two generations of neoclassicists found themselves out of the spotlight and sometimes out of a job.

But at the same time, a third train of thought in music seemed to contradict all the other camps. In his 1949 "Lecture on Nothing," composer John Cage declared, "I have nothing to say / and I am saying it / and that is poetry / as I need it." In the spirit of a Zen openness to the world, Cage rejected the whole past agenda of music: logic, emotion, meaning, beauty, form, and on and on. Any sound whatsoever (and even better, silence) he declared to be music. Cage began to compose by chance methods involving throwing dice, turning on radios, consulting the ancient Chinese book of prophecy, the *I Ching*. Cage and his disciples came to be called the *aleatoric* movement (from the Latin *alea*, "dice"). It had a wide influence; for some, the pursuit of meaninglessness appeared to be a way out of the disastrous ideologies and agendas of the past.

It seemed that the aleatoric ethos was ultimately contrary to the serial school—it certainly was to the neoclassical. In practice, however, there grew a rapprochement between serialists and aleatoricists. After all, they made similar kinds of sounds, they worked outside the mainstream of concert life, they were all generally denoted as "avant-garde," and they often had an attitude of indifference unto hostility toward the bourgeois concert-going public and to popular culture.

All this had an air of authenticity and inevitability. For many postwar composers in Europe and America, after the manifest death of the old tonal system, serialism appeared the only alternative to musical anarchy, the avant-garde the best antidote to cultural boredom and stagnation. But as the 1950s gave way to the 1960s, an abiding problem refused to go away: not enough people were buying tickets to hear avant-garde or serial music. It didn't put the backsides in the seats. By then much of Stravinsky was standard repertoire, Bartók catching on. But despite these occasional successes, the more revolutionary side of the musical equation could not find its way firmly into the mainstream. Then came the Vietnam War, and in its aftermath a new wave of revolution and reaction—a political reaction that is still ongoing as of this writing.

Perhaps inevitably, among younger American composers there arose a rebellion against the last generation's rebellion. In 1964, as the "counterculture" emerged and beards and protests sprouted across the United States, Terry Riley wrote a chirping, hypnotic, semi-aleatoric piece called *In C*. That work and its fellows came to be called the *minimalist* school, led by composers Steve Reich and Philip Glass. This movement fled as far as possible from academic serialism to an utter simplicity and transparency of means. Minimalism's relentless babble and beat rose, among other sources, from pop music. The success of minimalism had the effect of opening up a gigantic tract of musical territory between serialist arcana on the one hand, and five-note, hour-long minimalism on the other. Most composers of the last fifty years work somewhere in that middle territory. At the same time, from the 1960s on, the once somewhat well-defined realms of "popular," "classical," and "avant-garde" music, of "high" and "low" art, began to blur. They have been merging ever since.

In 1974 leading Japanese composer Toru Takemitsu, visiting at Yale, told me: "We are free now." He meant free from ideologies of tonal vs. atonal, of stylistic consistency, even of popular vs. classical. It was in the same period that another composer said, approximately, "It's hard to make a revolution when, two revolutions ago, they already said anything goes." The end-of-century *postmodern* movement seemed to revel in the impossibility of doing anything truly new. Instead, postmodern artists indulge in ironic games with the past, mixing and matching and mismatching among the arts once divided into "high" and "low."

In effect, what the serialists of the 1950s feared came to pass: musical composition has evolved into a kind of dynamic anarchy that voraciously consumes every movement of the past. Some credit for this goes to the ubiquity of modern media, which preserves everything. It becomes harder to envision the future when the past is before our eyes and ears all the time. There is less of a natural ebb and flow of artistic evolution when every movement tends to stick around indefinitely.

More recent developments in new music, as they always do, have taken contrasting directions. On the one hand, there is a kind of postpunk rambunctiousness that has been dubbed "aesthetic brutalism." On the other, in the United States, there are composers grouped around the Atlanta Symphony Orchestra, dubbed the "Atlanta School." This group offers listeners a warm embrace; it's been called "the new niceness." Among the Atlanta School composers is **Jennifer Higdon**, whose lushly neoromantic **Violin Concerto** won the 2010 Pulitzer Prize. On quite another hand, a school of *spectralist* composers explore different kinds of musical organization based on the acoustical properties of sound. Have a listen to **Gérard Grisey's** growling, whistling *Partiels*, from 1975.

Thus my quick survey of modernism, postmodernism, and whatever period we're in now. How to summarize it? The best way I can think of is as follows. For some years I taught at a conservatory in which at one point there were thirty-three student composers and five composition teachers. These thirty-eight composers wrote in thirty-eight distinct ways. Of the composers older and younger at my school, none wrote exclusively serial music, none were mainstream minimalists, none regularly involved with Cagean aleatoric procedures, none sounded much like Schoenberg or Stravinsky, some wrote both tonal and atonal pieces, only a few were detectably neoromantic or postmodern or close to the 1960s–1970s avant-garde. Yet every one of those influences were present in their work, in kaleidoscopic and unpredictable ways. That is what I mean by "dynamic anarchy." It has its dangers, but also its potentials.

There are a lot of composers to cover in this section, more than in any other period. Maybe that's because history has not yet finished its winnowing. Or it may be that because of modern media—radio, recordings, the easy availability of the entire repertoire online—fewer and fewer composers will fade away at all. As a lesser-known composer myself, whose stuff appears on YouTube and Spotify and hopefully will linger online forever, I'm not going to complain about that.

Chapter 25

CLAUDE DEBUSSY (1862–1918)

In the 1920s in Riceville, Tennessee, a little red-dirt south-
ern town beside the train tracks, my mother played
Debussy on piano a decade after he died. He was one of the
last composers of classical music whose works would be uni-
versally recognized and adored, played by young and old in
parlors everywhere. Yet Debussy was also one of the most radical composers who ever lived. His training was grounded in
the past, yet in his work he threw much of what he had learned
out the window: the melodies, the harmonies, the forms, the
attitudes.

Unlike many of the modernists who followed him,
Debussy set out not to shock but to intoxicate, not to provoke
but to seduce. "I love music passionately," he said, "and because
I love it I try to free it from barren traditions that stifle it. It is
a free art . . . an open-air art, an art boundless as the elements,
the wind, the sky, the sea!" He was a fierce enemy of abstrac-
tion: "There's no need for music to make people *think*! . . . It
would be enough if . . . they felt that for a moment they had
been dreaming of an imaginary country."

Claude-Achille Debussy was born in Saint-Germain-en-
Laye, France, his father a china salesman and his mother a

seamstress. He began studying piano at age seven and by age ten had advanced so remarkably that he was accepted into the Paris Conservatoire. He studied at that notoriously conservative school for eleven years, though he proved a generally recalcitrant and free-spirited student. Stories abound of Debussy shocking his professors by breaking musical rules wholesale. He got away with it because nearly everybody understood his brilliance. Outside school his life was already adventurous. For three summers starting in 1880 he traveled around Europe as pianist for Nadezhda von Meck, the celebrated patroness of Tchaikovsky. At age eighteen he started an affair in Paris with Blanche Vasnier, a married singer, that went on for eight years.

In 1884 Debussy wrote a cantata polite enough to win the Conservatoire's Prix de Rome, which required a three-year residence in Rome. He found he despised the city, his fellow students, the accommodations, and the food. Dutifully he composed his required residency pieces, which the professors decried as "courting the unusual." "I am too enamored of my freedom, too fond of my own ideas!" he wrote in a letter. After only two years he fled back to Paris and Blanche. There were other women in those days, too; as a young man Debussy was a bohemian of the more profligate variety. One mistress threatened suicide if he left her; another, whom he married in 1899, did shoot herself when he left for a new wife, but she survived. Debussy himself was beset by suicidal thoughts.

In 1890 he wrote what would become his first famous piece, though he only published it (much revised) in 1905: *Clair de Lune* (Moonlight), for piano. The piece is archetypically Debussy: languid, dreamlike, full of subtle perfumes, in harmony and melody and pianism a work of the most remarkable originality.

Living in the high-bohemian district of Montmartre in Paris, Debussy was caught up in the arts scene of the late-century French fin de siècle, a period when romanticism had become overripe and Western culture was stumbling toward the catastrophes of the next century. Still, the fin de siècle was fertile for the arts all over Europe. Debussy hung out with the Symbolists, writers whose founders and heroes included Edgar Allan Poe and the poets Baudelaire, Verlaine, and Mallarmé. One of the group gave an appropriately opaque summary of their goals: away with "plain meanings, declamations, false sentimentality and matter-of-fact description . . . scenes from nature, human activities, and all other real world phenomena will not be described for their own sake; here, they are perceptible surfaces created to represent their esoteric affinities with the primordial Ideals." (Aha . . . What?)

Based on a famously nebulous and erotic poem of his friend Mallarmé, in 1891–1894 Debussy wrote what was at once his most famous orchestral work, his first masterpiece, and the inauguration of musical modernism: *Prélude à l'après-midi d'un faune* (Prelude to the Afternoon of a Faun). In Mallarmé's poem a faun from ancient myth lies dreaming of his lovemaking with a nymph. Debussy places his version in a new tonal world: a sighing melody in the lowest range of the flute, whose silken sexiness had never been explored before. The piece unfolds like a waking dream, harmonies drifting and unresolved, melodies like the breathing of wind, rhythms spreading loosely around the barline, the strings and harp like diaphanous veils, the form as free yet inevitable as rock sculpted by flowing water.

The singular, utterly fresh, entirely revolutionary style of *Faune* sounds so familiar, natural and inevitable that it is easy to miss what a complex and difficult synthesis it was. For *Faune*, Debussy drew on an enormous range of influences. At the Conservatoire he had been steeped in the mostly Germanic past. For a while he involved himself with Wagner, studying the scores and making a pilgrimage to Bayreuth. Beyond that there was the long history of French music, from the little character pieces for harpsichord of François Couperin to the subtle harmonies of Debussy's older contemporary Gabriel Fauré. The Russian masters of the time played a part in his influences as well: Rimsky-Korsakov, Mussorgsky, Tchaikovsky.

Debussy found even more exotic influences in Paris: the gnomic and harmonically innovative pieces of Erik Satie, one of the grand eccentrics of the day both in his antiromantic music and his person. Among his titles: *Pieces to Make You Run Away, Veritable Flabby Preludes (for a dog)*. And there was the enchanted exoticism of the Javanese gamelan Debussy encountered at the Paris Universal Exposition of 1889, a languid and exotic music that seemed to wipe away everything he had been taught. Perhaps that music ringing with gongs completed his break from the past, from classical forms and its attendant rules and regulations. Now he largely put Beethoven aside; Wagner became for him "that old poisoner . . . a beautiful sunset that was mistaken for a dawn." By a creative alchemy of singular genius Debussy forged this mélange of influences into a musical personality that seemed to have come out of nowhere fully formed.

Because of his tendency to compose pieces portraying wind and water and people and events, critics labeled him an impressionist, after the contemporary French painters who worked outdoors and attempted to capture the elements on canvas. Debussy hated the label but it stuck, and soon the younger Ravel joined him as the other founding father of musical impressionism.

Despite Debussy's distaste for it, "impressionism" is as good a label as any for him, as shown in his next great orchestral work, *La mer*, (The Sea) from 1903–1905. It amounts to a three-movement symphony, but is something far from the usual—meaning Germanic—idea of what constituted a symphony. It is a series of portraits of the sea in motion. "From Dawn to Noon on the Sea" gradually lays out a broad expanse, then sails into a journey. Part of the effect of the piece is Debussy's unprecedented use of the strings. They shape changing colors and textures, supplying an atmosphere over which winds and brass sing rhapsodic melodies. "Play of the Waves" is a more lively movement of shifting, shimmering sonorities. "Dialogue of the Wind and the Sea" begins with a squall, then gradually transforms toward a soaring, rapturous finish.

Debussy's ability to paint the world with music was incomparable, but like the Symbolists he was not interested in mere portrayal—he aimed for something more spiritual and poetic. It did not trouble him that he had actually never sailed on the sea; the sea in his imagination was more important. Meanwhile, though he had spent exactly one day in Spain, he wrote a remarkable work inspired by that country, the three-movement *Ibéria* for orchestra. (Likewise his contemporary Edgar Degas painted dance classes for years without ever having seen one.) The first of *Ibéria*'s three movements, all of them based on dance, begins with an explosion of castanets; the finale turns the string section into a kind of superguitar.

In his piano music Debussy remade the instrument in the same way and same spirit as Chopin had: new figures, new colors, new kinds of singing on an instrument that inherently resists singing. For a start, take in the **Preludes, Book 1.** Each of its miniatures is named: "Dancers of Delphi," "Puck's Dances," the American-tinged "Minstrels." Perhaps the centerpiece is "The Sunken Cathedral," based on the old myth of a cathedral sunk in the sea that daily rises to the surface with bells ringing, organ playing, priests chanting. Accordingly, the piece swells gradually to an immense climax, its grand effect based on a novel technique: the middle pedal of the piano sustains bass notes while pealing chords sound above, creating piano resonances no one had explored before.

Finally, try Debussy's opera *Pelléas et Mélisande*, based on a Symbolist play with a medieval setting by Maurice Maeterlinck. Prince Golaud stumbles on the weeping Mélisande in a forest, her crown fallen in a spring. We never find out who she is or where she came from. She returns to his castle with him; they marry. She spends much of her time with his young and ingenuous half brother Pelléas, arousing Golaud's suspicions. Finally in a transport of jealousy he cuts both of them down. Debussy shaped this vaporous tale into tableaus from myth and dream. The premiere was done behind a transparent curtain. He once said that there was too much singing in opera, so he invented a unique kind of musical declamation for the singers that only occasionally flowers into lyricism. One critic called *Pelléas* "musical hashish"; it became a cult sensation among the young aesthetes of Paris. *Pelléas* is a work so otherworldly, so inimical to opera's usual dramatic and sentimental rigmaroles, so gothically Anne Rice–meets–David Lynch, that the ideal production would be mounted by a cast of masochists for an audience of vampires.

Debussy's last years were miserable. Through a long decline from cancer he kept composing as best he could. He died in Paris in March 1918, his passing hardly noticed in the flood of death from the war.

Among the great classical composers Debussy may have been the one least cooked by rules and formulas. The result was a new art, one of ambiance and evocation and mystery. At the same time he was among the most fastidious of craftsmen, with the patience, skill, and genius to realize new kinds of creative ambition, which he pursued with moral fervor. "I wish to sing of my interior visions with the naïve candor of a child," Debussy said. "It is bound to offend the partisans of deceit and artifice. I foresee that and rejoice at it."

More Debussy: Nocturnes for orchestra; *Estampes* for piano; the sonatas for violin and cello.

Chapter 26

Richard Strauss (1864–1949)

R ichard Strauss was born to a wealthy and prominent musical family. He revealed himself as a prodigy at a very young age, saw quick and spectacular success, and for decades enjoyed a pleasant and profitable career as composer and conductor. In his early work he is late-romantic in voice, but pushed that stylistic envelope to the brink of dissolution. Then he stepped backward instead of forward. He began his career as a bomb-throwing revolutionary and ended his long life outmoded and politically compromised. Perhaps Strauss didn't mind that much. He was not worried about expressing his soul or his vision but, rather, interested in reveling in his gifts, making a lavish income, and enjoying his success. His work endures because in his compulsion to seize his audience he wrote some of the more vivacious, compelling, sometimes provoking music of his time. That the titanic opening of his *Also sprach Zarathustra* has become a cultural icon would perhaps have amused him; he would have appreciated the royalties even more.

Richard Georg Strauss was born in Munich, his father the principal horn of the court orchestra, his mother an heiress of Schorr, the still-famous brewery. His father's tastes were conservative—he particularly loathed Wagner. In his early work, Strauss followed suit and adopted a comfortably neo-Brahmsian mode. By age eighteen he had composed some 140 pieces, some of them for orchestra. By age twenty he was assistant conductor of the famed Meiningen Orchestra. He would conduct widely for the rest of his life.

But behind his father's back Strauss developed a great passion for Wagner, which changed the course of his life and work. On the advice of an older friend he abandoned classical forms and took up the Lisztean genre of the tone poem, a.k.a. symphonic poem. That led to the 1889 *Don Juan* and worldwide fame—or rather, for a while, a mingling of fame and infamy. The piece is already pure Strauss: it seems to explode out of the orchestra, seizing the audience by the throat. He never really lets you take a breath.

Strauss was a natural with the orchestra, writing for it in constantly changing colors and textures. Pursued more meticulously than any before him, his symphonic poems are virtual operas for orchestra, their stories portrayed with enormous musical/visual imagination. Musical progressives adopted him as their hero; Brahms called him "the chief of the insurrectionists." Conservatives lambasted him for his rambling, post-Wagnerian harmony, his relentless nervous energy, his negation of the cherished idea of instrumental music as "pure" and "abstract." But Strauss was a fine craftsman, his music does make internal sense, and the music easily dominates the stories. After all, beside Wagner, his other musical hero was Mozart.

Soon he premiered his first opera, *Guntram*, also in a post-Wagnerian vein, and married its leading soprano, Pauline de Ahna. A hyperdiva and grand eccentric, she more or less ran Strauss's life from then on, which he appeared to appreciate over the fifty-five years of their marriage. She kept him on a short allowance, so he took to playing cards with his orchestral musicians and fleecing them regularly. Said conductor Hans Knappertsbuch: "I knew him very well. I played cards with him every week for forty years and he was a pig."

In 1898 came Strauss's second blockbuster symphonic poem, **Don Quixote**. Here his tone-painting went in even more crafty directions: the attack on the windmills, the bleating sheep and flying horses. Underlying it all was Strauss's covert classical side; the music is laid out in the old genre of a theme and variations. Here and elsewhere in his symphonic poems you can find some of the greatest fun in the repertoire, a quality in which the concert hall is sometimes deficient.

Then Strauss turned back to opera, with a vengeance. He took up Oscar Wilde's deliriously decadent play *Salome* and lavished his tone-painting skills on its most notorious elements: Salome smooching the decapitated head of John the Baptist, and of course her ecdysiastical "Dance of the Seven Veils." *Salome* was widely condemned as blasphemous and immoral, was banned in Vienna, and made a sensation as intended. From the gratifying proceeds Strauss built a dream villa in Garmisch, where he and his wife lived the rest of their lives.

In the 1930s, Strauss like all contemporary artists faced the advent of totalitarianism and worldwide conflagration. Each dealt with the cataclysm in his own way. With the Nazis, at first, Strauss took the path of cooperation. Privately he called them a bunch of savages, but as the leading German composer of the time (at least for a regime that called modernist music "degenerate") he was offered a position as head of the Chamber of State Music, and he took it. He lasted in the post for two years, but friction with the Nazi Party, including

his defense of his Jewish librettist Stefan Zweig, led to his re-
moval. From that point he tried to fade into the woodwork for
the rest of the war. Whatever Strauss's culpability, postwar
tribunals did not bring charges against him as they did with
some other artists.

In 1909 came *Elektra*, his first partnership with the great librettist Hugo von Hofmannsthal. This story, based on the
ancient Greek epic of Agamemnon, the Trojan War, and the
bloody aftermath, reached a level of ferocity and hysterical
near-atonality that took audiences' breaths away.

In the next decades Strauss and Hofmannsthal had five
more collaborations, above all the exquisite *Der Rosenkavalier*.
Elektra did not mark the end of Strauss's great work, but it was
the last time he was called a bomb-thrower. Schoenberg and
Stravinsky were already in the wings. Strauss's style calmed
down to something more backward-looking, but still rich and
individual.

This being a book mainly about instrumental music, I'll
recommend another symphonic poem. *Also sprach Zarathustra* is an evocation of the philosopher Nietzsche's mystical
treatise of that name. Most of *Zarathustra* is not particularly mystical; rather, it is lushly and mellifluously Viennese-
romantic. It was a modestly popular repertoire item when
filmmaker Stanley Kubrick took up its opening "Dawn of
Man" segment for the colossal opening of *2001*. *Zarathustra*,
or that opening anyway, became a culture-wide symbol of
achievement, sold cars on TV, whatever. When the Boston
Red Sox unrolled their first World Series banner in eighty-
some years, it unrolled to "The Dawn of Man."

At one point Strauss himself declared, "I may not be a first-rate composer, but I am a first-class second-rate composer!" In a time whose most exciting musical voices were the likes of Stravinsky, Schoenberg, and Bartók, Strauss never departed again from his comfortable late-romantic style. His 1945–1946 *Metamorphosen* for twenty-three solo strings shows that in his eighties he could still wield that style in a work of great beauty, vitality, and nostalgia. The piece has no stated program, but many feel that it amounts to a memorial for what the Nazis destroyed in German culture. After the war Strauss wrote in his diary, "The most terrible period of human history is at an end, the twelve year reign of bestiality, ignorance and anti-culture under the greatest criminals, during which Germany's 2000 years of cultural evolution met its doom."

In 1948 came his farewell to music and to life, the *Four Last Songs* for soprano and orchestra. These four meditations on death are calmly beautiful, without bathos or sentimentality. Here his handling of the orchestra is at its most subtle and lovely. In September 1949 Strauss died in Garmisch, a relic of an earlier time, compromised but unbowed.

More Strauss: *Till Eulenspiegel's Merry Pranks; Salome; Elektra; Der Rosenkavalier.*

Chapter 27

Maurice Ravel (1875–1937)

For most of us destined to be lovers of classical music, one of our most marvelous memories is the first time we heard Maurice Ravel. It's like music that has always existed in some pastel Neverland. When as a teenager I first heard *Pavane for a Dead Princess*, I swooned as I rarely have for any music. And all this came from a man given to keeping his life and emotions to himself, and not much interested in putting them into his music, either.

Ravel was a splendid melodist and possessed one of the most refined ears for harmony and instrumental color of any composer. No matter how traditional his materials, no matter what his influences, he never sounded like anybody but himself. As a craftsman Ravel was so fastidious that in his time he was sometimes accused of being all technique and no feeling. Rather, he believed that technique and emotion worked together. (When somebody suggested he should write an orchestration textbook, Ravel replied that he would only be willing to write a book about his mistakes.)

He was born in a village called Saint-Jean-de-Luz, his father Swiss and his mother Basque. There was a certain sense during his career that he inherited his precision from his father and his sensibility from his mother, including a lasting interest in all things Spanish. His parents were highly cultivated and encouraged their son's gift for music. He was accepted into the Paris Conservatoire at age fourteen and stayed there off and on for sixteen years, despite being an indifferent student who seems to have annoyed most of his professors. Ravel was not actively rebellious but simply went his own way without much caring what anybody thought.

By the time he left the Conservatoire for good in 1905 he had already written two of his finest works and been the subject of a major musical scandal. That year the jury of the Conservatoire declined for the third time to give him its leading award, the Prix de Rome. This drew attention, as Ravel was already an admired composer in France, already paired with the well-established Debussy. Eventually they would be called founders of the impressionist school. The uproar over the Prix de Rome rocked the cafés of Paris, and the backlash was intense enough that the director of the Conservatoire was forced out.

The first major work of Ravel's is **Pavane for a Dead Princess**, a miniature whose exquisite sighing melodies and distinctive perfumed harmonies announced the presence of a genuine new voice. As with several of his pieces, Ravel wrote it first for piano and later orchestrated it. Then in 1903 he finished the astonishing **String Quartet**, a work ravishing from beginning to end, which seems from its first moment to take the medium Haydn first perfected and make it into something freshly invented—the same old four instruments sounding like a whole new world of color. The quartet also shows Ravel's attachment to old forms and genres and the tonal world that went with them—but to those old keys and harmonies he added tints and tinctures distinctly his own.

In 1899, the year of the *Pavane*, he and Debussy both had the same transformative experiences at the 1889 Paris Exposition Universelle, where they heard the splendrous colors of new Russian orchestral works conducted by Nikolay Rimsky-Korsakov, and the exotic sounds of a Javanese gamelan. The latter music, dreamy and languid and ringing with gongs, had nothing do with the forms or melodies or harmonies they had learned at the Conservatoire. It gave both men a new vision of the possibilities of music, a new sense of freedom and daring.

Although Ravel would often be accused of building his style off Debussy, the reality is that he learned from any number of sources throughout his career, Debussy among them. Another inspiration for both men was the puckish Erik Satie, who wrote harmonies by ear rather than by rule. All of them in their own fashion turned away from the heart-on-sleeve grandiosities of late romanticism. Debussy and Ravel were friendly for a while, but when opposing factions formed around each of them, they found it best to keep their distance. Whatever the politics of the time, their mutual influence on the music that followed them has been incalculable. To mention one example: classic American songwriting from Gershwin on would be unthinkable without impressionist harmony.

As a person Ravel was relentlessly private, fastidious, dandyish in his dress, completely sunk in his work. Given his slight figure and chiseled features, one observer said he looked like a well-dressed jockey. His sexuality has been a subject of long and unresolved debate. He composed slowly, pursuing a perfection he knew he could never reach. "I did my work slowly, drop by drop," he said. "I tore it out of me by pieces."

All the same he had strong friendships, the early ones formed around a collection of young aesthetes dubbed the

"Apaches" (Hooligans), indicating a collection of outcasts strange and a little scary, enthusiasts for the new and outré in ideas and arts. One of the presiding deities of the Apaches was Edgar Allan Poe, whose bizarre and fantastical imagination and concise craftsmanship Ravel cited as a major influence (so did Debussy).

Ravel was also a terrifically generous man, always open to the new. Among the Apaches for a while was the young Igor Stravinsky. When the premiere of his *Le sacre du printemps* helped touched off the legendary concert-hall riot, amid the melee of screams and fistfights stood Ravel crying, "Genius! Genius!" Stravinsky said that Ravel was the only one to understand the *Sacre* from the beginning; his other friend Debussy was rather frightened by it. When George Gershwin asked him for lessons, Ravel concluded he might influence the brilliant young American too much and reportedly told him, "Why would you want to be a second-rate Ravel when you're already a first-rate Gershwin?"

Ravel's mature works have achieved a kind of iconic status, partly because there are so few of them relative to other important composers. For a sampling of the mature piano works, start with **Gaspard de la nuit** from 1908, famous both for its enchanted atmosphere and for its outlandish difficulty. It is a work revered and feared by pianists everywhere. The elusive shimmer of the beginning hardly sounds like a piano at all, going further than Debussy in exploring new sonorities on piano. The movements of the piece are based on three eerie fin-de-siècle poems. Ravel said of it, "My ambition is to say with notes what a poet expresses with words." So, to describe the piece, the first lines of each poem: (1) "Listen!—Listen!—It is I, it is Ondine who brushes drops of water on the resonant panes of your windows lit by the gloomy rays of the moon"; (2) "Ah! that which I hear, was it the north wind that screeches in the night, or the hanged one who utters a sigh on the fork of the gibbet?"; (3) "Oh! how often have I heard and seen him, Scarbo, when at midnight the moon glitters in the sky like a silver shield on an azure banner strewn with golden bees."

From early on few questioned Ravel's status as a supreme orchestral colorist. The most famous of the orchestral pieces is *Daphnis et Chloé* from 1912, based on the old Greek tale of destined lovers. It was written for Sergey Diaghilev and his Ballets Russes, then in their prime as the most innovative and influential dance troupe of the century—perhaps the last time avant-garde art was grand, sexy, and profitable. The music for *Daphnis* is in Ravel's most voluptuous vein, its opening portrayal of sunrise sounding like something beyond an orchestra, or an orchestra on some planet of eternal springtime. As a ballet it flopped, but the two concert suites Ravel extracted, especially No. 2, soon became audience favorites and have been so ever since.

Then there is the inevitable *Boléro*, based on the traditional Spanish dance, consisting entirely of two alternating themes over a relentless drum rhythm. It begins quietly and swells in the orchestra over seventeen minutes to a manic conclusion. Ravel was modest about the piece, calling it "orchestration without music," and never comfortable over what a gigantic hit it was. He once said with bitter irony, "I've written only one masterpiece—*Boléro*. Unfortunately there's no music in it."

La valse (The Waltz), also originally written for ballet, is a vision of Viennese waltz that seems heard through pastel vapors in a dream. It builds to a climax of shocking violence that tears the waltz apart. Some took it for a symbol of what was happening in Europe as war approached. Ravel did his best to squelch the idea, insisting it was only "an ascending progression of sonority."

In his later years he moved to a small town and lived as a bit of a recluse, his health damaged by his service in World War I as a truck driver. Still, there was a triumphant tour of America in the 1920s, where he could bask in his love of American jazz at its source. He called jazz the most important musical development of the century. Its colors can be heard in some of his late music including the "Blues" movement of his Second Violin Sonata.

Ravel's later instrumental music pulled back from the lush textures of his middle period to more distilled and fresh sonorities partly rising from his respect for both Stravinsky and Schoenberg. An example is *Le tombeau de Couperin*, a tribute to the French baroque harpsichord master, written for piano and orchestrated in 1919. The material is as mellifluous and sensuous as his always was, but his orchestra now is as lucid and refined as burnished silver.

Ravel was sadly reduced in his last years by a mysterious brain ailment. Still hearing music in his mind but unable to write it down, he lapsed into near silence, though still received friends to the end. He had to have known that his music had soared beyond the old scandals and partisan squabbles to become fixed in the ears of the world, one of those things that remind us how exquisite the world can be sometimes.

More Ravel: *Rapsodie espagnole;* Introduction and Allegro; the opera *L'enfant et les sortilèges;* his orchestration of Mussorgsky's *Pictures at an Exhibition.*

Chapter 28

IGOR STRAVINSKY (1882–1971)

For some reason, the history of creative eras often forms around a central duo of artists who are not only giants in themselves but sometimes contrasting embodiments of the time: Bach and Handel in the musical baroque, Mozart and Haydn in the classical period, Picasso and Matisse in modern painting. In modern music, it was Stravinsky and Schoenberg. For most of his career Stravinsky was the more popular of the two, his work moving quickly into the mainstream repertoire (though he got his share of slings and arrows). Schoenberg was the scary and controversial one, who can still rouse bitter debates.

In all his manifestations, whether the surface of the style was voluptuous or austere, Stravinsky was an artist of great focus and clarity. Here's an experiment: line up the following pieces of his and listen to the first minute or two of each one: *Pastorale, The Firebird, Petrushka, Le sacre du printemps, Les noces, L'histoire du soldat, Symphonies of Wind Instruments, Pulcinella, Symphony of Psalms, Agon.* As you'll notice, the stylistic range is so vast it's almost shocking. What they have in common, however, is that they all immediately define their sound worlds, from the Russian pastels of the early *Pastorale,*

the bustling carnival scene of *Petrushka*, the keening high bassoon of *Sacre*, the exotic wailing and chanting of *Les noces*, all
the way to the trumpet fanfares and chattering basses of *Agon*.
Stravinsky's career formed a record of kaleidoscopic transfor-
mations informed by a single creative temperament.

Igor Fyodorovich Stravinsky was born in Oranienbaum
near Saint Petersburg, son of a famous operatic bass. He
studied piano in his youth but at first showed no particular
inclination to music. He got a degree in law and philosophy
in Saint Petersburg while playing piano on the side. By then
he was studying with the Russian orchestral master Nikolay
Rimsky-Korsakov, who developed in Stravinsky one of the
most original imaginations for instrumental color in history.
Brilliant orchestration is a Russian specialty; to that tradition Stravinsky would add what he learned from Debussy and
Ravel, two superb colorists. The kind of budding personality
Stravinsky had as a student is seen in the sweetly undulant
little **Pastorale** from 1907 (originally for piano, later a small
group).

Talent aside, it was really a stroke of luck that made Stravinsky's career. In 1909 the ballet impresario Sergey Diaghilev
happened to hear his orchestral *Scherzo fantastique* at a Saint
Petersburg concert. Impressed, Diaghilev hired Stravinsky for
some arrangements, then in 1910 commissioned him for a full-
length ballet. Stravinsky was twenty-eight; the ballet was *The
Firebird*. Just before the Paris premiere Diaghilev was talking
to somebody and pointed across the room to Stravinsky, saying something to the effect of: "Take a look at that young man.
A week from now he's going to be famous." He was right. The
ballet proved a sensation, likewise the music. This joining
of Diaghilev's revolutionary Ballets Russes with its dazzling

costume and scenic designers and a dynamic young Russian composer would have historic results.

The story of a Firebird and a sorcerer was taken from Russian folktales. *Firebird* begins with basses whispering an enigmatic theme, muttering trombones, a slithery texture of string harmonics. It already sounds like nothing else. Stravinsky's music paints the story in polychrome colors, in twitterings and surgings. In the dance of the wizard Koschey there is a hair-raising rhythmic intensity that would only intensify in Stravinsky's later music. To this day *Firebird* remains his most popular work. In his old age somebody offered him what today would be the better part of a million dollars to write another piece like it. Stravinsky declined. "It would cost me more," he said.

In those years he was absolutely on fire. In 1911 came another work for the Ballets Russes, **Petrushka**. The story was largely Stravinsky's: Petrushka, a traditional puppet seen at Russian carnivals, is brought to life by an evil magician and suffers at his hands. At the premiere it proved if anything a still bigger sensation than *Firebird*. In the title role was the legendary dancer Vaslav Nijinsky. The music is a fantastically varied canvas, beginning with the bustling carnival and including a ballerina, a dancing bear, a hurdy-gurdy with a broken note, delicious extended solos for flute and trumpet, stretches of irresistible sonic delight from the orchestra. In what otherwise might feel disjointed, part of the consistency of the piece is that all of it is based on a single combination of chords, C major and F-sharp major, what would be dubbed the "*Petrushka* chord." Stravinsky had a remarkably inquiring ear; he would spend much of his life tinkering with traditional harmony in constantly fresh ways. (A certain number of people, including me in my twenties, go through a *Petrushka* phase, during which we listen to it all the time.)

Stravinsky began on a high plane with *Firebird*, topped it with *Petrushka*, and in 1913 topped it again with one of the most astonishing feats of musical imagination in history: **Le sacre du printemps** (The Rite of Spring). Again the basic story of the ballet was Stravinsky's. In a primeval Russian village we watch the various rites and dances of spring. At the end a virgin is chosen for a sacrifice: she must dance herself to death. The story was perfect for ballet, perfect for the dancers and designers of the Ballets Russes, perfect for its time, perfect for Diaghilev who wanted his company always to be in the forefront of innovation. *Sacre* is one of those epochal works that gave a shot in the arm to the entire art of music, the kind of thing Beethoven had once achieved with the "Eroica" Symphony.

At this point Paris was at the center of a revolutionary fervor in the arts, some of which involved a sophisticated primitivism. Picasso developed cubism partly from his encounter with African masks. Stravinsky applied the same train of thought to *Sacre*. From the eerie bassoon wail that begins it, the piece is a revolution in sound and in its very conception, but a revolution founded on a return to the primeval. Winds twine like vines, strings pound like percussion, French horns howl like elk in heat. Animating it all is the Stravinskian rhythm, relentless and ecstatic, an inexorable pulse often articulated by changing meters. For rehearsals Stravinsky made a piano four-hand version which is sometimes performed; hearing it, one realizes how raw and elemental the music actually was before he clothed it in fantastical orchestral garb. It is one of the few revolutionary works in any medium that never loses its capacity to astonish. The choreography was by Nijinsky, who was equally determined to revolutionize his art. There is a reconstruction of most of the dance, with original sets and costumes, and I highly recommend seeking it out on video. Nijinsky's choreography is virtually antiballet, the dancers' movements hunched, ungainly, spasmodic, but with a strange beauty. When you listen on recordings, give the piece your full attention and turn it up loud.

Stravinsky had written *Sacre* in some kind of ecstasy, writing a friend, "It seems to me that I have penetrated the secret rhythm of spring." When he and Debussy read over the piano four-hand version, an observer recalled, "We were dumbfounded, overcome by this hurricane which had come from the depths of the ages, and which had taken life by the roots."

The first performance of *Sacre* was instantly legendary: it sparked the most demented audience riot ever seen in a theater. Everybody who was anybody in Paris was there and expecting something prodigious, and they got it. From the strange opening notes there was murmuring, which escalated to shouts as the ballet began. Soon the audience had descended to a donnybrook complete with fisticuffs between pros and antis—Maurice Ravel in the middle of the fray crying "Genius! Genius!" It is hard to say whether the outrage was provoked more by the music or the dance, though before long the uproar had overwhelmed the music. Backstage, with Stravinsky holding his coattails, Nijinsky was standing on a chair screaming numbers to his dancers to keep them on the beat because they could not hear the orchestra. At dinner afterward, Diaghilev crowed, "It's exactly what I wanted!" Stravinsky, I suspect, was horrified. It was as if the world had crushed his ecstasy.

With *Sacre* Stravinsky completed another revolution that Debussy and Ravel had begun: putting aside traditional forms and thematic development in favor of tone color as a central element, defining its character and form. To put it another way, Stravinsky reversed the traditional relationship of content to form. In the past form was central, the content subordinate. The main point of a work was the whole. In Stravinsky and much music following him, the power of the ideas is the central issue; the form is looser, there to serve the content.

By age thirty-one Stravinsky had produced three works that together changed the face of music and placed him at the forefront of musical innovation, the equivalent of Picasso in painting, Rodin in sculpture, and later James Joyce in literature. (In Germany his corevolutionary Arnold Schoenberg was in his maturity, eliciting his own riots.) Stravinsky's face became famous, its odd angles forming a kind of modernist icon in itself. There were attempts by other composers to echo *Sacre*, but really nobody else had the chops to do it. Meanwhile Stravinsky had no intention of repeating it either. To some degree he probably considered the work an end rather than a beginning; the only place to go now was to retreat to something smaller. Perhaps the boiling imagination of his early years had settled down. I have always wondered whether the rabid audience response to *Sacre* inflicted a wound on Stravinsky's spirit that never entirely healed. In any case, he would not lay himself out like that again.

But if that was indeed the case, there was nothing rational about his response. One of the most radical works in history, *Sacre* got plenty of abuse but still conquered the world very fast. After a concert performance a year following the premiere, Stravinsky was carried through the streets of Paris on the shoulders of a cheering crowd. And of course, some twenty-five years later the piece graced Walt Disney's *Fantasia*, accompanying a rumpus of dinosaurs. (Stravinsky claimed he never approved using the piece for the cartoon, but he did; the letter exists.)

Still, Stravinsky had one more seismic work to go. After *Sacre* he began another primitivistic but more stripped-down piece for chorus and instruments. Written in Russian but usually known by its French name **Les noces** (The Wedding), it is a portrait of a Russian village wedding in some undefined past. A draft of it was done by 1917, then began a long period of uncertainty concerning the instrumental forces. Stravinsky tried full orchestra, bagged that, then experimented with player pianos. Finally in 1924 *Les Noces* reached its final, desiccated form for chorus, soloists, four pianos, and percussion. Premiered as a ballet, it is equally a concert piece. For each of his first three ballets Stravinsky had created a singular style, and now he did it again: brusquely chanting choruses, incantatory vocal solos. Its total effect is preminimalist and mesmerizing, including the text: "Combing her tresses, her bright golden tresses, combing her tresses . . . " and so on. I was fascinated by this piece from high school on, but didn't really understand it until I heard it live. In flesh and blood it is breathtaking, like being caught up in some primordial ritual. (When the wedding party gets drunk, it's also pretty funny.) The ending, the bridegroom lovingly praising his bride, is truly moving.

Stravinsky would continue to reinvent himself, if never again on the astounding level of those four works. When World War I appeared, he began to cut back his forces and his ambitions. The first fruit of this later period was the little *L'histoire du soldat* (The Soldier's Tale) from 1918, a parable about a soldier, a violin, and the devil. The forces are a septet of instruments including percussion, and three characters— Soldier, Devil, Narrator. The music is quirky, ironic, bone-dry, at the same time full of unflagging rhythm and captivating melody. Most celebrated for his rhythm and harmony, Stravinsky was a fine melodist when he let himself indulge in it.

After the war Stravinsky molted again, but this time he stuck with the new aesthetic for decades. He turned away from the Russian background of his earlier music and stories and reached further back to the past. The first signature work of what came to be called his *neoclassic* period was *Pulcinella*, an exhilarating reimagining of pieces by the baroque composer Pergolesi. It was commissioned by Diaghilev; at the 1920 premiere the sets were by Picasso. On this eighteenth-century framework Stravinsky lavished his most incandescent orchestration, also his signature harmony and rhythm. Listen to the *Pulcinella* Suite first; then, if you like, move on to the complete ballet.

Stravinsky pursued his new style in works chaste and sometimes almost chastened. "My music is not free from dryness," he said, "but that's the price of precision." In the larger musical world Stravinskian neoclassicism became the era's leading influence, especially on French composers, but on Americans as well, among them George Gershwin and Aaron Copland. Neoclassicism was embraced as a more popularistic alternative to the "difficult" modernists who lined up behind Arnold Schoenberg. Yet in the first years of his neoclassic music, Stravinsky got some of the worst, most insulting reviews of his life, from critics who accused him of betraying the revolution he had achieved with *Sacre*. One critic called *L'his-toire* and *Pulcinella* "poor, half-starved things." Young French avant-gardists booed them in concerts. In any case, an endur-ing conflict had appeared in twentieth-century music, which amounted to two visions of the future: the neoclassicists be-hind Stravinsky, the atonal composers behind Schoenberg.

Stravinsky and his first wife and children sat out World War I in Switzerland. After the war he lived in France for nearly twenty years, composing and performing as pianist and con-ductor. Diaghilev died in 1928 and his ballet company evap-orated. Stravinsky embraced Christianity, and on a Boston Symphony Orchestra commission produced in 1930 what I call the finest religious work of the twentieth century, **Sym-phony of Psalms.** From the crunching E minor chord of its beginning to the answering cascades of woodwinds and its second-movement fugue, the piece is firmly in his austere, somewhat remote neoclassic style. But with a lovely *alleluia* in the "Laudate dominum," the piece warms with exquisite har-monies until the sustained trance of the end, intensely spiri-tual and unforgettable.

By this point Stravinsky was preaching a doctrine that music was incapable of expressing definable emotions, but his work and his responses to other music (he was generous to other composers) were hardly consistent with that philosophy. At one point he became fascinated with Charles Ives's *Decora-tion Day*; he declared it a masterpiece, its ending the saddest he knew. So much for music's inability to express things.

In 1940, with his first wife dead and war raging across Europe again, Stravinsky married his mistress, the painter

Vera de Bosset, and they moved to Hollywood. World War II Hollywood saw a strange scene mixing movie stars and leading European expat artists, among them Arnold Schoenberg. He and Stravinsky had once been friendly, but by this point they were the heads of two mutually hostile camps and had retreated to sniping distance. Schoenberg and Stravinsky both flirted with the idea of doing film music, but it never happened.

In the middle 1950s, after finishing his grandest neoclassical effort, an opera in the spirit of Mozart called *The Rake's Progress*, Stravinsky had a creative crisis. Between 1953 and 1957 he had been working on the ballet **Agon**, and in the middle of composing it he came to feel that his neoclassic vein was played out and he did not know where to go. He resolved the crisis in a completely unexpected way. *Agon* begins briskly with neoclassic trumpet fanfares, but soon another voice intrudes: Stravinsky began using a Schoenbergian twelve-tone row.

His great rival had died in 1951. Now with Stravinsky taking up Schoenberg's method the musical world reeled. In terms of popularity, commissions, and academic positions, the compositional scene had been dominated for decades by neoclassicists such as Aaron Copland, who was also of the "Americana" school. Stravinsky's defection upended the status quo and led to the triumph of serialism in the academy. As for *Agon*, it is a vibrant piece, full of fresh orchestral colors, showing how personal was his adaptation of his rival's technique. Stravinsky wrote serial music for the rest of his life.

In the 1950s and 1960s the world came to know Stravinsky in interviews and documentaries, an old man witty and fascinating, a raconteur, a passionate devotee of music, love, and strong spirits. On film during a sea voyage, he holds up his cocktail and declares, "I am nevair seasick! I am sea-droonk!" He died in New York in April 1971. For his resting place he wanted to return to the triumphs and excitements of his youth: at his request he was buried in Venice beside Diaghilev. I still have a newspaper headlining his death. Like many musicians I felt the loss personally. All of us wondered when somebody would step up to fill his shoes. To date, I think, no one quite has.

Chapter 29

Arnold Schoenberg (1874–1951)

One day a stranger asked Arnold Schoenberg if he was *that* Schoenberg. "Somebody had to be," Schoenberg replied wearily. "Nobody else volunteered, so I answered the call." Schoenberg shared a Germanic conception of history with many of his contemporaries, who held that history only goes forward, and some people are destined to be agents of history. That's how Schoenberg saw himself as an artist, and how his followers saw him and his methods for many years to come.

In a way, starting an essay on Schoenberg in these terms is not fair to him, because he saw his music not as primarily historic or messianic, but above all as expressive. At one point he wrote that he wanted to be, "sort of like Tchaikovsky, but better." Composers tend to discover Schoenberg in terms of technique and method; audiences are advised to discover him in terms of intensely expressive music, whether the terms are of love, loss, suffering, or joy. As he also put it: "My works are not *twelve-tone* compositions, they are twelve-tone *compositions*." That a great many of his disciples over the years did not follow that model is not his fault. His atonal works have gradually worked their way into the edges of the mainstream; years ago I saw a standing ovation in Boston for his Piano Concerto as rendered by Mitsuko Uchida. Still, it is taking Schoenberg and his two towering pupils Berg and Webern much longer to enter the mainstream than their compatriots Stravinsky and Bartók.

Arnold Franz Walter Schoenberg was born in in Vienna, son of a shoe salesman. The family struggled, but they were musical like many Austrian families—two of Arnold's brothers became professional singers. He began writing little pieces at nine years old and took up the cello. For a while he played Jewish tunes with a Vienna street band that included the later celebrated violinist Fritz Kreisler. He never attended a conservatory because he could never afford it. While working a day job in a bank in 1895 he took a few lessons with composer and conductor Alexander von Zemlinsky, a Brahms protégé and progressive composer.

Schoenberg's early String Quartet in D Minor, in late-romantic style, was warmly received in Vienna and found the approval of Brahms. His first masterpiece, and one of the remarkable works of its era, came in 1899: *Verklärte Nacht* (Transfigured Night), for string sextet. It is based on a poem by the high-Viennese poet Richard Dehmel: during a nocturnal walk a woman confesses to her lover that she bears another man's child, and in the rapturous ending he forgives her. At the time the music was too much for the Viennese, but this darkly surging, often ecstatic, dreamlike work has long been Schoenberg's most popular, one of the pieces that people who don't like Schoenberg like. To get the full, spine-chilling effect, I suggest the composer's string orchestra arrangement.

For a while Schoenberg got by composing and arranging popular songs for a cabaret. Finally, with the help of Richard Strauss, he found the first of his several teaching positions. Soon he gained another powerful mentor and champion in Gustav Mahler. In 1904 Schoenberg placed a newspaper ad offering composition lessons; among those who responded were Alban Berg and Anton Webern. Together, they would spearhead what came to be called the Second Viennese School of composers (the First Viennese School being Haydn, Mozart, and Beethoven). While he was still in his late-romantic, post-Wagnerian style, in this period Schoenberg produced two enormous works, the tone poem *Pelleas und Melisande* and the cantata *Gurrelieder*. The latter, begun in 1900, had a wildly successful premiere in Vienna in 1913, but by then he had moved so far beyond the work that he refused to acknowledge the applause.

In the last movement of his Second String Quartet No. 2 of 1907–1908, Schoenberg, who had stretched late-romantic chromatic harmony until it broke, found his path into atonality. Appropriately the music breaks out of tonality—for an entirely expressive reason—on the line "I feel the wind from other planets." There followed a quiet but profound revolution in the **Three Piano Pieces of Op. 11**, started in 1909, only a dozen years after Brahms died. In its time, this was indeed music from another planet, but if you get on their wavelength these are intimately expressive pieces.

In Vienna and around Europe, this was the shadowed and heady time of the fin de siècle, when in the arts romanticism had gone overripe. In Austro-Germany, anti-Semitism and its allied politics of blood and iron were rising ever higher. As I say earlier, this era of profound cultural malaise forced artists into new and hyperbolic places: the music of Schoenberg, the paintings of Egon Schiele, Ernst Ludwig Kirchner, and Max Beckmann. Added to that was the revolutionary vision of the human unconscious evoked by Freud. He painted the

basement of our mind as a murky underworld of primeval irrationality, violence, and sexuality, over which rationality and
civilization float tenuously. Especially in German lands, all
these forces acted on artists in powerful and productive ways,
if not always in cheery directions.

All this is embodied in Schoenberg's two shattering works
of 1909 and 1912: **Five Pieces for Orchestra** and *Pierrot lunaire*, among the greatest of his free-atonal, high-expressionist
period. Like Stravinsky's *Sacre*, they have never lost their
punch. The first of the Five Pieces, "Premonitions," grows
from explosive energy to something of monstrous tread, and
ends on an ominous clock-tick. It was entirely appropriate
for its time, as Vienna slid toward horrors to come. Equally,
the movement might be a journey into the more unnerving
regions of the Freudian unconscious. Here is the Schoenbergian expressionist orchestra at its most lurid, with screaming
trumpets and savage trombones. The second movement, "The
Past," is absolutely contrasting in its veiled gentleness, though
there is a touch of anxiety. In some ways the most remarkable
movement is "Summer Morning by a Lake," in which the most
refined orchestral colors wash through soft, slow-changing
harmonies. Here is the first orchestral illustration of what
Schoenberg named *Klangfarbenmelodie* (tone-color melody),
in which the sheer color of the sound is in the foreground. The
third movement is another nervous one. The piece ends on
"The Obbligato Recitative," in which a keening melody is surrounded by kaleidoscopic washes of orchestral color. It is hard
to imagine how this music hit listeners who had grown up
on Brahms and Beethoven, especially in Vienna where many
music lovers could have known Brahms in person. But from
early on Schoenberg had his champions among performers,

including Arnold Rosé, concertmaster of the Vienna Philharmonic, who in his youth championed Brahms and in his later years Schoenberg.

Pierrot lunaire (Moonstruck Pierrot), for soprano and five players, was conceived in the old form of a *melodrama*, essentially poetry recited to music. Schoenberg decided to join Albert Giraud's poems more closely to the music by writing down the speaker's rhythms and to a degree her pitches. Here he invented *Sprechstimme* (speaking voice), which in practice has a kind of innate strangeness. Giraud's poems themselves a definition of the fin de siècle—moonstruck, eerie, incipiently violent, all applied to the classical clown figures of commedia dell'arte: Pierrot, Columbine, Cassander, et al. This was, after all, the era of Oscar Wilde and Aubrey Beardsley and their atmosphere of cryptic and elegant decadence.

"The wine that man drinks with his eyes / Spills into the waves at night," it begins. In "The Sick Moon," moonlight becomes ominous: "You nocturnal, deathly-sick moon, / There on the black pillow of the sky, / Your gaze, swollen with fever, / Enchants me like an alien melody." I have to quote "Mean Trick" whole:

Into the polished skull of Cassander,
While his cries split the air,
Pierrot the hypocrite tenderly
Bores with a trepan!

Then he tamps down with his thumbs
His genuine Turkish tobacco
Into the polished skull of Cassander,
While his cries split the air!

Then he twists a perfumed pipestem
Into the gleaming bald spot,
And complacently he smokes and puffs
His genuine Turkish tobacco
From the polished skull of Cassander.

I'm quoting the text at some length because the music is the vibrating embodiment of its disquieting ambience. Early on some called the poems blasphemous, to which Schoenberg responded, "If they were musical, not a single one would give a damn about the words. Instead, they would go away whistling the tunes." Who knows whether he really meant it. Later he insisted that he was actually a traditionalist, with no revolutionary intentions. Perhaps there is something to that, but it was more likely a red herring, or maybe a bruised retreat from so many years of attacks. To my mind there is no question that in these years both Schoenberg and Stravinsky had revolutionary ambitions, though both later denied it.

The critical attacks Schoenberg endured were relentless throughout his life. For a while in Vienna he and his disciples formed the Society for Private Performances, by invitation only, critics not allowed. It was the first time in history a concert series was organized to keep people out. Meanwhile Schoenberg's finances remained shaky; in pursuit of work he went to Berlin, then came back to Vienna for a short period of military service during World War I. After the war, having winged it in his free-atonal years, he developed a new discipline, the twelve-tone method—which we have discussed some already.

The essence of the twelve-tone method is this: everything in a piece, both "horizontally" in terms of melody and "vertically" in terms of harmony, is based on a single theme, of a particular kind: an arrangement of the twelve notes of the chromatic scale; that is, all the available notes, into a pattern called a *row*. To erase tonality, there is a rule (often broken in practice) that no note in the row can be repeated until the whole row has been heard. There are four basic forms of the row: the original; the *retrograde*, which is the row backward; the *inversion*, the row upside down; and the *retrograde inversion*, the row upside down and backward. All these are traditional thematic treatments known to composers since the Renaissance, now applied to quite different material. All forms of the row can be transposed at will; that is, the same interval pattern of intervals but starting on any note. Schoenberg had already decreed a "liberation of the dissonance," meaning that dissonance and consonance were to be considered equal, and dissonance no longer required to resolve. In practice, he and his disciples tended to write steadily dissonant harmony.

Schoenberg expected his invention to conquer the Western musical world, to become the new common practice, and for a while it sort of did. He and his disciples wrote theoretical pieces about the method in an attempt to convert others. As a result, among those who didn't like it, twelve-tone acquired an air of cold intellectualism, and plenty of its adherents since have conformed to that stereotype. The reality is that whatever his technique, Schoenberg usually wrote lightning fast, depending on inspiration. He said only afterward did he look back and figure out what he had done technically. For one example, he sometimes wrote several numbers of *Pierrot* in a day.

In regard to the anti-atonal strain that was virulent for decades and has not yet disappeared, a point needs to be made. First, nobody is required to like anything, and enjoying atonal music is not a litmus test for good musical taste or for one's attitude toward modernism as a whole. Beyond that, I think most concertgoers understand that music has the right to dark, tragic moods in vocal music—an oratorio about the death of Christ, a tragic opera. But there seems to be an assumption that in purely instrumental music the expression should be restricted to things pleasant, cheerful, uplifting, noble, maybe comic now and then—all those Beethovenian qualities. No. Music is a serious art, like literature and drama and poetry, and like those arts it lays claim to the full range of sound and of human experience and emotion, from the lightest to the darkest. Shakespeare's *King Lear* is no fun at all, rather overwhelmingly despairing, and likewise Webern's Six Pieces for Orchestra.

Meanwhile, in their expressionist period, Schoenberg, Webern, and Berg were writing portraits of their own inner lives and of the culture around them, which was increasingly violent and alarming. That the three of them have largely been taught and viewed in terms of technique and innovation is partly their own fault, because they all wrote dispassionately about their technique. But the members of the Second Viennese School should be viewed like all other composers, as coming from a place and time, and largely in terms of emotion. I'm sure all three composers would agree with me. To put it another way: to make atonal music purely a technical and intellectual matter and remove its psychological and cultural implications amounts to gutting the music.

When the Nazis came, like most of his fellow Jewish-born Germans who could, Schoenberg fled. In Paris he defiantly reconverted to Judaism. He ended up in California, for years teaching at UCLA. It would seem the least likely place in the world for him, yet like many of his fellow artistic émigrés he was embraced by the Hollywood set. He and George Gershwin became friends and mutual admirers, pianist Oscar Levant studied with him, he played tennis with Harpo Marx, he became a Ping-Pong fanatic. He flirted with doing movie music and could have used the money, but when he demanded an extravagant salary and artistic control of the picture, that was the end of that.

Much of the time in America Schoenberg spent on his massive opera *Moses und Aron*, an intensely felt statement of faith both religious and artistic. He never finished it. Of Schoenberg's American pieces I'm going to recommend just one, the **Violin Concerto**, from 1936, one of the greatest of the century in its genre. By this point Schoenberg was settled into his twelve-tone method and had left most of the agitated atmosphere of expressionism behind—though an echo of it lingered. The concerto begins on a note of troubled lyricism, then something more ill-omened intrudes. Regarding the Violin Concerto, I'm going to do something hardly anybody does with Schoenberg's instrumental music: relate it to the real world. I think the concerto is one of his several responses to the catastrophe in Europe. In it we hear two conflicting forces: the first, as in the beginning, a matter of individual feeling, passionate emotion tinged with unrest; the other voice is steely, marchlike, menacing—it is war. In other words, in its implications Schoenberg's Violin Concerto is a dialectic between individual feeling and the monstrous, impersonal mechanism of war. In the end, war overwhelms the individual, just as it did in the real world during the next years.

Thus Schoenberg. Whatever his standing with the public, which has evolved over the years and I think will, or should, end with his being part of the familiar repertoire, he had incalculable influence on future composers.

More Schoenberg: Chamber Symphony No. 1; Piano Concerto; *Erwartung*.

Chapter 30

Charles Ives (1874–1954)

C harles Ives is the irreplaceable maverick of American music, writing everything from sentimental Victorian songs to the wildest pandemonium, but he was a maverick more by default than intention. The boggling spectrum of styles and techniques he wielded in his music, itself a mirror of his country's prodigal diversity, did not evolve quickly or capriciously. Ives was a teenaged organ prodigy when he began composing in familiar forms and genres: songs for the parlor, band marches, polite pieces for local musicians and singers. At the same time, his bandmaster father, George Ives, bequeathed his son an inquiring and adventurous spirit regarding the materials of music. Any combination of notes at all was acceptable, his father said, if you knew what you were doing with them. That was surely the first time a budding composer had ever been handed that kind of freedom, and Ives knew what to do with it. So, while the young Ives was writing conventional music for immediate use, he was privately experimenting with music in two keys at once, free harmonies, conventional chords stacked up together, and other unprecedented techniques.

Charles Edward Ives was born in the hat-making town of Danbury, Connecticut. He studied piano and organ intensively in his youth and took his first professional church-organ job at age fourteen. In 1898 he graduated from Yale, where he studied with the leading American composition teacher of the day, German-trained Horatio Parker. Parker brushed aside Ives's musical experiments, but he taught his student a great deal about the shaping of large works. At the same time, in college Ives played ragtime piano at parties and local theaters, and at the keyboard amused his friends with what he called "take-offs" of football games (he was a lifelong sports fan), fraternity initiations, and the like. From college on, most of his work was program music picturing a story or an event. Vivacious, funny, unpredictable, "Dasher" Ives was a popular man on the Yale campus.

After college, facing the reality that the music he wanted to write would not earn him a living, Ives got a job in the life insurance industry in Manhattan. He turned out to be good at that, too. In the next decades he rose to the top of the profession, a founding partner in the largest insurance agency in the country. At the same time he composed at white heat nights and weekends and vacations. He was likely in some degree manic-depressive, but more the former than the latter.

Ives absorbed and responded intensely to everything he heard. To him, all music was an avatar of the eternal human spirit that lies beneath it. Every kind of music excited him if it was earnest and authentic, whether it was a Bach fugue, a Brahms symphony, a gospel hymn, a barroom ragtime, a town band on the march. Much of his music would involve quotes of familiar American tunes—hymns, marches, patriotic songs: music of the people. He had a particular love for the enthusiasms and quirks of amateur musicians, who played for love rather than money, and he translated even their mistakes into his music. "Bandstuff," he told one of his long-suffering copyists. "They didn't always play right & together and it was as good either way." As he matured as a composer he found continually new ways to interweave the myriad conventional and radical voices he had at his command—a larger range of style and technique than any composer had ever wielded before. "Style," he wrote, "has been too narrowly conceived of."

In practice, the young Ives had a traditional side grounded in his formal training, on which he based his early large works such as the European-style First Symphony, and the exploratory side that for years was expressed in small experimental pieces. Here is an example of each. Starting in his teens he drafted a series of experimental choral psalm settings, each a study of a particular technique. First came the precocious little **Psalm 67**. It is nominally in two keys, G minor in the men and C major in the women, but in practice it is a prophetic essay in what the future called polychords, meaning juxtapositions of common harmonies. The effect is a strange, lush, sui generis wash of sound.

Symphony No. 2, finished around 1902, is in form and harmony comparatively well behaved. It begins with a dark-toned fugue and goes on to movements in more or less standard layouts. But there are two quite special things about it. First, now and then it bursts into a literal quote of European music, mainly bits of Brahms, Bach, and Tchaikovsky, as if a window were briefly opened into the past. Ives used musical quotes for his whole career, but rarely so baldly as in the Second. Here the quotes stand as a symbol of his intention to join the European symphonic tradition with the voice of the American people. That is the other thing about the Second, it is the first large concert work in history with a distinctly

American voice. That is one of Ives's historic achievements that went unnoticed for a long time. The Second would have to wait nearly fifty years for its premiere by Leonard Bernstein and the New York Philharmonic. It's a lovely and ebullient piece, full of echoes of Stephen Foster, with a finale like a grand fiddle tune.

As he rose in the life insurance industry around the turn of the century, Ives also held important posts as a church organist and choir director, writing proper Victorian-style pieces for services. By 1902 he'd had enough of musical convention and felt driven to explore his most far-reaching ideas. He quit his last church position and became, for two decades, a virtual private composer. In that period, essentially every professional musician to whom he showed his more advanced music told him he was crazy. It takes phenomenal courage to carry on in a situation like that. Only when European modernist music arrived on American shores in the 1920s did listeners begin to have some context for his sounds. But Ives had wielded modernist techniques from tone clusters to atonality long before anyone else, and with no knowledge of or connection to modernism. The most accurate historical category for Ives is "Ivesian."

One of the first fruits of his new freedom was *The Unanswered Question*, drafted in 1906 and put into final form decades later. Here Ives first applied collage technique to music. It has three layers, roughly coordinated. A haunting background of strings represent the "Silence of the Druids." Over that a trumpet repeatedly intones the "Perennial Question of Existence." With increasing fury, a group of winds attempts to answer the trumpet's question. Finally the trumpet asks the question one last time, answered by an eloquent silence. For Ives, a question was better than an answer. A question, he said, got you further and higher than stopping at certainty and building barricades.

It was after his 1908 marriage to Harmony Twichell, daughter of a prominent Hartford minister, that Ives reached his maturity, when he began to apply his most advanced ideas to big, ambitious works. He wrote, "One thing I am certain of is that, if I have done anything good in music, it was, first, because of my father, and second, because of my wife." To Harmony, Charlie and his music were the same, so she loved them both. Intensely religious people (Harmony more conventionally so than her husband), they developed a kind of theology around his music: their love was a particle of divine love, and his music would be their way of spreading that love into the world.

Which is to say that Ives is fundamentally a religious composer, however madcap he can be sometimes. He also believed that there was not enough laughter in the concert hall, a situation he intended to remedy. An example is his hilarious *Four Ragtime Dances* from around 1902, in which the popular style is vandalized and scandalized in an almost cubistic way, all of it covertly based on gospel hymns (try *Ragtime No. 4* first). Ives's intention in these pieces was not to sully the sacred with dance tunes but rather to declare that each in its way is holy. By then African American ragtime had become a vital part of his voice.

Here are three works from Ives's maturity that show his range, his vigor, his revolutionary technique, no less his grounding in tradition, his wit, his spirituality (sometimes all those things on the same tumultuous page). *Three Places in New England* is one of the works he called a "set," meaning a collection of semi-independent pieces joined by a programmatic idea. The dreamlike first movement, "The St. Gaudens on Boston Common," is his response to the famous sculpture depicting the first black regiment of the Civil War. The movement is a joining of slow march and a sort of proto-blues. Next, "Putnam's Camp" is a wildly comic evocation of that Revolutionary-era campground near Danbury; in it Ives fondly conjures the image of amateur bands falling off the beat and playing wrong notes with gusto. Last, "The Housatonic at Stockbridge" was based on a trip he and Harmony took to that village in autumn, shortly after their marriage. Walking along the river, they heard a hymn from a distant church. In a magical stretch of tone-painting, Ives's Housatonic conjures the flowing river and the autumnal colors; over them floats a lovely hymnlike tune. The movement reaches a whirling, ecstatic climax that is a rapturous vision of love human and divine.

The symphony *Holidays* is a larger set, its theme four American holidays that also evoke the four seasons. First is "George Washington's Birthday," starting with an evocation of bleak winter in complex murmuring string textures, the second part a rollicking barn dance to warm things up. "Decoration Day" (today's Veterans Day) begins with an image of dawn in quiet string harmonies, then moves to a poignant slow march recalling townspeople walking in solemn procession to the cemetery; there amid a haze of strings we hear "Taps" intoned over the graves of the Civil War dead. Then comes a boisterous march back to town—but when Ives writes a march it's more than a march, it's the whole parade, with cheers and multiple bands going by. "The Fourth of July" is the most riotous of the *Holidays*. Ives recalled his hometown's Fourth as a spectacle of bands, fire engine bells, drunken bandsmen and spectators, and the grand finale of fireworks. All that is in the music, finishing with a full-orchestra explosion. The richly sonorous "Thanksgiving" finale is based on organ pieces written in his twenties, his church-organist days, when Ives was already using sophisticated polytonality. In music rich with folk tunes and autumnal colors, the movement builds to an exalted choral conclusion.

If you've absorbed the above, maybe you're ready to take on Ives's most challenging, deepest, greatest work: the **Fourth Symphony**, finished around 1924. It is one of the most ambitious, innovative, uproarious, concrete, at the same time spiritual works of the century. In the first movement, with its craggy and searching opening followed by a flowing hymn, the chorus introduces a "Traveler," which is to say a pilgrim, and the transcendent "glory-beaming star" he seeks. The ensuing journey is life from high to low, comic to prophetic. The grand pandemonium of the second movement Ives called the "Comedy." It is his version of the old symphonic scherzo, in part a portrait of modern urban life. For Ives that meant turn-of-the-century Manhattan; he called the city "Hell Hole," but he also retained an irrepressible fondness for its teeming vitality.

A traditional fugue in C major, the spacious third movement is set in a New England church, but that formal and doctrinal stop in the symphony's pilgrimage is not its conclusion. When it arrives, the mystical finale is a luminous fabric of whispering, finally jubilant voices, at the coda resolving into the hymn that has been singing beneath the symphony's surface all along: "Nearer, My God, to Thee." That is where Ives wanted to bring his listeners. The Fourth Symphony is Ives's most far-reaching exploration of his vision of life and music, in a work of universal religion. At the end the music seems to evanesce into the stars, still searching.

Ives wrote, "The fabric of existence weaves itself whole. You cannot set art off in a corner and hope for it to have vitality, reality, and substance." We can sense his larger point and method in, of all places, the "Comedy" movement of the Fourth Symphony. Amid its masses of sound tumbling and crashing in air, the sharp-eared can discern something remarkable: all these teeming, shouting, drunken and riotous voices are somehow moving together. That is what Ives was getting at. Each of us on our own path, with myriad stumbles and detours, traces the transcendent purposes of the divine, and all of us are headed in the same direction.

Ives suffered a debilitating heart attack in 1918. Over the next decade his composing drifted to a halt. In his last twenty-five years he was essentially an invalid, afflicted with severe diabetes. He still played piano, tinkered with his scores, saw to his expanding reputation as best he could, and used his fortune not only for his own music but in support of new music around the country. In his ailing age he remained as gloriously eccentric as ever. From beginning to end Ives was a kind of ongoing, one-man Event. He died in May 1954, his music still being discovered, the Fourth Symphony years from its triumphant first performance by Leopold Stokowski and the American Symphony Orchestra.

More Ives: String Quartet No. 1; Orchestral Set No. 2; collections of songs including "General William Booth Enters into Heaven."

Chapter 31

Béla Bartók (1881–1945)

I n the panoply of Western classical music there is an abiding emphasis on central Europe westward; most of the familiar repertoire hails from Austro-Germany, Italy, France, and England. That is part of the importance of Béla Bartók: with a unique voice that rose from the musical soul of his native Hungary, he is an invaluable seasoning among the supreme composers of the twentieth century. He was a man of deep convictions fiercely held, and at times there is a kind of primeval fierceness in his music. Beneath that is a profoundly humanistic core. History regards him as one of the last of the great nationalist composers, but in fact Bartók disavowed nationalism, having seen firsthand how that spirit was tearing Europe and his country apart. He imbued his style with music he gathered in the countryside, but he always intended to be a universal composer.

Bartók was born in the provincial Hungarian town of Nagyszentmiklós, and first studied piano with his mother. As a child he was painfully shy and for years afflicted with a miserable skin condition. He composed and performed from early on and ended up in the Royal Academy of Music in Budapest, where he developed into an outstanding pianist. His composition came along more slowly. In 1903 he produced the tone poem *Kossuth*, exalting the leader of Hungarian nationalism, in a late-romantic style owing much to Liszt and Richard Strauss. Due probably to its patriotic subject as much as to its music, the piece found considerable success.

Bartók's real inspiration began when he and his composer friend Zoltán Kodály set out on an expedition into the backcountry to study and gather the music of Hungarian peasants. They had realized that the long-standing European tradition of "Hungarian" or "Gypsy" music was a popular style that had little to do with authentic folk music, which was wilder and freer in rhythm and tonality than what people heard in the city. The two men went on repeated excursions that stretched over years, determined to absorb the folk spirit and adapt it in their work. Each in his own way, that determination brought both to their maturity as composers.

In 1907 Bartók became a professor at the Royal Academy in Budapest and stayed there for twenty-seven years. He only taught piano, however—he did not believe composition could be taught, and refused to do it. Later his conviction about teaching composition would cause much trouble for himself and his family. At the academy, Bartók was a much-respected teacher and performer. He spent his summers gathering folk music in the countryside and began to publish what became a significant body of ethnomusicology. Handsome and exotic of face, with blazing eyes, Bartók was slight and never really well, but he was still a tireless hiker and field researcher. His spirit was made of steel. In personality he was dour, taciturn, largely a closed book. There is a story that when he was first teaching and still living with his mother, he brought a young female student home for a piano lesson. The lesson seemed to keep going, so finally his mother asked what was up. "We're married," Bartók replied tersely.

His 1908 String Quartet No. 1 is a splendid piece, the beginning of a set of six that came to be called the greatest quartets of the century, but it has little trace of the folk influence that would shape his later work. His haunted and haunting 1911 opera, *Duke Bluebeard's Castle*, is more folk-tinted. It is the old fable about a duke whose wives seem to vanish into oblivion. Then Bartók discovered Stravinsky, who, he said, "taught me daring." In 1919 he finished the garish and exquisitely decadent pantomime *The Miraculous Mandarin*, which is not yet in his mature voice but shows his assimilation of Stravinsky in general and *Le sacre du printemps* in particular. Meanwhile he also absorbed the influences of Schoenberg and the impressionists Debussy and Ravel. From these apparently contradictory sources Bartók synthesized a voice at once eclectic and intensely personal. His melodies even when utterly chromatic still sound Hungarian, and he developed an approach that has been called "chromatic tonality": even when the melody and harmony are quite free, there is generally an underlying sense of a home pitch. As he once said about a passage: "I wanted to show Schoenberg that you can use all twelve tones and remain tonal."

Bartók's harmonic voice was one of the broadest of all composers, enfolding everything from ferocious dissonance to traditional chords, the latter always handled in fresh juxtapositions. Added to that was a tremendous rhythmic energy, often expressed in the rhythms and meters he had learned from Hungarian and Romanian folk music. He had an unprecedented interest in finding fresh sounds in old instruments: glissandos on timpani, violin played with the wood of the bow, the "Bartók pizzicato" that snaps a string off the fingerboard. Especially in terms of exploring new sounds his influence has been tremendous, yet few people have since written using Bartók's compositional techniques. There is, I think, a simple reason for this: where Schoenberg and his school wrote extensively about their twelve-tone method and so created a composition movement, Bartók rarely said or wrote anything about his techniques. He believed composers needed to find out their methods for themselves. The sources of one's style did not matter, as long as they were authentic and vital. To hear all these forces in play, listen to Bartók's **Fourth String Quartet.** This is a piece that seems to have risen from some primal rite, so old it is new. You will not forget its driving, jabbing rhythms and its fantastic blocks of sound—it seems impossible that these are the same four string instruments that Haydn once wrote for. Much of this music is pure, unbuttoned excitement, except for the slow movement in Bartók's "night music" style, seeming to be made of drifting breezes and the sounds of birds and insects. (Bartók was a nature lover, and that informed his music, too.) I once heard this quartet in an old church in a New Hampshire mill town. It was a mainstream chamber concert, and many of the audience if asked would probably have said they didn't like dissonant modern music. The performance was blistering, the dissonances howled, and at the end the audience jumped up and roared approval.

In the two decades after World War I Bartók thrived as a composer and wrote most of his greatest work, which garnered mounting attention and acclaim. As a pianist he was in demand all over Europe. In the twenties he made an extensive tour of the United States, playing the traditional repertoire and his own work. His singular style, his dissonances, his tendency to treat the piano as a percussion instrument got their share of critical brickbats. When one critic branded him "barbaric," Bartók retaliated by writing a pounding piano piece called *Allegro barbaro*.

From his great period I'm going to recommend four pieces in quite different directions. *Cantata profana* (Secular Cantata) from 1930, his only large choral work, is not that well known, I suspect, because it's kind of scary for the singers. Done sensitively and well, it's one of his most powerful pieces. (I have to add that I'm not too satisfied with any of the current recordings. Of those available, I guess I recommend Pierre Boulez and the Chicago Symphony Orchestra—his usual lucid if chilly job.) The story is a folktale: the nine sons of a father go hunting, and in pursuit of a stag they are themselves magically transformed into stags. The father, searching for his sons, sees them and is about to shoot when the eldest cries to his father that it is them. The father begs his children to return home, but the eldest says, no, we can no longer live with men, we must live in the forest and drink from cool streams. The dialogue of father and son and the soaring final chorus are among Bartók's most moving pages. This is music of forests and brooks, and throughout a demonstration of what a marvelous melodist Bartók was. No matter how much his themes were founded on folk music, he never quoted them but always wrote his own.

The **Divertimento for String Orchestra** from 1939 is one of his more immediately appealing works, beginning with a delicious folk dance and ending with a breathtaking romp. In the middle is, I suspect, a response to the approach of war and chaos in Europe: a moaning, relentlessly rising lament like some kind of banshee howl. Another irresistible outing is the

Piano Concerto No. 2, from 1930–1931, utterly fresh in sound, outgoing and jubilant in temperament.

In 1936 appeared Bartók's greatest work, and one of the greatest of the century: **Music for Strings, Percussion, and Celesta**. It begins with an enigmatic chromatic theme that sounds like the distant murmur of wind; it becomes a long-unfolding fugue of absolutely original, gripping effect. After one of his most striking "night music" movements, the finale is a giddy whirlwind, its climax a transformation of the work's opening theme into a heart-filling humanistic anthem. Here and elsewhere Bartók sometimes uses traditional forms, such as the fugue, but he also finds his own patterns in symmetrical handling of notes around a central pitch. He creates large-scale symmetries with analogous movements straddling a central movement, and symmetrical proportions sometimes related to a number pattern called the Fibonacci series, which is done by adding two consecutive numbers to get the next one: $1 + 1 = 2$, $1 + 2 = 3$, $2 + 3 = 5$, $3 + 5 = 8$, and so on. The Fibonacci has a mystical dimension, because it is related not only to the "Golden Mean" of ancient Greece (which determined the proportions of the Parthenon), it is also found in natural phenomena from plants to nautilus shells to spiral nebulae.

Threatened by the slide toward tyranny and war in Hungary and across Europe, in 1940 Bartók and his new young wife, Ditta, originally another piano pupil, fled to New York. Bartók had powerful admirers in the United States and was offered several jobs teaching composition. Here his steely resolve set in: he would not accept a composition position. The result was that he and his family lived on the verge of financial collapse. Friends got him a job at Columbia University pursuing his folk research, but it was hardly enough to live on. Here and there he had a piano concert. His composing fell to nothing. He was depressed, tormented by the traffic and radios of the city, suffering from a mysterious ailment.

By 1943 he was seriously ill and languishing in a sanitarium. There his fortunes changed. Into his room strode legendary Boston Symphony Orchestra conductor Serge Koussevitzky, carrying a commission. No, Bartók said; I'm sick, I can't compose. The conductor refused to listen, laid a check on the table, and left. Somewhere Bartók found the strength and inspiration for a big new work, what became the **Concerto for Orchestra.** It is at once manifestly in Bartók's voice, at the same time an audience-grabber from the mysterious whispers of its opening, through stretches of passion and humor (including a wicked satire of Shostakovich's Seventh Symphony), to the full-throated Hungarian festival of its ending. Within a decade or so of its premiere by the Boston Symphony Orchestra, it had become one of the most popular works of the century.

The concerto also began a remarkable rush of work in what Bartók knew were his last months. His disease turned out to be leukemia, and its progress was unrelenting. The end came in September 1945 as Bartók was frantically trying to finish his Third Piano Concerto, which he hoped to leave for his wife to perform. When the ambulance came he had finished everything but the last seventeen bars. He begged them to let him finish, but they dragged him away. Before his last breaths he said to the doctor, "I'm only sorry to be going with my luggage full." There was so much more he had wanted to do.

He was a singular man, with a singular voice in his art. Many who knew Bartók considered him some kind of saint. He let little of himself out except that remarkable music, full of nature and wildness and ferocity and joy. He's a model of those artists who see the whole of life from tragic to exalted in an absolutely individual way. He will remain inimitable and irreplaceable.

More Bartók: Concerto No. 2 for Violin and Orchestra; Piano Concerto No. 3; Sonata for Two Pianos and Percussion; String Quartet No. 5.

Chapter 32

DMITRY SHOSTAKOVICH (1906–1975)

I n Russia of the 1930s, after dictator Joseph Stalin had
made it clear that artists who gravitated to the avant-garde
were going to find their lives on the line, Dmitry Shostakovich
became for the world the virtual face of Soviet composers. But
that prestigious role made his position more precarious rather
than less. He had been something of a brash young man, a
provocateur, but in 1936 after an outraged Stalin walked out
on a performance of his rowdy opera *Lady Macbeth of Mt-
sensk*, a newspaper article declared that if he kept on this path
"things could end very badly." That did not mean loss of job
or commissions—it meant a bullet in the back of the head.
So began for Shostakovich a cat-and-mouse game with the
communist regime that he survived for over forty years. In the
process, submitting here and risking his neck there, he left to
the world an indelible record of tyranny and suffering.

Dmitry Dmitriyevich Shostakovich was born in Saint
Petersburg in 1906. In the aftermath of the Russian Revolution of 1917 he shone as both composer and pianist at the
Saint Petersburg Conservatory. He gained international attention for his Symphony No. 1, and soon was issuing puckish
works known for their "wrong-note" approach to traditional

harmony, and their atmosphere of satire, parody, and sometimes grotesquerie. Meanwhile in the late 1920s into the 1930s he churned out a great deal of musical hackwork for film and stage. To this point he seemed to have little interest in being serious or profound. Then came the newspaper article "Muddle Instead of Music," denouncing *Lady Macbeth*. The opera and his still-unheard Fourth Symphony were banned. Thereafter his life and work, whether he wanted or not, got very serious indeed. (Stalin, you see, was highly involved in the arts and convinced of their importance to society. That's why he murdered so many artists he considered bad influences, and/or he just didn't like their stuff. In general, when politicians get interested in the arts, artists better run.)

What Shostakovich did in response was kind of unbelievable. He issued a symphony, submissively declaring it "a Soviet artist's reply to just criticism." Anyone else would have written a nicely patriotic work, perhaps one extolling Stalin's socialist paradise. Instead, the 1937 **Symphony No. 5** was Shostakovich's most ambitious and finest to date. It flew around the world and remains one of the most popular symphonies of the century. The stern proclamation of the opening announces an epic work, in tone if not in length. The first movement is tragic, building from quiet lyricism to shattering climaxes. Here is where the ambiguity of instrumental music comes into play, and the game that artists of any integrity must engage in under a totalitarian regime. Are those climaxes a matter of stern heroism, as Stalin would wish them to be, or transports of anguish and rage? The second movement scherzo moves between a stern march and mocking interludes. For the third movement, Largo, Shostakovich wrote an expansive, beautiful, exquisitely sorrowful movement led by the strings. What

then should we make of the brassy finale? Is it a march of
sometimes baffling banality? Is it a paean to the implacable
strength of the Soviet worker and soldier? Or is it a send-up
of the slaughter and hypocrisy of Stalin's Russia? Cat and
mouse. In any case, the symphony did the trick. The premiere
gained a standing ovation that went on for over half an hour.
The newspaper reviews, whose direction came from on high,
were glowing.

When the Nazi onslaught arrived in 1941 Shostakovich was
teaching at the Leningrad Conservatory. Stalin's message
went out: every citizen was to do his and her duty in the war;
peasants were to grow food, soldiers to fight, artists to create and inspire. Shostakovich became a volunteer fireman in
the siege of Leningrad, during which he witnessed first hand
the most terrible things humanity is capable of wreaking and
surviving. From that experience he wrote the Seventh Symphony ("Leningrad"), which became a worldwide symbol of
Soviet resistance to the Nazis. However inspirational it is as
a symbol, musically it is one of his lesser large works. (Bartók,
having heard the "Leningrad" on radio in the United States,
razzed it mercilessly in the Concerto for Orchestra.)

In a way the war allowed Soviet artists to extend their pal-
ettes, because they were expected to respond to tragedy and
violence. One of Shostakovich's great works from the war
years is the 1944 **Piano Trio No. 2**. Shostakovich, who un-
usually for Russians was no anti-Semite, heard a story that SS
soldiers had danced on the graves of their Jewish victims. That
image seems to have sparked the haunting dance of death in
the finale of the Trio, whose main theme is a Jewish melody.

From the first movement on the music is stark, at times brutal, rhythmically relentless, and absolutely compelling. It is one of the most memorable creative artifacts of the war.

Much the same can be said of the **Violin Concerto No. 1**, from 1947–1948, though its emotional world is not so single-minded. For a first movement, it has a spacious and grand Nocturne, melancholy in tone but with a good deal of warmth and lyricism. For second movement there is one of Shostakovich's scherzos operating between wry and demonic. The third movement takes shape around the old genre of the passacaglia, weaving gorgeous melodies over a repeated bass line. The "Burleska" finale is nervous and driving, verging at times on hysteria. See whether you can find a video of the great David Oistrakh, for whom the concerto was written, executing with astounding aplomb the enormous, finally berserk finale cadenza that seems to mount until splinters fly from the violin.

It was in 1948, while Shostakovich was working on the violin concerto, that the second great blow of his life fell. As the cold war settled in, Stalin decided to bring Soviet composers to heel. Out of the blue, at a Communist Party congress, a row of composers, starting with Prokofiev and Shostakovich, were summarily condemned for "formalistic distortions and antidemocratic tendencies alien to the Soviet people." They had, in short, written music deemed not relevant to factory workers, not in the orbit of "socialist realism," which is to say: propaganda.

By that point everyone knew artists in all disciplines who had disappeared. Now, as Stalin intended, the terror was complete for everyone. Shostakovich put the Violin Concerto in a drawer. He was handed an apology to read in an act of public humiliation. Afterward, he said to friends, his voice rising to a shriek: "I read like the most paltry wretch, a parasite, a puppet, a cut-out paper doll on a string!" For the time being most of his work was banned; he was dismissed from the Conservatory. It was around this point that one began to see Shostakovich's life engraved on his face: fixed, ravaged, revealing nothing. Shortly after that, Stalin sent him to America on a tour. Shostakovich knew, and Stalin knew he knew, that artists returning from these tours often found themselves shot. It was maybe a little joke on Stalin's part, to give the doomed a vacation first.

But Shostakovich wasn't shot. He returned to Russia and got back to work. Gradually the bans were lifted, his music was heard again, he returned to teaching. After Stalin died in 1953, official pressures eased considerably, but not entirely.

Still, Shostakovich managed to have a full life. He was gregarious, generous to his students, a perfervid soccer fan who traveled widely to see matches. He still composed with enormous facility, for well and ill: his facility sometimes outran his judgment. In music as in life, he believed in just sticking it out. When a student came to him saying he was having trouble with a second movement, Shostakovich told him, "You should not be *worrying* about the second movement. You should be *writing* the second movement." When authorities told his student Sofia Gubaidulina she was treading a "mistaken path," Shostakovich told her, "I think you should stick to your mistaken path."

In the Soviet era, chamber music was generally safer for composers, perhaps understood to be a more private expression than their big works. In recent years, Shostakovich's fifteen string quartets have come to be seen as masterworks of the twentieth century, second only to Bartók's. Here, if anywhere, he said what he wanted, how he wanted. They were his private rebellion.

The genesis of the **String Quartet No. 8** was another humiliation. In 1960 Shostakovich was pressured into joining the Communist Party, something he had resisted for years. His son remembered him weeping in despair, saying he had been blackmailed. Shostakovich resolved to write the Eighth Quartet and then to kill himself. He wrote it in three days. Its main motif is made from notes taken from his name: D–S–C–H, in German notation the pitches D–E-flat–C–B. (He used that motto in other pieces as well.) Here they are the first notes in the quartet, and never far away in the rest of it. They form a mournful presence, heard over and over in a haunted but riveting work. The second movement is as savage as a quartet can get. Here and elsewhere Shostakovich seems to be working by indirection, implying things too terrible to speak, in trances of sorrow or explosions of rage and derision. In any case, after the piece he did not kill himself, and the Eighth became his most popular quartet. It is in the **String Quartet No. 13** that he perhaps came closest to what he had witnessed and felt. This is music of bleak directness and unutterable sadness. It is like coming on a pile of dry bones in a forest.

I believe that of the leading twentieth-century Russian composers, Prokofiev is the finer artist of the two—his technique, his judgment, his range outstrip Shostakovich. But I also believe that Shostakovich is the more important of the two. More than his colleague, Shostakovich witnessed the cataclysm of midcentury before his eyes, felt it and lived it. Of the artists who worked in the midst and the aftermath of

Stalin and Hitler and resonated with it, he was the one with the most vision and the most talent. That makes Shostakovich an irreplaceable witness for his age. We need to be reminded, to feel in our hearts and minds, what tyranny can wreak, and what of humanity can be saved from it.

More Shostakovich: Symphony No. 9; Symphony No. 13 ("Babi Yar"); Piano Concerto No. 1; String Quartet No. 10; Quintet in G Minor for Piano and Strings.

Chapter 33

Benjamin Britten (1913–1976)

E ven as Benjamin Britten ascended to the leading position among British composers in the 1940s, he remained
something of an enigma, traveling on his own path. Like most
of his country's composers he was a thoroughgoing eclectic in
his work, but his influences played out in distinctive ways. In
a time when the leading international composers were revolutionaries on the order of Schoenberg and Stravinsky, or trying
to be, Britten remained a tonal composer, a melodist in the
traditional sense.

A good deal of his work was highly Anglican sacred music.
Yet he learned from everybody, including the above composers. His opera *The Turn of the Screw* is based on a twelve-tone
theme, but sounds nothing like Schoenberg. He absorbed folk
music while rarely sounding folksy. He wrote works inspired
by Japanese theater and Balinese gamelan. All the while, in his
person he maintained a cool distance from the public and a
gruff professionalism, making few statements about his work
or about music in general. His homosexuality, his obsessions,
his insecurities remained more or less hidden in plain sight.

He was born Edward Benjamin Britten, Baron Britten of
Aldeburgh. He composed from childhood and at twelve began

studying with the well-known composer Frank Bridge. After a stint at the Royal College of Music, in the 1930s he did a good deal of work in theater, film and radio, and became close to poet W. H. Auden, who helped him come to terms with his sexuality. When the war broke out he sailed for the States, where he wrote his first opera, *Paul Bunyan*, to an Auden libretto. He was already living with his lifetime partner, tenor Peter Pears.

After much soul-searching, Britten sailed back to England in 1942, in the middle of the war. But he had already made a considerable impression in the United States, which led to a commission from the Koussevitzky Foundation for what became the opera *Peter Grimes*. Premiered in 1945, this bleak but electrifying story of a fisherman and his doomed boy apprentice was an international success and placed Britten in the first rank of opera composers and composers in general. In reputation it remains one of the towering operas of the twentieth century. Its leading role, like all Britten's leading tenor roles, was written expressly and lovingly for Peter Pears.

For an introduction to Britten, I propose two pieces. The first is the 1937 work that more or less announced him to the world as a formidable new presence: ***Variations on a Theme of Frank Bridge***. Brash, witty, melodious, engaging from beginning to end, "conservative" (complete with a concluding fugue) yet fresh and distinctive in voice, it forms a fond memorial for his teacher. The other piece is his collection **Four Sea Interludes from *Peter Grimes***. Here Britten shows off his strength and originality in orchestral color and tone painting: the luminous melancholy of "Dawn," the pealing Sunday "Morning," soulful "Moonlight," raging "Storm." All these are scenes any number of composers have painted, but nobody did them like

Britten. (For more of his orchestral music, of course you can try his *Young Person's Guide to the Orchestra* based on an old Henry Purcell tune, a didactic piece introducing the instruments of the orchestra, that he made more delightful than it had reason to be. Britten loved children and wrote a good deal of music for them, usually with children as performers.)

On the boat as he returned to England in 1942 Britten produced one of his most beloved works, *A Ceremony of Carols*, eleven pieces for treble choir and harp based on Middle English poems (in their original spellings). It begins and ends evoking a church ceremony, in the form of a Gregorian Christmas chant. Between is some of the freshest and most appealing choral music of the century. He fashions a style with a certain archaic flavor to reflect the old poems. To quote one of the most enchanting of the pieces, "There is no rose of such vertu / as is the rose that bare Jesu . . . By that rose we may well see / There be one God in persons three." These pieces have become one of the familiar ornaments of the holidays; may they always be.

Finally I'll recommend what for me is his greatest opera, *The Turn of the Screw*, based on Henry James's elusive and harrowing ghost story. Here Britten was working not only with a powerful story by a great writer, he was also working within the circle of his own obsessions. Britten was a gay man with a longtime companion and never talked about it. He had feelings for young boys with which he struggled, and kept it under wraps. He wrote several operas about suffering or death or sexual feelings involving children, and nobody in his time seriously examined that, either. James's original *Turn of the Screw* had sexual threat in the center of the opera: a new governess of two children finds that they seem to be haunted and seduced by the ghosts of their dead servant and governess. In a good production *Turn of the Screw* is one of the most disquieting and riveting works the theater has to offer: the insinuating and unnerving melody with which Peter Quint calls to the children; the recurring refrain, taken from Yeats: "The ceremony of innocence is drowned." In the opera seduction and revulsion are merged in a singular way. By all means first take this in with a video of a production (there is an excellent film of it). You won't forget it. Here is as good a demonstration as any that music is not just an amusement, but a mirror of humanity in light and dark as profound as literature or drama or poetry.

Britten died in December 1976 in Aldeburgh, where he was born and where he founded an important music festival. He died shortly after completing his last opera, *Death in Venice*, from Thomas Mann's story about an old artist's fatal obsession with a young boy. Since then his life has been filled out in biographies and publications of his love letters to Pears, in stories of the personal and artistic insecurities he never escaped. I think that this stream of biography, which is ongoing, will only flesh out what was implicit in his music all along: anxiety, suffering, uncertainty, and immense human empathy.

More Britten: *A Simple Symphony; War Requiem; The Burning Fiery Furnace;* Serenade for Tenor, Horn, and Strings.

Chapter 34

AARON COPLAND (1900–1990)

Aaron Copland is one of those figures who gives a tincture of credibility to the American myth of the melting pot. A Brooklyn boy of Lithuanian-Jewish extraction (originally surnamed Kaplan), he grew up above his family's department store. He studied in Paris and returned to the United States as an avant-gardist. Only later did he become the quintessential American populist on the concert stage, his compositions grounded in the country's folk music but presented with a tremendous instrumental flair, learned from the Russian-born Stravinsky's Parisian style. Only, as they say, in America.

Growing up where and when he did, Copland said he could not imagine how he ended up as a composer. As a child he had piano lessons from his sister. By age fifteen, from random encounters with assorted music, he had decided he wanted to compose. He took some lessons in New York and at twenty-one was accepted into the new Fontainebleau School of Music, near Paris. There he became the first student of the brilliant Nadia Boulanger, who steeped him in Stravinskian neoclassicism and introduced him to conductor Serge Koussevitzky, who later with the Boston Symphony became a powerful advocate for Copland and other American composers.

(Boulanger went on to teach generations of Americans, among them Samuel Barber.)

Copland returned to the United States in 1924 with a commission for an organ concerto; Boulanger premiered it in Carnegie Hall. Then and for some time after, critics considered Copland a radical; he was writing fiercely experimental, sometimes political music. Searching for some kind of uniquely American voice, among his more austere works he also produced the jazzy, sardonic *Music for the Theater.*

In those years Copland was much involved in leftist politics, in 1935 winning a socialist song competition with his "Into the Streets May First." By that point in the middle of the Depression, his politics were taking him away from mainstream modernism. In a famous statement he said, "During those years I began to feel an increasing dissatisfaction with the relations of the music-loving public and the living composer . . . I felt that it was worth the effort to see if I couldn't say what I had to say in the simplest possible terms." This was the time of Grant Wood's painting *American Gothic* and other works that came to be called Americana. Copland became the standard bearer of that movement in music.

The new style began with a dazzling orchestral work based on Mexican folksongs: *El salon México*, from 1936. Here as if out of nowhere appeared the Copland sound: vivid orchestral colors founded on Stravinsky's neoclassic style but with an individual voice; athletic, intricately syncopated rhythms based on jazz but with a singular effect; an apparently effortless absorption of folk material that was foreign to Copland's background, but which he made his own. What he did should not have worked, but somehow it did.

There followed three legendary ballets, each on an American theme. *Billy the Kid* appeared in 1938. The story is based not on the real but the mythical outlaw. Copland's music evokes that mythical sense of the west, integrating familiar cowboy songs, such as "Goodbye Old Paint" and "Git Along Little Dogies." Try the suite Copland extracted from the ballet. The opening conjures grand drama and vast spaces. The "Mexican Dance" looks back to the jazzy syncopations of *El salon México*. After vivid bits of tone-painting in the "Card Game," "Gun Battle," and "Billy's Death," the conclusion returns memorably to the mythic voice. Here is American history on an epic tonal canvas that sounds timeless, but which Copland invented for himself. (After an early performance of the ballet, an old cowhand showed up backstage to say it was all grand except that he knew Billy, and he shot left-handed.)

Next came *Rodeo*, in 1942. Try the familiar four excerpts from the ballet: "Buckaroo Holiday," "Corral Nocturne," "Saturday Night Waltz," "Hoedown." This sort of thing was a formula for cliché and sentimentality, but the irresistible vivacity and freshness of Copland's execution made it a classic. You don't forget the sweet poignant grace of the waltz, the fiddle-tune ecstasy of "Hoedown." As with his models in Stravinsky and Mahler, Copland's iridescent handling of the orchestra is an indispensable part of the expression and excitement.

In 1944 came his masterpiece, a ballet on a commission from Martha Graham: *Appalachian Spring*. It is an unadorned story: a young couple marries and establishes a home in nineteenth-century Pennsylvania. Copland always owned a distinctive strain of heart-tugging pathos, and it is on moving display here. Best known is the orchestral suite he extracted, but like many musicians I prefer the original chamber version as it was written for the ballet. Here the warmth and intimacy of the scoring matches the intimacy and spirituality of the music: a quiet affirmation of plain living and plain virtues. The spacious opening clarinet solo is unforgettable; like Mahler, Copland could write that kind of thing as if there had never been a clarinet solo before. For material for the latter part of the ballet he perused a collection of Shaker songs, with historic results: his variations on "Simple Gifts," made an obscure tune from the collection famous. I suggest trying the original chamber version first, then go on to his full-orchestra arrangement, where he places the music in a plusher setting.

In the postwar years Copland became an icon. Having started as a musical and political radical of Russian descent, he ended up the Dumbledore of American music. He engaged in a great deal of outreach to classical audiences via radio programs and appreciation books, including *What to Listen for in Music*. He proselytized and performed as pianist and conductor, among other things giving historic premieres of Charles Ives. He wrote memorable music for films, including *The Heiress* and *The Red Pony*. He and Leonard Bernstein became the nucleus of a glittering group of gay composers and musicians, though in those days they had to keep their orientation under wraps. Copland downplayed his 1930s radicalism, though his pealing, pounding *Fanfare for the Common Man*, taken from his 1936 Third Symphony, echoed his political convictions.

After years of decline, Copland died in Tarrytown, New York, in December 1990. That his most celebrated music sounds so natural and inevitable is a testament to his artistry: he composed slowly and with great effort, somehow managing to forge from the variegated quilt of his experience a singular and enormously appealing voice.

More Copland: Third Symphony; *Lincoln Portrait*; *The Red Pony* Suite.

Chapter 35

György Ligeti (1923–2006)

In the 1970s I got a recording of György Ligeti's *Adventures* and *New Adventures* for a small group of instruments and "singers." I listened to it a lot, but had to wait ten years and hear those pieces performed live before I realized they're falling-down funny: absurdist chamber "operas" expressed by shouts, wheezes, squeaks, sighs, whoops, blitherings, bellows, and so on—everything but actual words. Before then it hadn't occurred to me that the avant-garde and the comic could cohabitate. They didn't teach you that in music school. Give them a try, and hear what I mean.

Ligeti's music sometimes is almost alarmingly funny, other times vivacious, mesmerizing, uncanny, touching, ironic, all the good stuff music used to do. It's characteristic of his individualism and rapport with the past that as a nominally "experimental" composer he could bring it all off. It was his genius to take the ideas and techniques of the late-century German experimental school and make them musical, which is to say, he humanized the avant-garde.

Ligeti was born in Transylvania, Romania, to a cultured Hungarian-Jewish family who ended up in concentration camps in World War II. His father and brother died there.

György managed to escape from a slave-labor camp and walked home to find his home was gone. After the war he studied music and settled into a teaching and composing career in Budapest.

Having survived the Nazis, Ligeti now had to contend with the Soviets. In communist Hungary, writing strange chords could have nasty consequences. After the Russian clampdown of 1956 he precipitously fled Hungary and found himself broke and alone in Cologne, Germany. He was given a place to work in the studios of Cologne Radio, where pioneering electronic music was being put together with remarkably primitive means. In those days they edited tape pieces with scissors and generated sounds with old engineering equipment. Avant-garde icons Karlheinz Stockhausen and Pierre Boulez became his mentors and friends.

But Ligeti's path diverged from his mentors in important ways. In the 1960s and 1970s Stockhausen was the most visible of European avant-gardists. He decreed that every piece must constitute some kind of revolution. Ligeti needed models but didn't care for gurus and absolutes. Finding his voice in the heart of the European experimental scene, where ultrarationality was the answer to the war's irrationality and everything had to be justified by theory, he never fit the mold.

Responding to the horrors of midcentury he had experienced first hand, Ligeti went in a direction more about feeling than intellect. Like his colleagues Ligeti was all for innovation, but new forms and sounds were for him means and not ends. Meanwhile he had not just an undogmatic but a truly antidogmatic passion for everything musical, including Caribbean, central African, and East Asian traditions, and American minimalism of the Steve Reich and Terry Riley persuasion.

True, this kind of broad reach and eclecticism was not necessarily comfortable. "I am in a prison," Ligeti once said. "One wall is the avant-garde, the other is the past. I want to escape." He declared his later music to be neither tonal nor atonal. To hell, in other words, with both camps.

One form of escape was an all-consuming outlandishness. In his comic mode Ligeti was arguably the funniest composer ever, though his humor has an unsettling edge. His opera *Le grand macabre* is an exercise in apocalyptic madness, on the subject of the end of the world as a supernatural scam. Ligeti described it as "some kind of flea market half real, half unreal . . . a world where everything is falling in." Growing up where and when he did, Ligeti knew that implosion can be funny, but ultimately it's no joke. I won't recommend the whole opera for starters, but on YouTube or the like seek out his excerpt from the opera, called **Mysteries of the Macabre**, especially the performance by the marvelous soprano Barbara Hannigan with Simon Rattle conducting. It will, I promise, be one of the damnedest things you ever heard—or saw.

Ligeti's religious music has an unearthly aura that made it a natural fit for Stanley Kubrick's *2001: A Space Odyssey*. For me Ligeti's music remains the most sublime element of that transcendent film. Still, if the **Requiem** and *Lux aeterna* used in the movie resemble anything else, it's not apemen and monoliths on the moon, it's the ululations of mythical beasts, the sighing of lonely stars in forgotten nebulae, the ritual songs of wraiths. It's the most genuinely cosmic sacred music I know.

Another singular and overwhelming work is his **Violin Concerto**. Its hymnlike second movement climaxes with a chorus of ocarinas (that flute thing shaped like a potato) that manage to sound at once goofy and creepy, like a choir of nightmare cherubs. Here Ligeti opened a vein of intoxicating weirdness maybe music had never reached before. His experiments weren't ever trivial; he sought to express something beyond analysis, in the realm of the heart.

His hypervirtuosic Études for piano are spoken of with awe and fear in keyboard circles. Listen to Ligeti's favorite pianist, Pierre-Laurent Aimard, play the jazzy and ridiculously difficult *Fanfares*.

I heard Karlheinz Stockhausen give talks in Boston in the 1960s and 1970s, and in the 1990s saw Ligeti as a guest composer at New England Conservatory. Stockhausen was the image of the German modernist, proclaiming tidily arranged dicta about the imperatives of history. At the conservatory Ligeti simply charmed everybody. He had no theories to offer. He was unpretentious, witty in his scrambled English, and in contrast to Stockhausen's sharp features and burning eyes there was Ligeti's wonderful face of an old spaniel.

He told us that when his music was first being performed in European new-music festivals he had to hitchhike to the concerts. "I didn't have the money to buy a girl a cup of coffee." Then one day somebody told him, "Did you know there's a movie with your music in it?" Stanley Kubrick had simply ripped off his work for 2001. Ligeti duly sued Kubrick and in the end, he told us, received the grand sum of $3,000. "Do you like the movie?" somebody asked. "Yah, I really like it," Ligeti said. And of course, 2001 did for him what being on the cover of the Beatles' *Sgt. Pepper's Lonely Hearts Club Band* did for Stockhausen; it helped make him famous beyond the esoteric circles of the European avant-garde. His music has been in a number of movies since.

Ligeti died in Vienna in June 2006. For my money, he is the most interesting, most expressive, most important tonal artist to appear since Stravinsky died. Stockhausen was a great inventor in sound, but Ligeti was a great composer in a long tradition. I don't see any replacements on the horizon.

More Ligeti: *Nonsense Madrigals; Atmospheres; Lontano.*

Chapter 36

Further Modernist Listening

I'll start by noting that there are going to be more compos-ers here than in the romantic roundup, because in the last 115 years history has only begun to do its job of deciding who thrives and who fades. As of this writing all these composers have a presence in contemporary musical life. The difference in the past century is that now all music, all art for that mat-ter, can have a kind of immortality in media, especially the online media that has developed in the last quarter century. How that situation will affect the future of the arts for well or ill remains to be seen.

Sergey Prokofiev (1891–1953): By the time the Russian Revolution exploded in 1917, Prokofiev had completed two op-eras and two piano concertos. He was an ardent supporter of the new Soviet regime, writing a remarkable number of pieces in that year. In 1918 Prokofiev left Russia for a concert tour intended to be brief, but for various reasons he didn't see Rus-sia again for nearly ten years. He ended up in America for a while, his explosive New York debut recital earning him the title "Bolshevik pianist." He returned to the Soviet Union for good in 1932, where he found a much changed situation in the arts. Stalin had cracked down on modernism and brought the brilliant period of post-Revolutionary art to a sharp and brutal end. Yet for years, Prokofiev thrived under the watchful gaze of Stalin and his stooges. He joined the Composers' Union and wrote a cantata for Stalin's sixtieth birthday. He put aside dissonance and innovation, but the result was a new focus in his work and a still deeper involvement with his Russian musical wellsprings. In 1948 the Cold War was under way and, as we saw, Stalin decreed that artists were to be brought to heel once and for all. Despite their worldwide fame, Shostakovich and Prokofiev were not spared. Both men knuckled under, issued pathetic self-condemnations. It nearly killed Shostakovich, and if anything went worse on Prokofiev, who was already exhausted and ailing. For whatever reasons, from that moment on Prokofiev was less able to pursue his work in the Soviet Union than his compatriot Shostakovich. A Russian thinker once compared America and the Soviet Union this way: in America everything is possible and nothing is important; in Russia far less is possible and everything is important. Both Prokofiev and Shostakovich survived, each in his own way, and each in his own way did vitally important work under the worst of circumstances. Prokofiev had a vigorous, athletic side in allegros (listen to the hair-raising last movement of the Piano Sonata No. 7), a great gift for lyric melody, and he produced epic canvases in his large works. **Suggested listening:** "Classical" Symphony (No. 1); Piano Concerto No. 3; *Lieutenant Kijé*; *Peter and the Wolf*; Symphony No. 5. Piano Sonata No. 7.

Alban Berg (1885–1935): A student of Schoenberg and member of the Second Viennese School, Berg was a slow and painstaking worker; no composer of his stature has so few works in his catalogue, but all of them are important. Berg spent some eight years working intermittently on his greatest work, the opera **Wozzeck**. In this story of a tormented, doomed soldier and his mistress the expression is utterly individual, the tone ranging from deep tenderness to savage irony to a sense of incipient chaos. It remains the most admired opera of the twentieth century. By 1935 Berg was considered a leading Austrian composer, but he and Anton Webern had also been denounced by the Nazis as "degenerate artists" and Berg had lost most of his income. Berg was never really healthy; after completing his beautiful and elegiac **Violin Concerto** he died from an infected insect bite before he could finish his opera *Lulu*. **Suggested listening:** Three Fragments from *Wozzeck*.

Anton Webern (1883–1945): Another Schoenberg pupil and member of the Second Viennese School, Webern in his maturity wrote in mounting denunciation and growing obscurity, but shortly after his death transformed postwar music. Like Berg, Webern began writing free-atonal pieces and then followed Schoenberg into twelve-tone music in the 1920s. For my ear his early free-atonal work is his most communicative—puckish to deeply tragic, utterly fresh in sound. In his later twelve-tone works Webern became the most austere of them all, the most meticulous in his use of the technique. His pieces got shorter, more aphoristic, and lost the expressionistic intensity of his free-atonal years. The onset of the Nazi regime was a creative disaster for Webern as for so many progressive creatives, who were lumped together under the title "degenerate artists." Performances were banned and Webern had to turn to musical piecework to get by. His conducting and composing trickled to a halt; he was virtually forgotten as a composer. Just after the war he died in an accidental shooting by an American soldier. Ten years later, he and his relentless application of the twelve-tone method were the inspiration for an international school of "post-Webern" composers. One of them was Igor Stravinsky, who said of him: "Doomed to a total failure in a deaf world of ignorance and indifference, he inexorably kept on cutting out his diamonds, his dazzling diamonds." **Suggested listening:** Five Pieces for String Quartet; Six Pieces for Orchestra; Concerto for Nine Instruments.

Leoš Janáček (1854–1928): Janáček is an inspiration to struggling composers everywhere, because he worked in semi-obscurity much of his life and hit his stride only in his sixties and seventies—with the help of his yearning for a young woman, married and unavailable who nonetheless inspired him. In 1916, his nationalistic opera *Jenůfa* was performed in Prague to great acclaim. From then on, Janáček was the leading Czech composer and before long, in his sixties, an international figure. His music is saturated not only with the rich tradition of Moravian folk music, but also the culture's language. **Suggested listening:** *Sinfonietta; Glagolitic Mass;* the opera *The Cunning Little Vixen.*

Ralph Vaughan Williams (1872–1958): Vaughan Williams went through the Royal College of Music, studied with the German Max Bruch and the French Maurice Ravel. But instead of taking up the somewhat Brahmsian, late-romantic vein of Elgar, he turned to British folk music for inspiration and maintained that foundation, plus British church music and the like, for the rest of a long and productive career. **Suggested listening:** *Fantasia on a Theme of Thomas Tallis;* Symphony No. 4.

Sergey Rachmaninoff (1873–1943): Rachmaninoff raised himself from a troubled Russian childhood, in which his father impoverished and deserted the family, to become by the end of his teens one of the finest pianists in the world. He became a sensation after his melodramatic **Prelude in C-sharp Minor** for piano, written in 1892, went global. (Rachmaninoff, who never escaped the notoriety of that piece, came to hate it.) The 1901 Moscow premiere of what would become his most celebrated work, the **Piano Concerto No. 2 in C Minor,** cemented his importance on the world stage. At Juilliard it's called "Rocky 2," one of those peaks you must climb if you hope to be called a virtuoso. His fellow Russian Stravinsky appreciated his playing, his music not so much, and described Rachmaninoff the man as "a six-foot scowl." **Suggested listening:** *Isle of the Dead.*

Paul Hindemith (1895–1963): For some time Hindemith was considered one of the leading composers of his time, up there with Schoenberg and Stravinsky and Bartók. He rejected atonality, and became for many the necessary riposte to Schoenberg. During the 1920s he was considered one of the revolutionaries, his music marked by great energy and wit. They include his surreal chamber opera *Hin and Zurück* (There and Back), which gets halfway, then in both music and action goes in reverse until it reaches the beginning, like a film run backward. In the 1930s the Nazis lumped him into the "cultural Bolshevist" camp and banned his magnum opus, the opera *Mathis der Maler* (Mathis the Painter). In later years Hindemith calmed down into a craftsman issuing stacks of meticulously crafted works. **Suggested listening:** the symphony *Mathis der Maler; Symphonic Metamorphoses of Themes by Carl Maria von Weber.*

Edgard Varèse (1883–1965): Varèse has the distinction of being the prime inspiration for the midcentury musical avant-garde and the same for avant-rockers including Frank Zappa. From the beginning to the present, he has been in sound and reputation the prototypical modernist. I once heard a blistering performance of his *Amériques* by the Boston Symphony that I had to return to hear again, even though I don't really like the piece—what I appreciate is its rabid, in-your-face ferocity raging on for twenty minutes. **Suggested listening:** *Ionization; Amériques; Poème électronique.*

George Gershwin (1898–1937): Gershwin created some of the most beloved songs in American popular music and some of the same in works for the concert hall, a kind of all-embracing career that could only have happened in the United States. With insatiable curiosity and ambition he absorbed all the music around him, popular and classical, black and white, and remade it in his own voice. In his midteens Gershwin dropped out of school and went to work as a song plugger on Tin Pan Alley, spending his days at the keyboard playing tunes for sheet-music customers. At age twenty, reportedly during a ten-minute bus ride in Manhattan, he wrote "Swanee," which sold in the millions and remains a familiar standard. After that he never lacked for money and fame, but his creative ambitions went far beyond simple tunes. Nearly everybody who encountered Gershwin, from the music fan on the street to the most sophisticated musicians of their time, was astounded by his gifts. To repeat Ravel's line when Gershwin asked him for lessons: "Why would you want to be a second-rate Ravel when you're already a first-rate Gershwin?" *Porgy and Bess*, his masterpiece, is a seamless melding of traditional opera and Broadway into a story of great tragic power. **Suggested listening:** *Rhapsody in Blue;* Concerto in F; *An American in Paris; Porgy and Bess.*

Erik Satie (1866–1925): Satie is not by any stretch a great composer, but in his droll and eccentric fashion he made himself an important one, inspiring a row of more ambitious artists. Satie wrote his ballet *Parade* for veterans of the Ballets Russes (its score includes typewriters, milk bottles, and a foghorn; the sets were by Picasso). He was a friend and inspiration to Debussy and Ravel and the surrealists, whom he inspired with his whimsical names for pieces, among them *Vexations* and *Veritable Flabby Preludes (for a dog)*. Satie was a walking rebuke to all pretension. **Suggested listening:** *Gymnopédies* for piano.

Francis Poulenc (1899–1963): Poulenc often wrote with reference to French popular music, including many notable songs. His opera *Les mamelles de Tirésias* (The Breasts of Tiresias) was based on a farce by the surrealist poet Apollinaire. Before he turned to religious works in later life, most of Poulenc's music was unfailingly charming and piquant, the epitome of Parisian urbanity. **Suggested listening:** Sextet for Piano and Wind Quintet; *Gloria*.

Darius Milhaud (1892–1974): Milhaud was creatively involved with both French and American popular culture. The most celebrated result was the first jazz ballet or concert work (it preceded Gershwin's *Rhapsody in Blue*), which at its premiere was presented in boxy costumes as a "cubist ballet." **Suggested listening:** Aforesaid ballet, *La création du monde*.

Samuel Barber (1910–1981): Barber's music is generally so welcoming that one can forget what a maverick he was. He was neither a postromantic nor an Americana composer, neither avant-garde nor reactionary, but in some ways he drew on the whole musical culture of his time in a distinctly personal synthesis. His somberly beautiful **Adagio for Strings** has become a ubiquitous accompaniment for tragedies depicted in the media. **Suggested listening:** *Knoxville: Summer of 1915*; Piano Sonata; Piano Concerto.

John Cage (1912–1992): Cage is the trickster of modern music, which is not to say that he wasn't serious. Rather, for him the serious to the provocative to the wacky were part of the same cosmic continuum. He studied with Arnold Schoenberg and wrote twelve-tone pieces, but soon wearied of the formalism and sobriety of both the reactionaries and the avant-garde. He began to look for new sounds, divorced of questions of meaning and intent. Soon he began to plan his works by chance methods: flipping a coin, consulting the Chinese *I Ching*. What came out of this *aleatoric* method (*alea* being Latin for "dice") were such pieces as *Imaginary Landscape No. 4* from 1951, performed according to elaborate instructions for twelve radios tuned to different channels, so what comes out is whatever happens to be on the air. His legendary *4'32"* involves a pianist sitting at the keyboard for four minutes, thirty-two seconds, playing nothing at all. The "music" is whatever sounds the audience may, or may not, provide. Cage's aesthetic was widely influential, especially useful for composers with no talent, among whom he grouped himself, but he always managed to bring it off with more puckish bravura than anybody else. **Suggested listening:** Sonatas and Interludes (1946–1948) for "prepared piano." That means a piano whose strings have been decked with screws, rubber, plastic, bolts, and various other stuff to produce the most unlikely sounds. These were among Cage's early, planned, and precisely notated pieces. They're great fun.

Olivier Messiaen (1908–1992): Messiaen made a study of Eastern music, whose rhythms and tonalities became part of his work—along with the songs of birds, a lifelong fascination of his. Two more elements would mark Messiaen's mature music: his fervent Catholicism and his inborn synesthesia, a quirk of brain wiring in which you perceive two senses conjoined. In his case, he heard music in extravagant colors, and became a composer of inimitable and polychrome cast. **Suggested listening:** *Quartet for the End of Time; Visions de l'Amen; Chronochromie,* a big, rowdy orchestral work made almost entirely of birdcalls.

Pierre Boulez (1925–2016): Boulez emerged from the Paris Conservatoire a fire-breathing radical, preaching "total serialism" and issuing manifestos: "[A]ny musician who has not experienced . . . the necessity of [serialism] is USELESS. For his whole work is irrelevant to the needs of his epoch." And, "Schoenberg is dead"—because in Boulez's not remotely humble opinion, the inventor of atonality did not go far enough. For Boulez and his compatriots, serialism was an intellectual path to recovery from the madness of the war. At the same time, he and his generation of avant-gardists were much influenced by the aleatoric procedures of John Cage. **Suggested listening:** *Dérives 2*, in which he left behind some of his old ideologies to write music of fine propulsive energy.

Karlheinz Stockhausen (1928–2007): Stockhausen grew up amid bombing raids during the war, and associated the Nazis' ubiquitous military music with Germany's march into disaster. His own work would flee as far as possible from regular rhythm and traditional melody and harmony. Stockhausen spent many years proselytizing for the avant-garde, writing a great deal of technical and polemical prose, composing both electronic and acoustic music and sometimes uniting them. Something of a fanatic by nature, he declared that every piece must be a revolution in itself. In the 1960s he became famous as one of the faces on the cover of the Beatles' *Sgt. Pepper's* album, and part of its inspiration. **Suggested listening:** *Gesang der Jünglinge*; *Stimmung*; *Hymnen*. Important: read the liner notes or look up the pieces on Wikipedia.

Alfred Schnittke (1934–1998): Schnittke's postmodern, often poly-stylistic work, influenced by Ives among others, has been in vogue for years and remains formidable. For a taste, try the **Concerto Grosso No. 1**, which takes that old baroque genre and baroque style as a foundation on which to build one of the maddest works I know, with tenderness and ferocity, tonality and skewered tonality and atonality and raging chaos competing in a riveting aural nightmare. **Suggested listening:** Viola Concerto.

Giacinto Scelsi (1905–1988): Scelsi spent most of his life composing in obscurity, known only to a few disciples. For his later work he improvised on tape, and collaborators wrote out the results under his supervision. Near the end of his life he had some acclaimed performances and acquired champions, including the Arditti Quartet. **Suggested listening:** *Uaxuctum: The Legend of the Mayan City Which They Themselves Destroyed for Religious Reasons.*

Terry Riley (1935–): One of the founders of musical minimalism, Riley went the academic route, receiving a master's from the University of California before gravitating to studies in Indian music. He was equally involved with the counterculture of the Sixties and its music. All that contributed to his work, along with an abiding interest in midcentury jazz. Minimalism fled as far as you can get from the arcana of academic serialism, integrating elements of world music and American pop. Its form and processes are entirely on the surface, something a four-year-old can understand. Not long ago I stumbled upon a performance of his legendary *In C* in a museum, looking down from a balcony as smiling and dancing musicians made their way through the open-topped galleries and finally gathered below us for the conclusion. It was one of the most enchanting times I've ever had in a museum, and no other piece would have had that effect. **Suggested listening:** *A Rainbow in Curved Air.*

Steve Reich (1936–): Reich is another seminal minimalist. He went from being a philosophy major at Cornell University to musical studies at Juilliard and Mills College. From 1966 he headed his own ensemble. A good start with Reich is the tape piece **Come Out**, in which a phrase spoken by a black kid on the street is cycled over and over on multiple tape machines that become gradually out of sync until the phrase has transformed into a spellbinding soundscape. Reich's masterpiece, I think the masterpiece of all minimalism, is the 1976 **Music for 18 Musicians**. The piece has the trademark inexorable pulse, babbling repeated figures, and so on, but unlike most minimal pieces it is truly expressive, for me a long stretch of steadily renewing rhythmic invention with a pervasive undercurrent of brooding melancholy. If you get a chance to see it live, don't miss it. The music turns into a kind of theater, with musicians moving from instrument to instrument, women crooning into mikes, drummers alternating racing notes on both sides of a marimba. It's both a musical and visual treat.

Philip Glass (1937–): Glass studied philosophy in college, went on to Juilliard, and studied Indian music. A tireless self-promoter, he formed a group that played his relentlessly repetitious work on electric keyboards and winds—minimal, monotonous, and very loud. In the late 1960s the group acquired a cult status in New York. **Suggested listening:** his opera *Einstein on the Beach.*

John Adams (1947–): I call Adams a postminimalist because while he often makes use of the style's rolling repetitions and slow evolution, he places it in a broad stylistic palette whose influences range from romantic music to Charles Ives to pop music. **Suggested listening:** *Nixon in China; Shaker Loops.*

Conclusions

I want to say a bit about the contemporary phenomenon known as the early music movement. Through the history of Western music there has been a natural evolution in the types of instruments—say, the change from the gamba family of strings to the violin family—and technical improvements in existing ones, such as the nineteenth-century addition of keys to winds and of valves to brass. There have been some exceptions to this evolutionary rule; for example, the general agreement is that the string instruments made by the Stradivari family and a few others in the seventeenth and eighteenth centuries are unsurpassed. (Most of their instruments, though, were in the nineteenth century taken apart and refitted with longer fingerboards, to suit the requirements of the time.)

As with the evolution from the harpsichord to the piano with its greater range of volume and touch, there was a tendency to consider the various evolutions to be a matter of sainted Progress. At the same time, performance styles also evolved, and in the absence of recordings each historical era and region developed its own habits of playing. So, when the larger Bach pieces were rediscovered toward the middle of the nineteenth century, he was played on the instruments of the time and in the style of the time, which meant adding effects of volume, articulation, and phrasing to the music.

In the twentieth century, however, there came an interest in older instruments, and that in turn led to an interest in how those instruments were played. Classical groups sprang up here and there sporting recorders, shawms, lutes, and the like.

When the early music movement really came of age in the 1970s, the attitude was, "We're going to play music on the instruments the music was written for, in the style they were played in the time, as best we can ascertain." There was a degree of self-righteousness in this endeavor: *we're* more authentic than *you* are. As a new generation of musicians got busy mastering baroque violins and recorders and gambas and lutes and valveless horns and the like, scholars studied every performance treatise available, mainly ones from the eighteenth century, for clues about performance practice of the time.

I remember in 1977, the first time I heard a recording of an original-instrument orchestra, which was playing Mozart's G Minor Symphony. I was thunderstruck. The opening melody in octaves, which in a modern large orchestra had always sounded logy, here sounded lithe and lucid. I could clearly hear every part in the orchestra down to the second bassoon. It was thrilling, as if the music were reborn. An experiment: listen to a version of Handel's *Music for the Royal Fireworks* in the usual version for modern orchestra. Then listen to the original version played by an early music band—say, the Schola Cantorum Basiliensis. You'll find the original was rowdier and more fun.

Over the decades the early music movement spread steadily, until by the 1990s original instruments had largely claimed the baroque repertoire for itself and was making inroads in the classical period. We came to appreciate the sighing of strings played without vibrato and with convex bows rather than modern concave ones, the sound of gut strings rather than metal, the mellow sheen of gambas, and of course, the tinkling of the harpsichord. The revival of Renaissance and medieval instruments opened up a large and wonderful repertoire that had been rarely and only tentatively heard before. Meanwhile, the performing style that grew up in the movement favored smaller bands, leaner textures, faster tempos. There was a general tendency to pull back on emotional expression, on the theory that it was too romantic, not baroque enough.

The triumph of the early music movement, though, also exposed its limitations and delusions. No matter how many treatises we study, we really can't know what Bach and anybody else before modern times sounded like playing their stuff. Many vital things are not possible to know at all, so the musicality and imagination of performers has to step in. Eventually the early music movement owned up to this reality by pulling back on claims of "authenticity" to the more modest, "historically informed performance" (HIP). In that guise, the skinny-and-zippy HIP style of performance spread into mainstream concert halls and modern instruments.

Nobody I wager today questions the value of all this. It's manifestly worthwhile to hear the sounds a composer wrote for, in some semblance of the performance practice of his time. In addition to research, original instruments in themselves can reveal a great deal. Beethoven complained mightily about the limitations of the pianos he had to work with. All the same, he wrote music geared for those pianos, as you discover if you hear the music on period instruments. The first movement of his "Moonlight" Sonata is directed to be played with the sustain pedal down the whole time. Because the resonance of a modern instrument is much longer than Beethoven's piano, that can't be done today—it would sound like a tonal traffic jam. You have to find some way to fake it. Hearing Beethoven's "Appassionata" Sonata on a piano from his time, you realize he's exploiting registral contrasts that don't exist on modern pianos. His pianos had boomy low registers, fairly mellow middle registers, and bright high registers, and they sounded more woody than modern pianos because their frames were wood rather than steel. On a period piano, the maddened end of the "Appassionata" sounds as if the music is tearing the instrument apart, and that's an important element of its emotional effect.

These matters remain highly complicated. The more you recognize the complications, the more the idea of authenticity dribbles away. For one example, yes, Mozart usually worked with orchestras having ten or twelve strings, but he himself said that if he had his way, his orchestra would have had fifty violins. The idea that skinnier sounds and faster tempos are always better has led to performances where there are no slow tempos at all; everything boogies along like a dance. I submit that this isn't "authentic"; it's inexpressive and unmusical. Meanwhile, the *setting* of music is enormously different now than in the past. Most music today is played in concert halls. In Mozart's day, chamber music was played in private music rooms, piano sonatas in private. Nobody has proposed to revive that—or the fact that a great deal of music played in the past was done with little or no rehearsal. Most performances before the nineteenth century would probably sound to our ears, in a word, lousy.

What I'm saying is that the early music style is not authentic so much as it is simply a modern playing style for early music. For me, the relentlessly fast tempos often heard these days can tear the guts out of the music. In any case, styles change. The steady, metronomic approach to tempo that appeared in the earlier twentieth century, replacing the flexible tempos of romantic playing, is still largely the norm. Eventually somebody will seriously listen, for example, to how Mahler played his own work—there are recordings of him on piano—and absorb his style of flexible tempos into a new approach to late nineteenth-century music.

As a teacher, how would I grade the early music movement and its influence? In terms of reviving original instruments, I'd say A, if not A+. In terms of its effect on the playing of baroque and classical repertoire, I'd say B+, if I was feeling generous. The enrichment the movement has given to music is unquestionable. But ends remain more important than means. "The best history has to give," said Johann Wolfgang von Goethe, "is the enthusiasm it arouses."

In any case, the early music movement is an indelible part of the continuing evolution of Western classical music, which has to evolve to retain its vitality and importance and relevance. Ours is the broadest, most kaleidoscopic musical tradition in the world, with over a millennium of constant exploration and renewal. In it everyone can find places and passions. What is necessary is to continue the journey, to find new places and new passions.

So, there's our tour of Western music from eons back to a few years ago. How do I, as a composer and writer, add all this up? Music is here to enjoy, to love, to be fascinated and moved and instructed and amused and scared and exalted by. I believe that a composer's job is to provide those experiences for us. If and when audiences for classical music are ready to be moved by myriad voices and languages, when audiences are as excited about hearing something *new* as they were in Mozart's day— then music will thrive. The works being composed today are part of an ongoing experiment in that direction.

To finish, I want again to take note of the stupendous scope of the music I've talked about. One of the great virtues of Western music is not only its enormous technical journey from monody to polyphony to homophony, from evolving tonality to evolving atonality, triads to tone clusters, simplicity to complexity, a small palette of colors to an enormous palette, austere to impassioned, calculated to crazed. It has also shown an ability to absorb into itself ideas and voices from around the world, and from popular music and jazz, while still remaining itself. For me the incomparable breadth of reference and style over the past millennium may be the most remarkable aspect of Western classical music. Of course, we haven't seen the end of that evolution and never will.

What do I foresee in the future? I decline to speculate. A recent study found that when it comes to prognostication, there's no difference between prophecies of the future and random outcomes. Whatever happens, it will not be what anybody predicted, unless by accident. What we can say is that the human spirit is endlessly creative, and musicians like all artists will keep doing what they do. In the process they will continue to reveal beautiful, sublime, enchanting, provoking, frightening, fascinating, exalted, comic, rude, marvelous things. Whether presented in terms of sounds, strings, brass, stone, wood, canvas, film, paint, or what have you, in the end art is all made of the same inexhaustible material as the human spirit.

SUGGESTED FURTHER READING

I suggest checking out these books online—some are for general readers, others (notably the classic Rosen, *The Classical Style*) require some technical knowledge.

Berlioz, Hector, and David Cairns, *The Memoirs of Hector Berlioz*.

Bostridge, Ian, *Schubert's Winter Journey: Anatomy of an Obsession*.

Frisch, Walter, *Music in the Nineteenth Century*.

Gardiner, John Eliot, *Bach: Music in the Castle of Heaven*.

Geiringer, Karl, and Irene Geiringer, *Haydn: A Creative Life in Music*.

Hamm, Charles, *Music in the New World*.

Hanning, Barbara Russano, *Concise History of Western Music* (5th ed.).

Hogwood, Christopher, *Handel* (rev. ed.).

Lederer, Victor, *Debussy: The Quiet Revolutionary*.

Melograni, Piero, and Lydia G. Cochrane, *Wolfgang Amadeus Mozart: A Biography*.

Orenstein, Arbie, *A Ravel Reader: Correspondence, Articles, Interviews*.

Rosen, Charles, *The Classical Style: Haydn, Mozart, Beethoven*.

Schumann, Robert, *Schumann on Music: A Selection from the Writings*.

Shaw, George Bernard, *Shaw on Music*.

Shawn, Allen, *Arnold Schoenberg's Journey*.

Simms, Bryan R., *Music of the Twentieth Century: Style and Structure*.

Stravinsky, Vera, and Robert Craft, *Stravinsky in Pictures and Documents*.

Swafford, Jan, *Beethoven: Anguish and Triumph*.

Swafford, Jan, *Charles Ives: A Life with Music.*
Swafford, Jan, *Johannes Brahms: A Biography.*
Wagner, Cosima, *Cosima Wagner's Diaries: An Abridgement.*
Walker, Alan, *The Chopin Companion.*
Watson, Derek, *Richard Wagner: A Biography.*

INDEX

Jan Swafford is a composer and music scholar and the author of acclaimed biographies of Beethoven, Brahms, and Ives, as well as *The Vintage Guide to Classical Music*. Swafford has also written on music for *Slate*, *Guardian International*, and *Gramophone*, among others, and has done commentary for NPR and the BBC. He has written program notes for the symphonies of Boston, Chicago, Cleveland, San Francisco, and Detroit. In addition to his writing, Swafford is also an award-winning composer whose work has been performed around the country and abroad. He studied at Harvard and the Yale School of Music, taught composition, music history, and theory at The Boston Conservatory, and has taught at Tufts, Harvard, Hampshire, Boston University, and Amherst. His website is janswafford.com.